Aging Families and Caregiving

Aging Families and Caregiving

Edited by

Sara Honn Qualls
Steven H. Zarit

WILEY

John Wiley & Sons, Inc.

Copyright © 2009 by John Wiley & Sons, Inc. All rights reserved.
Published by John Wiley & Sons, Inc., Hoboken, New Jersey.
Published simultaneously in Canada.

Library of Congress Cataloging-in-Publication Data:
 Aging families and caregiving / edited by Sara H. Qualls, Steven H. Zarit.
  p. cm.—(Wiley series in clinical geropsychology)
 Includes bibliographical references and index.
 ISBN 978-0-470-00855-3 (cloth alk. paper)
  1. Social work with older people. 2. Family social work. 3. Aging parents—Care.
4. Adult children of aging parents. 5. Caregivers—Family relationships. I. Qualls, Sarah Honn.
II. Zarit, Steven H.
 HV1451.A37 2009
 362.6–dc22
                     2008036139

Printed in the United States of America.
10 9 8 7 6 5 4 3 2 1

Contents

Contributors

Patti Auxier
HealthSouth Rehabilitation
  Hospital
Colorado Springs, CO

Elaine A. Blechman, PhD
Department of Psychology
University of Colorado, Boulder
Boulder, CO

Rosemary Blieszner, PhD
Department of Human
  Development and Center for
  Gerontology
Virginia Polytechnic Institute and
  State University
Blacksburg, VA

Diane L. Elmore, PhD, MPH
American Psychological
  Association
Washington, DC

Melissa M. Franks, PhD
Department of Child Development
  and Family Studies
Purdue University
West Lafayette, IN

Dolores Gallagher-Thompson, PhD
Department of Psychiatry and
  Behavioral Sciences
Stanford University School of
  Medicine
Stanford, CA

Nancy Giunta, PhD
University of California,
  Berkeley
School of Social Welfare
Berkeley, CA

Clayton Lewis, PhD
Coleman Institute for Cognitive
  Disabilities
University of Colorado,
  Boulder
Boulder, CO

Weiling Liu, PhD
Veterans Affairs Palo Alto Health
  Care System
Pacific Graduate School of
  Psychology
Palo Alto, CA

Tara L. Noecker, MS
Department of Psychology
University of Colorado, Colorado
    Springs
Colorado Springs, CO

Margaret P. Norris, PhD
Private Practice
College Station, TX

Sara Honn Qualls, PhD
Department of Psychology
University of Colorado, Colorado
    Springs
Colorado Springs, CO

Andrew Scharlach, PhD
University of California,
    Berkeley
School of Social Welfare
Berkeley, CA

Mary Ann Parris Stephens, PhD
Department of Psychology
Kent State University
Kent, OH

Ronda C. Talley, PhD, MPH
Centers for Disease Control and
    Prevention
Atlanta, GA

Michael Williams, PhD
Caring Family, LLC
Louisville, CO

Judy Zarit, PhD
Private Practice
State College, PA

Steven H. Zarit, PhD
Penn State University
University Park, PA

Preface

AGING FAMILIES AND CAREGIVING

Families are so important within the lives of older persons that they often are part of mental health assessment and treatment, whether explicitly or implicitly. Families are *hidden victims* of devastating diseases such as Alzheimer's disease (Zarit, Orr, & Zarit, 1985) and are the primary caregiving service providers of older adults (see Chapter 4, this volume). Yet, families are so much more than caregivers to older adults. They are the primary social network for older persons, accounting for nearly all of the confidants reported by older adults (see Chapter 1, this volume). Families receive both emotional and instrumental support from older adults who have provided similar assistance throughout the entire lifespan of their offspring. Families give back more than they receive only when parents reach very late life. In short, families of older adults are linked in complex, reciprocally beneficial, and challenging relationships that are powerful and meaningful.

This book is included in Wiley's Clinical Geropsychology series precisely because families are so critical to the well-being of older adults. The book series parallels and grows out of an annual Clinical Geropsychology conference held in Colorado Springs each summer (www.uccs.edu/geropsy). The conference provides advanced training to experienced mental health providers seeking postlicensure learning opportunities related to geriatric mental health. About midconference, the presenters built on the conference curriculum to create the content of the book you hold in your hands. The annual "author dinner" has become a highlight of the conference because it offers experts in the field the opportunity to build a book that can guide clinicians who are relatively new to geriatric work. Essentially, the entire set of presenters engages in the same task that the cochairs faced in structuring the conference: how to focus what is known in a very large field into the background knowledge underlying clinical skills.

Each year, creative perspective shifts occur as the presenters brainstorm, challenge each other, and ultimately hone in on a structure and suggested authors. Each presenter tackles a chapter or two, and other experts are asked to bring additional expertise to the project. What you have is a remarkable compendium created by outstanding scholars and clinicians.

The structure of a book always reflects a creative process. The editors of each book in this series could describe the unique challenges to summarizing each entire field in a way that is useful to practicing clinicians. The first book on *Psychotherapy for Depression in Older Adults* (Qualls & Knight, 2006) took up the challenge of summarizing a vast and growing literature in a way that was practical for clinicians treating depressed older adults with complex presentations of symptoms and in contexts that extend far past our empirical research base. The interdisciplinary nature of a rapidly emerging new field was the challenge of the second book, *Changes in Decision-Making Capacity in Older Adults: Assessment and Intervention* (Qualls & Smyer, 2007). The book you hold addresses yet a different challenge: building an empirically based approach to clinical work with older families despite the extremely limited base of clinical outcome research.

Much of the foundation for clinical work with older families can be found in the family development and family caregiving literatures. To date, few studies have examined specific methods for intervening with aging families to benefit either the older members or their families (see Chapter 7 for S. Zarit's review of that literature). Because the beginning point for clinicians is to learn about how older adults age within families, the first two chapters of this book are devoted to orienting clinicians to the family contexts of aging (Blieszner, Chapter 1) and the structures and functions of aging families (Fingerman et al., Chapter 2). Who is included or implied in the term *later-life family*? What do families actually *do*? Without understanding this developmental background, clinical care risks misunderstanding the immediate caring context.

Caregiving is a primary context in which clinicians will encounter the families of older adults, so three chapters review the key components of the caregiving literature that clinicians need to know. Crowther and Austin review effects of culture on family caregiving in Chapter 3;

Stephens and Franks describe families' process of providing care to persons with chronic illness in Chapter 4; and Liu and Gallagher-Thompson review the effects of caring for persons with dementia on their family members in Chapter 5. Each chapter summarizes a vast and confusing literature, providing structure that offers clinicians a framework for engaging families effectively in their practice.

The second section of the book addresses clinical services for families engaged in care of an older person. J. Zarit provides a rich clinical introduction to assessment and intervention with caregiving families encountered in clinical practice in Chapter 6. S. Zarit reviews the empirical research literature, drawing conclusions about how clinicians might use that literature to guide their work in Chapter 7. Qualls and Noecker describe a family therapy intervention designed specifically for caregiving families in Chapter 8. Finally, Norris addresses the complex issues that arise in working with family caregivers within long-term care residences in Chapter 9. These chapters are rich with clinical illustrations, guidance, tips for practice, and encouragement to persevere in the face of significant clinical complexity.

The next section of the book provides the background in social services and policy that clinicians need to know in order to practice effectively with older adults and their families, who almost inevitably will need more than just mental health resources. Among the more vexing tasks of expanding practice to work with any new population is figuring out the "lay of the land" of services that various clients will need. The topography of geriatric social services is shaped by policy and regulation at the federal, state, and local levels. Elmore and Tally provide a fascinating overview of federal policy issues that influence family care for older adults and clinicians working with caregiving families in Chapter 10. Auxier provides a practical guide to the diverse array of services available within most communities in Chapter 11. Giunta and Scharlach address variations and trends across states in the funding and structuring of social services in Chapter 12. The complex interplay among federal and state regulations ultimately shape the richness and format of local services and thus are key components of the knowledge base needed by geriatric mental health providers.

The final section of the book represents an emerging area of knowledge for mental health providers—the use of technology to improve quality of care and quality of life. Two chapters explore innovative approaches for addressing key challenges in family caregiving that have been developed by psychologists working across the boundaries of basic science and business solutions. In Chapter 13, Williams and Lewis describe a technological approach to helping elders participate in the electronic-communication network used by family members without requiring the elder to learn to use a computer or even a cell phone. The simple fax-type machine allows elders to submit handwritten materials, photographs, or other family artifacts that are scanned and sent to family members' e-technology of choice. Williams and Lewis have developed rich behind-the-scenes support systems to facilitate communication, if desired by users. These are but two of a myriad of technological innovations available to promote independence among family members and elders, support care demands, and foster well-being during the elder-care phase of family life. Other solutions are highlighted by organizations such as the Center for Aging Services Technologies that attempt to make technology more accessible to providers who can pass them along to families.

The first challenge addressed in Chapter 14 is managing multiple care providers, keeping good records, and advocating for coordinated care, which are some of the more complex challenges faced by family caregivers. Electronic health record systems are a hot area of innovation intended to support providers in providing higher quality of care, yet patients and families often are kept outside the official record-keeping system. In Chapter 14, Blechman provides an excellent orientation to the different types of electronic records, their strengths and weaknesses for older adults and their caregiving families, along with an introduction to a new technical solution to these challenges. She introduces characteristics of the next generation of electronic records by demonstrating how her person-centric personal health record extends beyond archiving to support coordination of care among diverse and dispersed health, social service, and residential providers. The second challenge is keeping older family members well-integrated into informal family communication channels that are increasingly occurring through technologies not yet embraced by most elders.

Finally, S. Zarit addresses the future of family caregiving in the Epilogue.

We hope you find this book challenges some of your assumptions, opens doors to new ways of practicing, and provides useful information that will influence your clinical practice. Regardless of the setting in which you provide services, or the services you provide to older adults, we hope this book helps you always *think family* when working with a client or patient in clinical practice.

REFERENCES

Qualls, S. H., & Knight, B. G. (2006). *Psychotherapy for depression in older adults.* New York: Wiley.

Qualls, S. H., & Smyer, M. A. (2007). *Changes in decision-making capacity in older adults: Assessment and intervention.* Hoboken, NJ : Wiley.

Zarit, S. H., Orr, N. K., & Zarit, J. M. (1985). *The hidden victims of Alzheimer's disease: Families under stress.* New York: New York University Press.

CHAPTER

1

Who Are the Aging Families?

ROSEMARY BLIESZNER

Adults typically grow old within multigenerational families. Ties with relatives are mostly positive experiences that supply companionship, provide numerous forms of support, and lend meaning to life. Of course, close relationships can include conflict and distress, as well. This chapter is introductory to the rest of the volume on interventions aimed at problematic aspects of late-life family ties. It sets the stage for the other discussions by focusing on the diversity of older adults' family structures and interactions. First is a detailed look at the definition of family for elderly persons, including illustrations of a range of family structures. Next is information about different types of old-age family ties. The final section addresses numerous personal, sociocultural, and historical influences on the nature of family interactions in the later years of life.

DEFINING OLDER ADULTS' *FAMILY*

Everyone has an intuitive idea of what the term *family* means; but when people articulate their views, many different perspectives become apparent. For example, individuals differ on how broad and permeable they consider the boundaries of family to be, with some viewing family as a fairly small and fixed group and others having a more encompassing and even shifting perspective on who is included. Understanding what people mean by *family* is crucial for psychologists because the definition influences who is important to patients, who is involved with them as they seek help, and who professionals consider when developing treatment and intervention plans.

Traditionally, anthropologists and sociologists used the term *family* to denote the nuclear family unit, composed of married partners and their children and situated within the larger kinship network (i.e., the group of all other relatives) (Adams, 1968). Another term for nuclear family is *family of procreation*, used to distinguish the married partners in each new nuclear family from their *family of origin*, comprising their parents and siblings. One problem with this traditional conception of family and its application in social science research and professional practice is that it marginalizes old people. That is, adult children belong to their parents' family of procreation, but their parents belong to the adult children's extended kin system, not to their family. This way of thinking about family leads some researchers and professionals to forget that old people both have relatives and are other peoples' relatives!

Another problem is that the traditional definition tends to pathologize family structures in African American, Native American, and other minority families that differ in composition from the mainstream patterns (Dilworth-Anderson, Burton, & Johnson, 1993). The chosen families of gay and lesbian persons who cannot legally marry are overlooked in the traditional definition (Savin-Williams & Esterberg, 2000), as are those of single adults (Amato, 2000; DePaulo, 2006). Families belonging to the minority by virtue of their racial ethnic group, class, single status, or sexual orientation often have open and fluid boundaries, with friends and neighbors (*fictive kin*), distant relatives, and older family members playing roles they might not play in traditional nuclear families (e.g., assuming parenting or caregiving responsibilities).

The U.S. Census Bureau perpetuates a narrow conception of family ("a group of two or more people who reside together and who are related by birth, marriage, or adoption"), which implicitly omits elders who reside in a different *household* ("all the people who occupy a housing unit as their usual place of residence") from that of their children, grandchildren, or siblings (U.S. Census Bureau, 2006). Although the Census definitions of family and household serve demographic functions, they are not very useful for capturing the essence of family that is most meaningful to people on a day-to-day basis: the functional and emotional aspects of relationships. Not only do the functional and emotional aspects of family ties often lend more meaning in everyday life than the formal structural dimensions do, they are also the chief reasons for individuals and families to seek assistance from psychologists. Even so, family interactions and the feelings family members hold for one another are connected to the different kinds of family structures, not dissociated from them. Thus, the purpose of this chapter is to provide an overview of important structural features of contemporary families in which older adults participate. Chapter 2 addresses specific family functions in greater detail.

We need to define family in such a way as to recognize old members as active participants. What is an alternative to the traditional definition of family as limited to the nuclear unit? Developing a definition that encompasses the experiences of older adults requires attending not only to the relatives with whom they interact regularly regardless of household status, but also to those who have psychological importance, even though they may be estranged or no longer living, and to fictive or chosen kin. With these considerations in mind, Victoria Bedford and I created the following definition of family: "A family is a set of relationships determined by biology, adoption, marriage, and . . . social designation, and existing even in the absence of contact or affective involvement, and in come cases, even after the death of certain members" (Bedford & Blieszner, 2000, p. 160). Our intention was to capture the experiences of many types of families and many personal perspectives, including both latent and potential family or family-like relationships. The implication of this definition is that it becomes crucial to ask individuals whom they consider to be part of their family, rather than assuming who belongs (which assumption would likely be based on the traditional nuclear family definition).

The necessity and importance of taking a broad perspective on family is illustrated by research that colleagues and I completed with older adults living independently in the community. We were curious about older adults' perspectives on contemporary family issues. We also wanted to learn about similarities or differences over generations in patterns of family life reflecting a continuum from traditional to nontraditional orientations. We coded as traditional or conventional the *ideal* nuclear family structure with its sequence of family events encompassing one heterosexual marriage, followed by birth of children, and enduring until the death of one spouse. Although this family type is often idealized by lay people, politicians, and professionals, it represents only 6% of the U.S. population (Jackson, Brown, Antonucci, & Daatland, 2005). In contrast, we coded any other pattern of family life as nontraditional or postmodern. Examples include families experiencing divorce, remarriage, gay or lesbian relationships, pregnancy before or outside of marriage, nonmarital cohabitation, singlehood, and the like (Allen, Blieszner, Roberto, Farnsworth, & Wilcox, 1999). We conducted detailed, in-depth interviews with 45 older women and men. We applied a comprehensive open-coding data-analysis process to transcripts of the interviews and used extensive verification procedures to identify themes related to family patterns.

We were not surprised to find that whereas 60% of the older adults had lived according to a conventional family model themselves, only 22% of their offspring had done so. Specifically, 15 female and 6 male elderly respondents reported the traditional pattern in their own lives but structural diversity in the families of their adult children. However, the other 24 cases reflected less typical patterns of family life. For 10 females and 4 males, both they and their adult children had nontraditional family structures, depicting the greatest complexity and variety of families in the sample. These families included as many chosen kin ties as legal and biological family ties, they portrayed egalitarian relationships, and they reflected adaptation to events and situations such as divorce, mental illness, incarceration, and death. For example, one man began rearing two young sisters-in-law right after he got married because his new wife's (and her sisters') mother died at that time. He considered those girls his daughters. Other elders and their offspring reared stepchildren or stepgrandchildren who were not biological kin, reared grandchildren after they thought their active parenting days were finished, or had friends playing more significant roles in their lives than their biological relatives. Atypically, another five females and one male reported that both they and their offspring had followed the conventional model of family life. Finally, most unusual of all were the four females who had experienced some type of structural diversity in their own lives but had children whose lives were conventional in that none had divorced and all were rearing their own children with their original spouses.

Contrary to ageist stereotypes, we found that the older adult participants mostly were accepting of nontraditional family patterns in their offspring's lives. Those who expressed intolerance of a certain lifestyle (e.g., biracial marriage, gay or lesbian partnership) actually had not experienced it within their own families. Moreover, some of the participants had themselves been living nontraditional lifestyles, demonstrating family structure heterogeneity in the older adult population. Thus, our findings show that older adults are not necessarily conservative or "set in their ways" and do not necessarily oppose social change. Based on their experiences, many clearly did not believe the traditional nuclear family is the only successful type of family life.

Discovering a wide range of family patterns across the generations in a sample drawn from small cities, towns, and rural areas in southwest Virginia suggests the likelihood of uncovering much diversity in the families of older adults from other locations, if researchers were only to ask the right questions. In fact, once a discussion starts about family (broadly defined), family history, and life events, elders often reveal very interesting situations and experiences that may not be apparent at first glance.

The information in this section provides a rationale for using a broad and inclusive definition of family. Research findings from a study of older adults revealed their acceptance of diverse family structures. The following section highlights typical family ties comprising older adults' family structures.

TYPES OF FAMILY TIES IN LATE LIFE

Depending on longevity of the oldest family members and spacing of successive generations, it is possible for contemporary families to contain four or even five generations for the first time in history. Thus, some older adults will still have surviving parents as the oldest generation in the family. Looking within their own generation, they are likely to have a spouse or romantic partner as well as siblings in their family. Succeeding generations probably include children, grandchildren, and possibly great-grandchildren.

Older adults with living parents assume regular responsibility for helping them to the extent they can, given their own functional health, geographic location, and financial circumstances. If they live close enough, they are likely to check on their older parents daily, prepare meals, provide shopping and transportation assistance, and complete household chores for them (Blieszner, Roberto, & Singh, 2002).

Although the majority of older men in the United States are married (72%), the proportion is smaller for older women (42%), who are more likely to be widowed (43% of older women vs. 14% of older men). Thus, over half (55%) of older adults live with a spouse, but nearly a third (30%) live alone due to widowhood, separation, or divorce (U.S. Census Bureau, 2007). Spouses and partners provide emotional support, companionship, and direct care to one another, and they help foster better physical and psychological health in each other (Connidis, 2001).

Sibling ties are a unique dimension of late-life family structure because siblings share potentially the longest-enduring close relationship of all (see Bedford, 1995). Studies using the National Survey of Families and Households show that adults tend to have at least monthly contact with their siblings for 60 or more years of adulthood and usually consider siblings as potential sources of support even if they do not actually help each other very often, particularly in advanced old age. Sister-sister relationships are strongest, and having living parents increases contact, affection, and exchanges of support among siblings (White, 2001; White & Reidmann, 1992).

Eighty percent of persons aged 65 years or more are parents (Connidis, 2001). Relationships with their adult children usually involve reciprocal exchanges of social and emotional support, shared leisure activities and companionship, and assistance with household chores throughout the adult years. Parents are more likely to provide financial assistance to their children than the reverse, however. As parents' functional health diminishes, they may receive more instrumental support and assistance from their children and grandchildren than previously. Next to spouses, adult children are most likely to provide elders with intense daily monitoring, meals, and numerous other forms of assistance.

Among the four-fifths of older adults who are parents, 94% have grandchildren and 50% have great-grandchildren (Giarrusso, Silverstein, & Bengtson, 1996). Grandmothers and grandfathers value their relationships with their grandchildren a great deal, although great-grandchildren seem less salient to them (Roberto, Allen, & Blieszner, 1999, 2001). Grandparents usually derive emotional satisfaction and a sense of generational continuity from interacting with grandchildren.

As indicated earlier, changes in mortality and fertility rates have led to families having fewer members in younger generations available to help with caregiving than in the past. Because such families may need assistance with caring for aged members, home health aides, who often spend quite a lot of intimate time with their clients and develop close relationships with them, represent a new category of fictive kin for old people (Piercy, 2000). Similarly, extended kin who would not ordinarily be primary care providers for old people with their own children may indeed be tapped to fill such a role for childless elders. In such cases, an older adult may elevate a more distant relative to a closer role in her or his family structure (e.g., "My niece is like a daughter to me. She would help me if I needed anything."). Finally, given current rates of divorce and remarriage, stepfamilies are increasingly common in the lives of older adults, leading to new questions within families about the obligations of steprelatives to help one another within and across the generations (Ganong & Coleman, 1998a, b).

The most common same-generation family relationships for older adults, then, are romantic and sibling ties; the usual multigenerational relationships are with children and grandchildren and, rarely, parents. Relatively little research has examined bonds of old people with their aunts and uncles, cousins, or nieces and nephews, although those relationships are important to at least some elders (Allen, Blieszner, & Roberto, 2008). Family ties depend not only on the composition of the family, but also on a host of personal, sociocultural, and historical influences, as discussed in the next section.

INFLUENCES ON OLDER ADULTS' FAMILY COMPOSITION AND EXPERIENCES

Personal characteristics of the individual members influence family experiences. So do cultural variations in the definition of family and family interaction patterns, historical and social changes, legal and policy matters, and the kinds of roles different family members play as they interact with one another.

Effects of Personal Characteristics

Being a woman or man, coming from a certain racial ethnic background, belonging to a particular socioeconomic class, preferring one or another sexual orientation, and enjoying good health or coping with illness or disability are key attributes that intersect with current age-group membership to define one's self-identity and place in society. These personal characteristics are socially delineated and have certain expectations and privileges attached to each. They create different opportunities and constraints for participating in society, and their effects are reciprocally influential and intertwined. Moreover, the meaning and influence of personal characteristics such as these change over time and differ across cultures (Allen, Fine, & Demo, 2000; Calasanti & Slevin, 2001). These influences on self-identity help shape family composition and experiences.

Although in the United States gender relations privilege men over women and race relations privilege Whites over Blacks, an example related to financial status in widowhood shows the impact of intersecting personal characteristics. In general, White widowers probably have more assets than White widows, as would be expected of White widowed persons overall compared to their Black counterparts. But Black widowers are likely to be worse off economically than White widows, and low-income Black women are the most economically disadvantaged of these four groups (Blieszner, 1993). These findings show the importance of considering multiple characteristics simultaneously rather than drawing conclusions based on assessment of only one feature at a time.

Contemporary society also privileges health over illness, youth over old age, and socially defined standards of beauty over perceived unattractiveness. If the focus is on these characteristics, gender privilege may not apply. Both old women and old men must grapple with the implications of changing bodies and increasing susceptibility to physical limitations in the context of ageist norms of youthful perfection. Still, the specific ways older adults experience changes in physical appearance and functional health, and the implications of those changes for psychological well-being, vary by gender, race, and sexual orientation (Holstein, 2006; Meadows & Davidson, 2006; Slevin, 2006).

As these two examples illustrate, intersecting social locations affect life experiences, sense of identity, opportunities for education and work, and many other important personal outcomes. This means that the members of a given family will have different experiences based on their gender and consequent pursuit of different opportunities while being subject to different constraints. It also means that families in the various socioeconomic classes and racial ethnic groups will have different chances and challenges in life.

Effects of Cultural Diversity

Given that the individuals comprising a family usually share a particular racial ethnic-group membership, the whole family is likely to resonate to the cultural norms prevalent within that group. Because these groups vary both within and between one another, their family structures and interaction patterns are likely to vary as well. In turn, the place of older adults within families and the degree of generational interdependence are a function of the attitudes and values of each subcultural group.

Recent analyses of family patterns reveal declining rates of marriage and remarriage, increasing rates of separation and divorce, and greater proportions of children living in single-parent households than was true for previous generations. Considering these trends, African American families have been changing much more rapidly than European American families. They are more likely than European American families to include extended kin and nonkin in their households, and the boundaries across families and households are more permeable than those of European American families. Moreover, African American families are more likely to be egalitarian, with flexible and complementary family roles (Taylor, 2000). But given diverse cultural heritage among persons descending not only from ancestors in Africa but also from those in Haiti, Jamaica, Trinidad, and other West Indian countries, many variations in these patterns can be observed among different Black families.

Latino families are also multicultural; this term refers to families of Mexicans, Puerto Ricans, Cubans, Central Americans, and South Americans. Nevertheless, scholars have observed a few general commonalities across these groups. For example, familism is prevalent, especially among Mexican families, leading them to value highly their family unity and solidarity within the extended kin network. Latino families have the largest concentration of offspring of all racial ethnic groups, and their children are less likely than those in any other group to live in nuclear families. Thus, the children and teenagers are socialized by multiple family members from multiple generations, not just parents, and learn a cooperative style of interaction. Recency of immigration to the United States is a key factor in determining the characteristics of Latino families, with more recent immigrants more likely to work in low-income jobs, to be separated from their extended kin and sometimes from nuclear family members, and to follow traditional family patterns such as male dominance in the household (Baca Zinn & Wells, 2000).

Asian American families include those of Chinese, Japanese, Korean, Filipino, and Southeast Asian descent. Although recognizing that variation exists among these groups as for other major cultural groups, studies show that Asian American individuals and families typically exhibit strong commitment to family, including accepting responsibility for care of elderly parents. Family members of all ages are usually included in family activities, rather than being separated by age group, and coresidence among adult children and at least one of their parents is common. Compared to European American families, Asian American families are more likely to emphasize higher levels of filial obligation and greater importance of shared decision making, and to have stronger mother-daughter bonds in adulthood (Hashimoto & Ikels, 2005; Ishii-Kuntz, 2000).

This section highlights only a few aspects of family values in a few U.S. cultural groups; many variations exist in the range of cultures found within the borders of this vast country. Each cultural group has its own views of the centrality of older family members in the affairs of the family as a whole, and each holds a perspective on where elders should live, what roles they should play in the family, and who should assist them. Individuals within the groups also vary, with some adhering strongly to traditions and others forging new family patterns. More information on cultural diversity among caregiving families appears in Chapter 3 of this volume.

Effects of Sociohistorical Time

Personal characteristics and families' cultural contexts intermingle with demographic shifts over time, adding to the mix of variables shaping intergenerational experiences (Hareven, 2001). Improved public health practices, better nutrition, and advanced medical technologies have contributed to greater longevity over time. With older adults living longer, families are likely to contain more generations than in previous eras, giving members opportunities to interact with multiple older or younger relatives to a greater extent than ever. These chances for crossgeneration involvement have potential both for enhancing the joyful aspects of family life and for increasing the sources of conflict (Mancini & Blieszner, 1989).

The movement away from the traditional nuclear family structure and the trend toward two-earner and single-parent households means that grandparents play a more active role in the daily lives of their grandchildren than in the middle of the previous century, when nuclear family households became the norm (Mueller, Wilhelm, & Elder, 2002). Today's grandparents often provide child care while parents work outside the home or assume responsibility for rearing the children of absentee parents. Reciprocally, increased life expectancy also means that family members surviving to old-old age are more likely to need care from younger generation members, including the possibility that several generations of family elders might need help simultaneously. But the emergence of the *beanpole* family (Hagestad, 1986; Bengtson, Rosenthal, & Burton, 1990), with more generations alive than in the past yet fewer members in each generation, suggests that the responsibility for elder care is shared across relatively fewer kin than might be the case with larger sets of siblings and cousins available (Jackson et al., 2005).

Both the proportion of never-married adults and the proportion of those who have not had children have increased over time (Saluter, 1995; Simmons & O'Neill, 2001). But marriage and parenthood are not prerequisites to family membership and the opportunities for support and happiness that family ties often provide. Indeed, nonmarried adults and nonparents do have family. Looking up the generational line, these individuals associate with their parents, aunts, and uncles; within their generation, they interact with their siblings and cousins; and looking downward, they have relationships with nieces and nephews. In addition, they often incorporate fictive kin into their personal family networks. Thus, contrary to stereotype, unmarried and childless elders are not necessarily lonely, unhappy, or lacking in emotional, social, or instrumental support. The key factor contributing to their well-being is whether the family pattern they experienced over the years corresponded to the one they preferred (DePaulo, 2006; Dykstra & de Jong Gierveld, 2004).

We see, then, that changing times and lifestyle patterns yield new family structures and situations for older adults (as well as for everyone else). New patterns require adaptation, but older persons are just as capable as anyone else of adjusting to the times, even though in the case of experiencing advanced longevity they are often forging a pathway without the benefit of family role models to imitate. Like younger people, they may need guidance on how to think about and cope with emerging family issues; also like younger people, they can benefit from professional intervention when any difficulties arise.

Effects of Legal and Policy Issues

Certain family patterns present unique challenges because of associated legal issues or policy restrictions. I have referred to one of them previously: situations in which grandparents take extensive or complete responsibility for rearing their grandchildren, often unexpectedly. Approximately 18% of older adults are grandparents living in households with one or more minor child, and 42% of them are responsible for rearing the grandchild(ren) (U.S. Census Bureau, 2003). Although becoming increasingly common, this is still an atypical family role for older adults. In many instances the grandparents assume custody to prevent their grandchildren from being fostered out of the family, but they do so at serious emotional and financial cost to themselves. Complicated legal and policy issues related to school-ing, health care, housing, and economic support attend this family pattern, particularly if the grandparents do not have legal custody of the grand-children. In addition, the middle generation of the immediate family may be absent, and the normative grandparent-grandchild relationships may be disrupted, requiring adjustment on the part of both the older adults and the minors (Hayslip & Goldberg-Glen, 2000; Henderson & Cook, 2005; Thomas, Sperry, & Yarbrough, 2000).

Another family structure in which legal and policy issues play a crucial role is that of lesbian, gay, bisexual, and transgender (LGBT) couples who engage in marital-like relationships. In states where these couples cannot legally marry, opportunities and protections related to income, housing, health care, and the like usually afforded heterosexual older persons as individuals and as partners are often denied. Legal and policy restrictions place older LBGT couples in types of economic and emotional jeop-ardy with which mainstream couples do not necessarily have to contend (de Vries, 2007; Harrington Meyer & Roseamelia, 2007).

As these examples show, legal and policy matters are not universally influential, but they affect particular groups of older adults differentially. Moreover, custodial grandparents or LGBT couples who are in the minor-ity because of race, class, health limitations, or other restrictions face additional complications related to those statuses on top of difficulties related to rearing grandchildren or having a minority sexual orientation.

Effects of the Multiplicity of Family Roles

Older adults engage in a wide range of family roles, including those that focus on relational ties and those that are task oriented. Depending on the number of generations alive in the family, relational roles may include romantic partner, parent, grandparent, adult child, grand-child, sibling, friend, neighbor, and comember of community organi-zations. Examples of task-oriented roles elders may play are caregiver, care receiver, worker or volunteer, organizer, social secretary, financial manager, chauffeur, housekeeper, and advocate. As with those who are younger, elders are highly likely to have responsibility for multiple roles simultaneously. Some of the overlapping roles might support each other, which enhances role performance and satisfaction. In contrast, other roles might interfere with each other, causing role conflict and distress or requiring more personal, social, or economic resources to manage. Like anyone else, when older adults have time for advance preparation or have models to use for guidance before assuming new roles, the transition is easier than when a role change occurs abruptly, without warning or preparation (Heckhausen, 2005).

The multiplicity of family roles in which older adults engage can contribute to sustaining their psychological well-being through having their social and emotional needs met and through supporting the needs of others as well (Baker, Cahalin, & Gerst, 2005; Weiss, 1998). This range of roles and attendant responsibilities can also contribute to experiencing stress and unhappiness if the demands are burdensome and interfere with health (Cohen, 2004) or if changing physical and mental capacities lead to a perceived loss of control in highly valued roles (Krause, 2007).

This section has highlighted some of the key personal and societal influences on family diversity among older adults. Constellations of influences intermingle with each individual's developmental trajectory, psychological maturity, social skills, and unique life experiences and events to affect interactions in both particular families and the subcultural groups they comprise.

CONCLUSION

This overview of family life in the later years demonstrates the utility of adopting a definition of family that acknowledges the full range of kin ties experienced by older adults. We have seen that elders are situated in an array of generations that may include their parents and is highly likely to include several younger generations. Their families usually contain relatives who are age peers as well, and fictive kin are often included. These bonds are sometimes conflicted but often provide extensive emotional, social, and instrumental support to older adults. Family relationships and support enrich older adults' lives and promote their health and well-being. The particular set of relatives and chosen family available to a given elder depends on a host of personal and societal variables that change over time and historical eras. Within the family, changing circumstances lead to changing roles, but most families respond adaptively. When troubles do occur, psychologists who consider all these dimensions and complexities of elders' family experiences when making assessments and designing intervention strategies are likely to find their work effective and rewarding.

REFERENCES

Adams, B. N. (1968). *Kinship in an urban setting.* Chicago: Markham.

Allen, K. R., Blieszner, R., & Roberto, K. A. (2008). *Reconstructing normal: How older adults reinterpret their relationships with family and friends.* Manuscript submitted for publication.

Allen, K. R., Blieszner, R., Roberto, K. A., Farnsworth, E. B., & Wilcox, K. L. (1999). Older adults and their children: Family patterns of structural diversity. *Family Relations, 48,* 151–157.

Allen, K. R., Fine, M. A., & Demo, D. H. (2000). An overview of family diversity: Controversies, questions, and values. In D. H. Demo, K. R. Allen, & M. A. Fine (Eds.), *Handbook of family diversity* (pp. 1–14). New York: Oxford University Press.

Amato, P. R. (2000). Diversity within single-parent families. In D. H. Demo, K. R. Allen, & M. A. Fine (Eds.), *Handbook of family diversity* (pp. 149–172). New York: Oxford University Press.

Baca Zinn, M., & Wells, B. (2000). Diversity within Latino families: New lessons for family social science. In D. H. Demo, K. R. Allen, & M. A. Fine (Eds.), *Handbook of family diversity* (pp. 252–273). New York: Oxford University Press.

Baker, L. A., Cahalin, L. P., & Gerst, K. (2005). Productive activities and subjective well-being among older adults: The influence of number of activities and time commitment. *Social Indicators Research, 73,* 431–458.

Bedford, V. H. (1995). Sibling relationships in middle and old age. In R. Blieszner & V. H. Bedford (Eds.), *Handbook of aging and the family* (pp. 201– 222). Westport, CT: Greenwood Press.

Bedford, V. H., & Blieszner, R. (2000). Personal relationships in later life families. In R. M. Milardo & S. Duck (Eds.), *Families as relationships* (pp. 157–174). New York: Wiley.

Bengtson, V., Rosenthal, C., & Burton, L. (1990). Families and aging: Diversity and heterogeneity. In R. H. Binstock & L. K. George (Eds.), *Handbook of aging and the social sciences* (3rd ed., pp. 263–287). New York: Academic Press.

Blieszner, R. (1993). A socialist-feminist perspective on widowhood. *Journal of Aging Studies, 7,* 171–182.

Blieszner, R., Roberto, K. A., & Singh, K. (2002). The helping networks of rural elders: Demographic and social psychological influences on service use. *Ageing International, 27,* 89–119.

Calasanti, T. M., & Slevin, K. F. (2001). *Gender, social inequalities, and aging.* Walnut Creek, CA: Alta Mira Press.

Cohen, S. (2004). Social relationships and health. *American Psychologist, 59,* 676–684.

Connidis, I. A. (2001). *Family ties and aging.* Thousand Oaks, CA: Sage.

de Vries, B. (2007). LGBT couples in later life: A study in diversity. *Generations, XXXI*(3), 18–23.

DePaulo, B. (2006). *Singled out.* New York: St. Martin's Press.

Dilworth-Anderson, P., Burton, L. M., & Johnson, L. B. (1993). Reframing theories for understanding race, ethnicity, and families. In P. G. Boss, W. J. Doherty, R. LaRossa, W. R. Schumm, & S. K. Steinmetz (Eds.), *Sourcebook of family theories and methods: A contextual approach* (pp. 627–646). New York: Plenum.

Dykstra, P., & de Jong Gierveld, J. (2004). Gender and marital-history differences in emotional and social loneliness among Dutch older adults. *Canadian Journal on Aging, 23,* 141–155.

Ganong, L. H., & Coleman, M. (1998a). An exploratory study of grandparents' and stepgrandparents' financial obligations to grandchildren and stepchildren. *Journal of Social and Personal Relationships, 15,* 39–58.

Ganong, L. H., & Coleman, M. (1998b). Attitudes regarding filial responsibilities to help elderly divorced parents and stepparents. *Journal of Aging Studies, 12,* 271–290.

Giarrusso, R., Silverstein, M., & Bengtson, V. L. (1996). Family complexities and the grandparent role. *Generations, XXII*(1), 17–23.

Hagestad, G. O. (1986). The aging society as a context for family life. *Daedalus, 115,* 119–139.

Hareven, T. (2001). Historical perspectives on aging and family relations. In R. H. Binstock & L. K. George (Eds.), *Handbook of aging and the social sciences* (5th ed., pp. 141–159). San Diego, CA: Academic.

Harrington Meyer, M., & Roseamelia, C. (2007). Emerging issues for older couples: Protecting income and assets, right to intimacy, and end-of-life decisions. *Generations, XXXI*(3), 66–71.

Hashimoto, A., & Ikels, C. (2005). Filial piety in changing Asian societies. In M. L. Johnson (Ed.), *The Cambridge handbook of age and ageing* (pp. 437–442). Cambridge, England: Cambridge University Press.

Hayslip, B., Jr., & Goldberg-Glen, R. (2000). *Grandparents raising grandchildren: Theoretical, empirical, and clinical perspectives.* New York: Springer Publishing Co.

Heckhausen, J. (2005). Psychological approaches to human development. In M. L. Johnson (Ed.), *The Cambridge handbook of age and ageing* (pp. 181–189). Cambridge, England: Cambridge University Press.

Henderson, T. L., & Cook, J. L. (2005). Grandma's hands: Black grandmothers speak about their experiences rearing grandchildren on TANF. *International Journal of Aging and Human Development, 61,* 1–19.

Holstein, M. S. (2006). On being an aging woman. In T. M. Calasanti & K. F. Slevin (Eds.), *Age matters* (pp. 313–334). New York: Routledge.

Ishii-Kuntz, M. (2000). Diversity within Asian American families. In D. H. Demo, K. R. Allen, & M. A. Fine (Eds.), *Handbook of family diversity* (pp. 274–292). New York: Oxford University Press.

Jackson, J. S., Brown, E., Antonucci, T. C., & Daatland, S. O. (2005). Ethnic diversity in ageing, multicultural societies. In M. L. Johnson (Ed.), *The Cambridge handbook of age and ageing* (pp. 475–481). Cambridge, England: Cambridge University Press.

Krause, N. (2007). Age and decline in role-specific control. *Journal of Gerontology: Social Sciences, 62B,* S28–S35.

Mancini, J. A., & Blieszner, R. (1989). Aging parents and adult children: Research themes in intergenerational relationships. *Journal of Marriage and the Family, 51,* 275–290.

Meadows, R., & Davidson, K. (2006). Maintaining manliness in later life. In T. M. Calasanti & K. F. Slevin (Eds.), *Age matters* (pp. 295–312). New York: Routledge.

Mueller, M. M., Wilhelm, B., & Elder, G. H., Jr. (2002). Variations in grandparenting. *Research on Aging, 24,* 360–388.

Piercy, K. W. (2000). When it is more than a job: Close relationships between home health aides and older clients. *Journal of Aging and Health, 12,* 362–387.

Roberto, K. A., Allen, K. R., & Blieszner, R. (1999). Older women, their children, and grandchildren: A feminist perspective on family relationships. *Journal of Women and Aging, 11,* 67–84.

Roberto, K. A., Allen, K. R., & Blieszner, R. (2001). Grandfathers' perceptions and expectations of relationships with their adult grandchildren. *Journal of Family Issues, 22*, 407–426.

Saluter, A. F. (1995). *Marital status and living arrangements.* U. S. Census Bureau. Retrieved February 6, 2008 from http://www.census.gov/population/ pop-profile/adobe/10_ps.pdf.

Savin-Williams, R. C., & Esterberg, K. G. (2000). Lesbian, gay, and bisexual families. In D. H. Demo, K. R. Allen, & M. A. Fine (Eds.), *Handbook of family diversity* (pp. 197–215). New York: Oxford University Press.

Simmons, T., & O'Neill, G. (2001). *Households and families: 2000.* U. S. Census Bureau. Retrieved February 6, 2008 from http://www.census.gov/ prod/2001pubs/c2kbr01-8.pdf.

Slevin, K. F. (2006). The embodied experiences of old lesbians. In T. M. Calasanti & K. F. Slevin (Eds.), *Age matters* (pp. 247–268). New York: Routledge.

Taylor, R. L. (2000). Diversity within African American families. In D. H. Demo, K. R. Allen, & M. A. Fine (Eds.), *Handbook of family diversity* (pp. 232–251). New York: Oxford University Press.

Thomas, J. L., Sperry, L., & Yarbrough, M. S. (2000). Grandparents as parents: Research findings and policy recommendations. *Child Psychiatry and Human Development, 31*, 3–22.

U.S. Census Bureau. (2003). *Statistical abstract of the United States: 2003* (Section 1. Population. No. 38, Persons 65 years old and over—grandparents, disability status, and language spoken at home: 2000). Washington, DC: U.S. Government Printing Office.

U.S. Census Bureau. (2006). *2006 American community survey.* Retrieved November 12, 2007 from http://factfinder.census.gov/home/en/epss/glossary_ f.html.

U.S. Census Bureau. (2007, June). *Older adults in 2005.* Washington, DC: Author. Retrieved November 12, 2007 from http://www.census.gov/population/ pop-profile/dynamic/OLDER.pdf.

Weiss, R. S. (1998). A taxonomy of relationships. *Journal of Social and Personal Relationships, 15*, 671–683.

White, L. (2001). Sibling relationships over the life course: A panel analysis. *Journal of Marriage and the Family, 63*, 555–568.

White, L. K., & Riedmann, A. (1992). Ties among adult siblings. *Social Forces, 71*, 85–102.

CHAPTER

2

<hr>

Functions Families Serve in Old Age

Karen L. Fingerman, Laura M. Miller, and Amber J. Seidel

Mary celebrated her 92nd birthday at a party with 43 people in attendance. She had a festive afternoon opening gifts and cards, talking with the guests, eating a piece of the full sheet cake necessary to feed the crowd, and watching young children scamper across the yard in a game of tag. It was not a particularly dramatic celebration in Mary's experience. In fact, the celebration was limited to Mary's immediate family, all direct descendants. Four of her living children, their spouses, her grandchildren, their partners or spouses, and an array of great-grandchildren gathered on a Sunday afternoon. A son and a daughter who resided out-of-town each called to convey their birthday wishes that day, and a grandson on active duty sent regards electronically via his father (Mary does not use e-mail).

After the party, Mary's eldest daughter, Cathy, and her husband drove her home to her apartment. Cathy and her husband had helped Mary purchase a new microwave oven earlier in the week, and Mary's son-in-law carried in the oven and began to set it up. Then, he used Mary's step ladder to change a light bulb while Mary and Cathy chatted. Cathy noticed a reminder note about a dentist appointment under a magnet on Mary's refrigerator and asked Mary if she wanted her to drive. Mary waved her hand and assured Cathy she would call one of the other children or take the senior cab service. Cathy and Mary decided to have lunch. Mary checked her calendar because her sister-in-law and niece were coming over one day that week, and she tries to limit her daily commitments due to waning energy. Cathy also had several conflicts involving her own grandchildren (Mary's great-grandchildren) that they had to work around. Mary was pleased to find a date to see Cathy and equally pleased when they started to leave, so she could rest after the busy party. Cathy noticed her mother was tired and grabbed the kitchen garbage on her way out the door.

Mary was going to watch TV, but realized there was a message from her sister, Alice. She called Alice back. Mary was the eldest in a sibship with four younger brothers and sisters. Not only did Mary make it to old age, but three of her siblings did as well. Mary's sister, Alice, who is 12 years younger, lives in town. They only talked briefly because Mary was to see Alice in a couple of days. Alice and Mary go to the hairdresser together every Tuesday, and Alice drives because Mary gave up her license 2 years ago.

Mary has achieved a perfect old age. She is surrounded by family who make her feel loved and who support her efforts to stay in her own home. Her children, grandchildren, siblings, and in-laws provide her with companionship and emotional support so that she is in a position to select the social events she has the energy to attend. Loneliness is never a problem. Mary has begun to grow weaker and frail in the past 5 years. Her family does the small tasks necessary to maintain a household that are just beyond Mary's reach: changing light bulbs, carrying trash bags to the dumpster, driving her to dentist appointments. They help her with issues that are outside common venues of knowledge for members of her birth cohort, such as using e-mail or purchasing a microwave oven. Her college-aged grandson used to come and change her VCR clock each October and April, but her niece recently helped her purchase a DVD player that does not need to be reset. And when health issues come up, be it a doctor's appointment or advice about treatment, one of Mary's children takes time off from work and helps her.

Mary is lucky to have such a large and stable family. Demographics were on her side. As a mother during the Baby Boom following World War II, Mary gave birth to seven children, six of whom are still living. Her seven children were not as prolific as Mary, but they still managed to produce 16 grandchildren, 10 of whom are grown and have children of their own. One of her children married three times and accumulated three stepchildren along the way. These children treat Mary as a step-grandmother; they do not offer her any specific help, but they remember her at the holidays. Granted, there is no way to intervene for older adults who lack Mary's fertile fortune. Further, family formation has undergone dramatic changes since the 1960s, and older adults in the future are unlikely to have the sort of highly stable network of grown siblings who are available to assist an aging parent (Hughes & Waite, 2006). Yet, Mary's situation sets up a contrast in comparison to the gaps that exist for less fortunate older adults and their limited progeny and step-progeny.

Genetics and a lifestyle that sustained health gave Mary a boost as well. Mary has no specific health problems per se, beyond some typical markers of decline characteristic of a woman over aged 90. Her eyesight is poor at night. She has osteopenia and also requires medication for elevated blood pressure. She finds that her energy level is waning and she tires easily. But on the whole, Mary fares better than many of her age-peers who suffer from cognitive or physical disabilities necessitating hands-on care with cooking, bathing, or getting to the toilet.

Mary's family members work together to provide Mary with support that can sustain an older adult to live independently. The family runs smoothly so that Mary's children cooperate rather than compete for Mary's affection or brood on past resentments (see Fingerman & Bermann, 2000, for a discussion of family systems in adulthood). They each take on small tasks on a frequent basis. In essence, Mary's siblings and her children and their families have formed together as Team Mary to spread out the necessary demands. In this manner, no one child, child-in-law, or grandchild feels particularly burdened by providing the total assistance Mary requires.

In this chapter, we discuss the help Mary's family members provide and when and why such support may be absent. At the onset, however, we provide a few caveats. Although we focus on Mary as a case of a person in need, she is something of an exception due to her advanced age. Despite accumulating health problems, most elderly adults are fairly independent until the final years of their lives. For example, Mary's daughter, Cathy, is 70-years-old herself, and one might consider her an *elder*. Yet, Cathy is busy helping her grown children by taking her grandchildren to activities and stepping up to do small tasks for Mary. Further, Mary's sister, Alice, recently turned 80 and she drives Mary to her hair appointment each week. This chapter will deal with the fuzzy ground of old age between being fully independent like Cathy and Alice, and requiring hands-on care. There is often a prolonged period of steady decline when families must deal with accumulating health problems and needs, but the older adult may not require daily complete assistance. We have referred to this period as the *transition to old age* (Fingerman, Hay, Kamp Dush, Cichy, & Hosterman, 2007). Mary falls in the transition to old-old age.

Second, this chapter will discuss children's support of elderly parents (i.e., intergenerational assistance of the aged). Again, offspring support to parents is somewhat anomalous in the chain of intergenerational relationships. Throughout life, and even in adulthood, most support flows from parent to child, rather than the other way around (McGarry & Schoeni, 1997; Zarit & Eggebeen, 2002). Thus, when adult offspring begin to help older adults, they may experience difficulties. Further, such intergenerational support pertains primarily to older adults who do not have spouses, especially widows. When an older adult does have a spouse, the spouse provides the vast majority of assistance. Support with daily tasks such as cooking and shopping are considered part of marriage and are unlikely to be considered in clinical discussions associated with aging. Thus, we limit our consideration of spousal support to coping with chronic illness, an area where even spouses often experience stress when trying to assist.

In the remainder of this chapter, we discuss the types of support families provide to older adults who are still residing in their homes. We first provide a brief overview of public programs that assist older adults and explain why families end up providing the bulk of daily help to older adults. Then, we consider the ways in which families may be effective in providing forms of support directly linked to psychological well-being, such as companionship, emotional support, stimulation, and interest in one's daily life. Finally, we turn to help with tasks and to tangible or financial support that may affect physical well-being more. Of course, psychological well-being and physical health are inherently linked, but for ease of presentation we consider emotional and instrumental or financial help separately.

NONFAMILIAL PUBLIC PROGRAMS TO ASSIST THE ELDERLY

Americans have relatively few public programs to assist older adults who wish to remain in their homes despite health declines. Western European countries (notably Sweden) typically provide a considerable range of government-sponsored services. Such programs include high-quality home health-care providers who assist with tasks such as shopping, rearranging the furniture to facilitate independent living, administering medication, and toileting and personal hygiene. In the United States, most of these tasks fall on family members. Unless elderly adults require skilled nursing care available in nursing homes, families have few options for public or paid providers. In the following we provide a brief overview of public programs that do assist older adults.

Two publicly funded programs address health care of older adults—Medicare and Medicaid. The two programs function differently and cover different groups of senior citizens.

Medicare is a health insurance program under the Social Security administration and Health and Human Services that provides reimbursement to physicians and hospitals for medical treatment of adults who are over the age of 65. Medicare is comprised of several parts: Medicare A, Medicare B, and Medicare D, or pharmaceutical coverage. In addition, many seniors opt to pay for Medigap, a private policy to cover expenses not covered through Medicare Part A or B. Medicare Part A is funded through payroll deductions. Individuals are eligible for Medicare A if they have worked for 10 years in a job with Medicare deductions and are over age 65. Medicare A only covers fairly urgent health-care needs, such as hospital stays, and does not cover routine care like check-ups, medications, oxygen for home use, or hearing aids. The other parts of Medicare cover a broader array of health-care services, involve voluntary enrollment, and require monthly payments from the older adults themselves. In some states, Medicaid will pay for older adults' Medicare B expenses or pharmaceutical needs if they are eligible for Medicaid.

Medicaid, a public policy program for the poor, includes two requirements that render the program undesirable to many families. First, Medicaid is an income needs-based program, which means that individuals must have few assets to be eligible. The program covers a variety of specific populations including children, the disabled, the blind, and pregnant women who meet the income requirements. For seniors, eligibility for Medicaid is limited to U.S. citizens and legal immigrants over the age of 65 who are persistently poor or who have become impoverished by long-term care spending. States administer Medicaid and set income thresholds, with many states setting qualifying monthly income below $800. Individuals also must have limited assets (below $2,000 in many states) and, further, they must contribute nearly all of their income to the costs of their care.

Medicaid is often the family's last resort in the process of seeking medical coverage for older adults who suffer from frailty or dementia. Medicare coverage of long-term care needs is limited to posthospitalization rehabilitative stays that cannot exceed 100 days, so older adults suffering disabilities cannot rely on Medicare for services. From the mid- to late-twentieth century, families had to "spend down" and give up the older adult's financial assets to qualify for Medicaid when the need for long-term care arose (O'Brien, 2005). Although the Medicaid system has implemented some attempts to fix these issues (e.g., allowing spouses to retain their homes), it still leads many older adults to give up their resources in exchange for benefits of Medicaid.

In addition, Medicaid has set up a system in which long-term care occurs in nursing homes, rather than at home. Such skilled care is inappropriate for an older adult like Mary, who is capable of residing on her own but needs a bit of assistance. And of course, one of the great fears of old age is ending up in a nursing home—no one *desires* this outcome.

Of course, alternates do exist and care of the elderly is not limited to extreme images presented in a stark choice between "urine-scented nursing home" of Medicaid versus "family members quit their jobs to care for mom." Innovations in nursing-home design and implementation have improved the quality of care in many facilities in the past 2 decades. Several new alternatives to traditional nursing homes integrate family members into life at the facilities and use gardens and pets or small home-like living units to make this residential care more comfortable and individualized (see Angelelli, 2006; Cohen-Mansfield, & Bester, 2006; Rabig, Thomas, Kane, Cutler, & McAlilly, 2006 for descriptions). Families may remain hopeful that such services are available in their area or that such nursing homes will become more widespread. At the moment, however, families do remain a mainstay of support, particularly for elders like Mary who would not belong in a skilled care facility.

Several states also have developed Medicaid-funded alternatives to nursing-home care for older adults who suffer impairments in daily activities (Feinberg & Newman, 2004). The idea behind such programs is to provide the type of in-home health care necessary for older adults to remain in the community rather than moving to a skilled nursing facility. Such programs are cost effective in the long run for states. Nonetheless, these programs require financial capital from the state to get started, and they tend to be underfunded and to have long waiting lists. The programs target persons who qualify for nursing-home placement based on their need for assistance with activities of daily life. People with less intensive disabilities, such as Mary, also require home-based care, but they cannot access these Medicaid waiver programs and thus the burden of care falls to family. Likewise, even in states that have these innovative programs, there is a shortage of at-home care services, and older adults often still end up in a nursing home. For example, the state of Indiana has a Medicaid waiver program that serves adults who have developmental disabilities as well as older adults in need of care. There are approximately 4,500 slots available for these waivers that provide in-home services. The waitlist for a Medicaid waiver slot is 2 to 3 years. Another Hoosier program intended to allow low- and moderate-income older adults to remain in their homes through home health services, Indiana CHOICE (Community and Home Options to Institutional Care for the Elderly), passed the state legislature unanimously years ago but never received *any* funding. The situation in Indiana is not atypical. In other words, even states that pay lip service to home care for the elderly still treat family care as a prerogative and obligation and the first line of defense for older adults.

For the financially well-off elderly, continuous care retirement communities (CCRCs) provide resources that can replace certain functions that families might otherwise provide for older adult relatives. Many of these communities are situated in large buildings or even on campuses with multiple buildings. The facilities typically include independent living apartments similar to what Mary currently has, assisted living units for older adults who require additional help with a limited range of activities, and nursing-home care for those who require skilled care. CCRCs may have a shared dining space, where older adults who live independently congregate for one or more meals a day. Although such communities meet many of the needs of older adults, including the ability to reside in the same facility as health declines accrue, CCRCs are more expensive than the average older adult can afford. Most communities require a large fee upon entrance to the facility of up to several hundred thousand dollars, followed by monthly payments (AARP, 2004).

Popular media also have reported a rising tide of community-based assistance, where older adults organize themselves to provide care for one another or purchase lower cost assistance from prescreened providers. For example, older adults in one neighborhood near Washington, DC banded together to deal with the demands of aging in their homes. They formed a community collective that organizes services for the elderly. Members can pay for a willing handyman who has been prescreened or have someone to check in on them during the snowbound days of winter (Gross, 2007). These communities are few and far between, however, and are primarily found in high-income areas. Informal neighborhood support has steadily declined over the past 30 years (Putnam, 2000). Whereas neighbors were a source of support for many older adults 30 years ago (Cantor, 1979), families cannot count on neighbors as a steady source of help with daily tasks today.

In the end, families are the mainstay of support to older adults in America. Government programs are poorly funded and in many cases badly implemented. Given constraints on the U.S. budget and the rising population of older adults, it is unlikely that this tide will turn in the near future. Western European nations are also facing budget constraints for their high-caliber programs, and it is unlikely that the U.S. government will mount such efforts. Private-pay expenses for the type of assistance Mary requires to remain at home are prohibitive for all but the wealthiest older adults. Moreover, Mary (and many older adults) prefers the help of family members to assistance from a paid stranger. Thus, the informal support of family members remains at the forefront of daily life for older adults who are in decline in the United States.

TYPES OF FAMILY SUPPORT

Family members do not suddenly arise like a phoenix at the end of life with outstretched arms. Rather, families exchange different types of support throughout life. In early life, parents are fully responsible for everything for their children, from clothing to burping. After children leave home, however, patterns of support become more complex, with different family members stepping in to provide different support at different stages of life. At one point, a mother may spend hours on the phone coaching her young-adult daughter through a car loan. At another point, the daughter may console her divorced mother over the break up of a romantic tie.

Researchers have devoted considerable attention to how and from whom adults get the support that helps sustain mental and physical well-being. Scholars conceptualize support in a variety of ways, but they typically focus on a few dimensions including: (a) information or advice (e.g., help with an important decision), (b) emotional support (e.g., ability to confide problems), (c) financial or material assistance,

(d) practical assistance (e.g., child care, transportation), (e) care when sick, and (f) companionship or shared leisure activities (Eggebeen & Davey, 1998; Silverstein, Gans, & Yang, 2006; Vaux, 1988; Vaux & Harrison, 1985). Needs for these forms of support are common throughout adulthood, but in late life the need for practical assistance may increase as physical health declines. Further, companionship and emotional support provided by a spouse may be absent following widowhood.

We consider these forms of support along with some lesser researched topics. For example, the modern American medical system can involve multiple specialists for a given health problem and places decision making with the patient. Thus, older adults may seek guidance from family with medical decisions (Fingerman et al., 2007; Roberto, 1999). Moreover, individuals may need assistance handling technology, such as purchasing equipment, using software, or configuring different forms of telecommunications. Research examining technological support is sparse, but the Pew Internet Survey recently included a question regarding help purchasing a new computer (Boase, Horrigan, Wellman, & Rainie, 2006). Nearly a third of the large national sample in that survey had turned to a close friend or family member for help with this task. Given the constant pace of advances in technology and features on gadgets, families may be a source of information for older adults regarding these newer technologies.

Conceptually, we might consider these different forms of support under two broader rubrics: (a) support that facilitates emotional or psychological well-being and (b) support that facilitates physical well-being. Clearly, psychological and physical well-being are linked, but it may be helpful to think about the ways in which families can listen to older adults, offer or receive advice, and provide companionship as distinct from the hands-on tasks or material support limited to those who are either nearby or who have financial resources to share.

Support that Facilitates Psychological Well-Being

Roughly speaking, there are three types of emotional functions we might consider with regard to relationships in late life. Feeling loved is an emotional function that is often overlooked in the general support literature, but that is of great value throughout life. A second function involves buffering against accumulating deficits and losses. Finally, older adults, like younger adults, enjoy engaging in activities with other people. Shared activities and companionship may help not only emotional well-being, but cognitive functioning as well.

The need to feel loved by others is a basic human need (Baumeister & Leary, 1995). As individuals age, they place greater emphasis on relationships that are close and meaningful (Carstensen, 2006). The proverbial deathbed wish for more time with family and less time at the office plays out as older adults' desires to be with their closest loved ones. Moreover, in general, older adults report that they have more positive ties with their family members and fewer problems in these ties than do younger adults (Fingerman, Hay, & Birditt, 2004). Thus, older adults are primed to enjoy their families and garner possible emotional benefits.

Having good relationships is beneficial to older adults. Older adults who have positive relationships with others also report better psychological well-being, even when faced with stressful events of late life. One study conducted in countries all over the world found that feeling a positive connection with only one or two people can offset the negative consequences of widowhood, financial strain, and illness in late life (Antonucci et al., 2002). Another study showed that elderly parents who felt close to even one of their children were less likely to die following widowhood; perceiving a strong bond with at least one child enhanced parental survival during a period of extreme stress (Silverstein & Bengtson, 1991).

Such high-quality relationships may benefit older adults through provision of emotional support. When people have someone who listens when they are upset and who cares about their thoughts and problems, they are less likely to report feelings of depression or anxiety (Ingersoll-Dayton, Morgan, & Antonucci, 1997; Newsom, Rook, Nishishiba, Sorkin, & Mahan, 2005; Rook, 2001). Yet, provision of emotional support to older adults can be challenging for family members. Family members can convey feelings of love to their older adult relatives via notes and cards or small gestures. Older adults may simply assume they are loved by virtue of their past relationships with these family members.

But family members face challenges in providing appropriate emotional support to older adults.

Differences in experiences and life roles can contribute to a lack of shared understanding. Elsewhere, we referred to *developmental schisms* to describe the discrepancies between parents and offspring that can generate tensions (Fingerman, 2001). Developmental schisms arise when family members differ in their values for their relationships, in their experiences, or in their current life situations. For very aged adults, like Mary, developmental schisms may or may not be a problem. In Mary's case, her daughter Cathy who is 70 is able to connect and relate to most of Mary's experiences and offer her emotional support. But Cathy may have difficulty getting similar support from her 40-year-old daughter. Cathy's daughter, Lauren, is busy with work, while Cathy is retired. Lauren has 3 teenaged children, each of whom has his or her own activities and social schedule, requiring supervision and transportation from Lauren. Cathy relates to Mary's health problems because she herself went through a bout of breast cancer 2 years ago. Lauren was solicitous and helpful to Cathy during her cancer, but Cathy did not want to impose on her daughter given the other demands in Lauren's life. And Lauren could not truly offer the emotional support Cathy needed at that time; Lauren simply did not understand how Cathy felt. For that, Cathy was fortunate to turn to her peers who had experienced similar health problems over the years.

Unfortunately, the ability to turn to peers diminishes by oldest old age as individuals outlive their age mates. In a study of adults over age 85, Johnson and Barer (1997) described conversations in which the very aged indicated they would trade time with a dozen grandchildren for just one good friend. Thus, young family members can be stymied in the inability to connect via shared experiences. Generational disparities may be particularly evident with regard to amusements, entertainment, and jokes. Young people cannot reminisce about shows or commercials they have never seen. Older adults are less interested in the hip music that younger generations gravitate toward. Young people do not relate to losses that are foreign to them and struggle to support aging family members through difficult transitions. Morgan (1989) found that widows felt their offspring misunderstood their feelings of weakness and vulnerability and, thus, were unable to offer the emotional support and comfort they needed. Many of these widows turned to one another for such solace instead.

Family members may also fall into old patterns of behaviors when new crises arise. Family systems theory has primarily focused on the systems and subsystems that can develop within families as parents raise children. Early patterns of resentment or of feeling underappreciated can arise anew when aging parents require help and multiple siblings and a spouse must negotiate who and how to provide that support (Fingerman & Bermann, 2000).

Structural barriers can also hinder the provision of emotional support in late life. When offspring reside far away from parents, the parties tend to report relationships of equally high quality as when offspring reside nearby parents (Lawton, Silverstein, & Bengtson, 1994). Yet, researchers have noted distant offspring confront difficulties providing practical assistance from far away (Ikkink, van Tilburg, & Knipscheer, 1999). Such distant offspring also may have a harder time providing emotional support to their parents. Although cheap long distance allows easy communication for sharing daily life and family events, telephone communication precludes physical contact such as hugs, kisses, and touches that conveys feelings of regard (Moss, Moss, & Moles, 1985). Further, the auditory nature of telephone communication does not provide access to visual facial cues involved in emotional sharing. Thus, offspring who live far from parents may have to work harder to provide emotional support during difficult times.

Further, distant offspring are not able to share the final form of emotional support we consider here—companionship and shared leisure activities. Researchers examining companionship between young adults and their parents report that the majority of parents and offspring are companions. Eggebeen and Davey (1998) examined companionship between adult children and parents who were over the age of 50. Of the sample, 69% of parents and 74% of the adult children reported mutual companionship. Companionship may be very different as adults grow older or move further apart, however. For instance, in the Berlin

Aging Study, adults aged 70 to 103 participated with others in leisure activities when they themselves did not experience difficulties performing daily tasks. However, if these older adults experienced difficulty with daily tasks, they often participated in leisure activities (e.g., television viewing) alone (Lang & Baltes, 1997). Likewise, when cognitive problems interrupt task competence, older adults may lack skills to arrange or engage in complex social or leisure activities.

But older adults who report few activities involving companionship do not necessarily suffer physical or cognitive problems. Research examining solitude among the well elderly is scant, but the desire for time alone may be greater in late life. Certainly, the desire for active leisure that demands energy, such as attending large parties, dampens in late life. Some older adults may experience a diminished need for companionship or shared activities with other people. In sum, needs for emotional connection and support remain, but the need for active companionship may diminish.

Not only do adults participate in leisure activities alone as they age, they also often become widows and therefore live alone. The American Changing Lives Survey shows that 61% of adults aged 65 or older live alone compared to 9% of middle-aged adults (Schnittker, 2007). However, 48% of adults 70 or older live alone without difficulty (Lang & Baltes, 1997). Yet, living alone does not necessarily generate loneliness. Researchers find that older adults are unlikely to report feeling lonely simply because they live alone (Schnittker, 2007). For example, adults in Berlin who lived alone reported feeling more independent (Lang & Baltes, 1997). In fact, the more social contacts they reported, the less independent they felt.

Nonetheless, because so many older adults live alone, research has examined how loneliness influences health and well-being (Cacioppo, Hawkley, and Berntson, 2003). Studies reveal that individuals who reported greater loneliness consumed more alcohol and experienced higher levels of perceived stress than those who do not feel lonely. Yet, adults who experienced a high level of loneliness engaged in the same number of physical activities as adults who experienced a low level of loneliness. Therefore, loneliness does not keep adults from doing activities that benefit their health (e.g., exercise), but it may contribute to more detrimental behaviors (e.g., increased alcohol consumption).

Support for Physical Well-Being

Family members are not simply a source of emotional grounding for older adults, but they also provide assistance with a range of tasks that sustain daily life. These tasks may place greater demands than providing emotional support in terms of time, material resources, and physical energy. Throughout adulthood, individuals depend on other people for help in daily life. Short people ask taller roommates to reach jars on the upper shelves, people going away on vacation have a neighbor bring in the mail, and as mentioned previously, spouses are engaged in an intricate dance in which one partner runs to the grocery store while the other partner pays bills. Typically, people try to reciprocate when someone does a favor—the person who had a neighbor bring in his mail in July uses his snow blower to help dig out the neighbor's driveway in December. Older adults may not be able to repay each favor tit for tat, however. Different accounting schemes may come into play.

Researchers have examined the balance sheets of family assistance. Social exchange theory suggests that adults generally attempt to give and receive reciprocally in their relationships. But exchange theory does not apply directly to cases like Mary's. Mary cannot return the support she receives from her family with comparable favors—and her family members do not expect her to do so. These family relationships have endured for decades.

Mary's children remember how much help she provided in the past, and they seek to repay longer term debts they feel toward her. Offspring typically step up to the plate more than other relatives because they feel beholden to their parents for what they received when they were younger. Such offspring frame the situation in terms of overall *equity*, considering the balance of favors over their lives (Silverstein, Conroy, Wang, Giarrusso, & Bengston, 2002). An elderly mother cannot help dig out the driveway in December, but she may have helped purchase that first snow blower for a young couple 20 years ago. Families who use exchange systems that tally early support can be very supportive in late life by giving the older adult some slack when they can no longer help in return. Yet, this system also has potential pitfalls.

For older adults who have divorced and remarried, available intergenerational assistance may be fragmented. If parents divorce when children are young, when the children later grow up, they tend to feel disenfranchised from their fathers and feel less obligated to offer support (Webster & Herzog, 1995). Likewise, remarriage can introduce complexities with regard to who should offer help to which older parent. If parents remarry in late life, their progeny may not view the new stepparent as a relative who warrants their time and resources. Although stepchildren do believe they should sometimes step in to support elderly stepparents, it is typically only when needs are dire (Ganong & Coleman, 2006), rather than with the type of everyday assistance Mary's children casually proffer.

Nonetheless, offspring may experience feelings of stress and strain in providing support to an older parent, particularly if they come from families with less available support than Mary's family. As is discussed in Chapter 4, the lifespan view of exchange (where offspring repay what they received as children) implies that offspring are available when parents require help. The time required to assist parents can conflict with the many other roles middle-aged adults occupy, including ties to their own grown children or demands at work.

We also note that feelings of obligation to care for elderly family members differ across ethnic groups. Researchers conducted a 10-year study of older adults from four ethnic groups in the United States: African American, Latino, Filipino, and Cambodian Americans (Becker, Beyene, Newsom, & Mayen, 2003). Older adults in the different ethnic groups talked about what they received from their grown children and what they expected to receive. The African American older adults tended to continue to provide care for the younger generations most often. African American older adults preferred to live alone, but they often offered their homes to younger relatives as a place to stay. By contrast, all but three of the Cambodian older adults resided with a grown son or daughter, and they expected the son or daughter to honor and care for them in old age as part of Khmer Buddhism. Nonetheless, the Cambodian older women were responsible for cooking, cleaning, and caring for children while the middle generation worked. The Latino older adults also often resided with their children, but they were often dissatisfied with their intergenerational ties. Latino older adults were the least likely in the study to report receiving financial support, but their cultural values led them to expect such support from their children. Likewise, a review of studies examining multiple cultures and ethnic groups revealed considerable differences in the stresses middle-aged adults experienced when providing hands-on care for the elderly (though information on everyday assistance was not specifically addressed; Janevic & Connell, 2001). In particular, White caregivers were more likely to be spouses than other groups (e.g., African Americans, Chinese, Chinese Americans, Koreans, Korean Americans, Latinos, residents of 14 European Union countries) and were also more likely to report feelings of depression.

In sum, individuals from different ethnic groups hold differing expectations about what family members should provide to aging parents. Moreover, even when family members hold similar views and expectations of support, the ability to provide such assistance in ways that are beneficial to both parties can present a tightrope dance.

Developmental schisms and tensions can arise when parents' health begins to decline. Offspring report ambivalence (i.e., feeling torn between positive and negative feelings) when their parents are in poor health (Fingerman, Chen, Hay, Cichy, & Lefkowitz, 2006). In one of our prior studies, we interviewed older adults who were relatively independent but who had experienced hearing loss, vision loss, and other chronic health conditions (e.g., arthritis). We then also interviewed their grown child who knew most about their health problems (Fingerman et al., 2007). The parents and their offspring reported that their relationships had improved in recent years and that they enjoyed one another more than ever. Yet, health problems also can introduce conflicting emotions. Grown children were surprisingly accurate in reporting their parents' health problems and ability to function independently, with offspring's reports matching closely with the older adults' medical records. In situations where the parents' health was declining and where parents were losing functional ability, offspring reported that they found their relationship more difficult, and offspring noted how much more they had to do for their parents than they had in the past.

Although people sometimes casually refer to such changes as a *role reversal*, the roles do not actually reverse. Caring for a parent is nothing like the experience of raising a child; the parenting experience is one of preparing a child for future independence. Offspring feel conflicted because they are doing tasks for a parent who used to be independent, but who is growing increasingly dependent. As offspring step up to help parents, they and their parents are admitting that parents are in decline and heading toward the end of life.

The parents' reactions to requiring help can add to offspring's conflicted feelings. Of course, there is considerable variation in how individuals cope with problems of aging, and some of that variability may reflect long-standing personality or relationship issues. Nonetheless, family members who are overly zealous in their attempts to help older adults may undermine, rather than enhance, the older adult's quality of life. Adults of all ages find unsolicited help to be generally unpleasant (Smith & Goodnow, 1999). Moreover, when older adults who are in decline receive assistance with tasks they could struggle to do on their own, they may lose functional abilities to perform those tasks in the future. Much evidence for this loss of abilities comes from research on the *disablement process* conducted in nursing homes, where nursing aids or assistants undermined the older adults' remaining abilities by doing daily tasks for them or by ignoring them when they did the tasks for themselves (Baltes, 1996). A study of this process in the community revealed a similar pattern, where family members did not provide appropriate responses to older adults' independent behaviors or they rushed in to provide too much support (Baltes & Wahl, 1992).

When older adults are relatively healthy, they may also feel irked by their grown children's efforts to assist or offer advice. In one study of very healthy older mothers and their grown daughters, the daughters were keenly aware of their mothers aging (almost every daughter mentioned something about her mother growing older during the interviews). The mother sometimes resented this interest in her aging because it made her feel less competent and perhaps made her think about future declines she might incur (Fingerman, 2001). Family help is not always detrimental to older adults, but the situation is complex. For example, a recent study revealed that when offspring worry more about their parents, the parents feel more irritated with those offspring, but they also feel more loved by those offspring (Hay, Fingerman, & Lefkowitz, 2007). Help may be essential to the survival of the older adult as is the case for Mary, but it is also emotionally challenging to give and receive that support.

Finally, we comment on an area of support that may require particular attention among older adults—the need for medical advice and assistance with the medical system. Typically, older adults are capable of making medical decisions, and their decisions reflect their knowledge, the disease, and their emotional attachments to others (Roberto, Weeks, & Matheis-Kraft, 2001). Yet, older adults face daunting demands to make such decisions, given that they typically have greater needs for medical care than younger adults do and that the systems they use are complicated. With age, adults also typically incur mild declines in processing abilities, which can carry over into increased difficulties dealing with new and intricate medical information (Park, Morrell, & Shifren, 1999).

Older adults confront problems seeking medical care because they must deal with systems that are both private (in terms of care providers) and public (in terms of Medicare assistance). Increasingly, older adults who suffer from cancer or other medical problems are forced to navigate among multiple specialists and care providers, in the absence of a central hub or generalist to help schedule appointments or offer referrals. Likewise, the Medicare system is very complicated, with a wide variety of choices and options that can tax older adults. When the new Medicare D, pharmacy plan came on board, many seniors had a difficult time figuring out which of the complicated plans would cover their myriad prescriptions. The government primarily provided Web-based assistance, despite the fact that over two thirds of adults aged 65 or older did not access the Internet (Demographics of Internet Users, 2007). Older adults may be dependent on their web-savvy offspring or even grandchildren to help them navigate decisions, paperwork, and health-care providers. Area Agencies on Aging also received funding to help counsel older adults. Nonetheless, news reports indicated that nearly half of older adults turned to their children for help figuring out which prescription plan to select (CBS news, 2005).

Furthermore, even after they obtain medical insurance and care, older adults benefit from family involvement. Individuals who have family support may experience health benefits due to the medical care they receive. Physicians often do not provide adequate care to patients who appear to be socially isolated (Cacioppo et al., 2003). Physicians report that they provide better medical care to patients whose families are involved. Research examining physician care points to the need to consider the family's role in helping older adults receive maximum benefits from their health-care providers.

CONCLUSION

Family is the mainstay of support for many older adults. Even individuals who are able to reside independently depend on family members for an increasing array of daily tasks and for emotional connection and support as they experience the transition to old-old age. Family members may experience a prolonged period, lasting for years, while the older adult gradually requires increasing assistance but is not eligible for formal or government-supported programs.

Even when older adults have easy-going personalities and loving families, providing assistance can be wrought with stress. A number of factors in modern American life introduce uncertainties and challenges for middle-aged adults who help elderly relatives. Smaller family sizes leave fewer individuals in any given generation to care for the generation above. In coming decades, families such as Mary's (who opened this chapter) will be rare. Marital dissolution generates complicated family forms in which norms for helping parents and stepparents may not be clear. Further, individuals who provide help face constraints of their own lives while trying to help their aging parent or relative. Dual careers and increasing commuting times leave less available flexibility for these adults to provide help on a daily basis without stretching themselves too thin. Helping the relative becomes another stressful obligation rather than incidental assistance that someone like Mary enjoys.

Psychological factors also play into the demands of assisting older relatives. Families are not formal providers who look at what they are doing with objectivity. Past resentments and patterns of interaction from an earlier stage of life may rekindle when an aging parent needs help. Grown children also may have difficulty understanding and empathizing with their parents' vulnerabilities, even when they wish to do so. Moreover, even under the best of circumstances, attempts to help the aging parent may go amiss if the assistance undermines the older adult's independence. Helping older adults maintain autonomy and providing just the right amount of assistance is a fine-tuned process.

In sum, given a dearth of formal or government-support systems in the United States, families are the mainstay of help. Families keep older adults in their homes when they begin to experience physical declines and social losses of old age. Even before they require hands-on care, older adults may need assistance with a variety of daily tasks. Healthy older adults turn to family members for advice regarding new technologies and for support navigating the medical system. Less healthy older adults require assistance with a myriad of daily tasks without yet qualifying for skilled nursing care. As families weave the fabric of daily life for their older relatives, they face an intricate array of challenges that may generate stress for those involved. For the fortunate few who have strong networks of relatives and friends nearby, old age can be a joyful and rewarding period, as exemplified in the case of Mary at the start of this chapter. For others, however, family patterns from the past taint interactions or new issues arise due to competing demands. Nonetheless, family support is part and parcel of the transition to old-old age. The tensions and rewards involved in that support are likely to become increasingly common in future years as more families face these issues.

REFERENCES

American Association of Retired Persons (AARP). (2004). *Continuing care retirement communities (CCRC)*. Retrieved August 20, 2007, from http://www.aarp.org/families/housing_choices/other_options/a2004-02-26-retirementcommunity.html

Angelelli, J. (2006). Promising models for transforming long-term care. *The Gerontologist, 46,* 428–430.

Antonucci, T. C., Lansford, J. E., Akiyama, H., Smith, J., Baltes, M. M., Takahashi, K., Fuhrer, R., & Dartigues, J. F. (2002). Differences between men and women in social relations, resource deficits, and depressive symptomatology during later life in four nations. *Journal of Social Issues, 58,* 767–783.

Baltes, M. M. (1996). *The many faces of dependency in old age.* New York: Cambridge University Press.

Baltes, M. M., & Wahl, H. (1992). The dependency-support script in institutions: Generalization to community settings. *Psychology and Aging, 7,* 409–418.

Baumeister, R. F., & Leary, M. R. (1995). The need to belong: Desire for interpersonal attachments as a fundamental human motivation, *Psychological Bulletin, 117,* 497–529.

Becker, G., Beyene, Y., Newsom, E., & Mayen, N. (2003). Creating continuity through mutual assistance: Intergenerational reciprocity in four ethnic groups. *Journal of Gerontology: Social Sciences, 58,* S151–S159.

Boase, J., Horrigan, J. B., Wellman, B., & Rainie, L. (2006). The strength of Internet ties. *Pew Internet and American Life Project.* Retrieved August 26, 2007 from http://www.pewinternet.org/pdfs/PIP_Internet_ties.pdf

Cacioppo, J. T., Hawkley, L. C., & Berntson, G. G. (2003). The anatomy of loneliness. *Current Directions in Psychological Science, 12,* 71–74.

Cantor, M. H. (1979). Neighbors and friends: An over-looked resource in the informal support system. *Research on Aging, 1,* 434–463.

Carstensen, L. L. (2006). The influence of a sense of time on human development. *Science, 312,* 1913–1915.

CBS news. (2005). *Bush pushes Medicare drug plan: Urges seniors to seek help if confused by new Rx drug benefit.* Retrieved August 20, 2007, from http://www.cbsnews.com/stories/2005/12/13/politics/main1123471.shtml

Cohen-Mansfield, J., & Bester, A. (2006). Flexibility as a management principle in dementia care: The Adards example. *The Gerontologist, 46,* 540–544.

Demographics of Internet users. (2007, June). *Pew Internet & American Life Project.* Retrieved October 4, 2007, from http://www.pewinternet.org/trends/

Eggebeen, D. J., & Davey, A. D. (1998). Do safety nets work? The role of anticipated help in times of need. *Journal of Marriage and the Family, 60,* 939–950.

Feinberg, L. F., & Newman, S. L. (2004). A study of 10 states since passage of the National Family Caregiver Support Program: Policies, perceptions, and program development. *The Gerontologist, 44,* 760–769.

Fingerman, K. L. (2001). The paradox of a distant closeness: Intimacy in parent/child ties. *Generations, 25*, 26–33.

Fingerman, K. L., & Bermann, E. (2000). Applications of family systems theory to the study of adulthood. *International Journal of Aging and Human Development, 51*, 5–29.

Fingerman, K. L., Chen, P. C., Hay, E. L., Cichy, K. E., & Lefkowitz, E. S. (2006). Ambivalent reactions in the parent and offspring relationship. *Journals of Gerontology: Psychological Sciences, 61B*, 152–160.

Fingerman, K. L., Hay, E. L., & Birditt, K. S. (2004). The best of ties, the worst of ties: Close, problematic, and ambivalent relationships across the lifespan. *Journal of Marriage and Family, 66*, 792–808.

Fingerman, K. L., Hay, E. L., Kamp Dush, C. M., Cichy, K. E., & Hosterman, S. (2007). Parents' and offspring's perceptions of change and continuity when parents experience the transition to old age. *Advances in Life Course Research, 12*, 275–306.

Ganong, L., & Coleman, M. (2006). Obligations to stepparents acquired later in life: Relationship quality and acuity of needs. *Journals of Gerontology: Social Sciences, 61*, S80–S88.

Gross, J. (2007, August 13). Elderly organize to meet problems of aging. *New York Times*. Retrieved August 27, 2007, from http://www.nytimes.com

Hay, E. L., Fingerman, K. L., & Lefkowitz, E. S. (2007). The experience of worry in parent-adult child relationships. *Personal Relationships, 14*, 605–622.

Hughes, M. E., & Waite, L. J. (2006). The aging of the second demographic transition. In K. W. Schaie & P. Uhlenberg (Eds.), *Social structures: The impact of demographic changes on the well-being of older persons* (pp. 179–211). New York: Springer.

Ikkink, K. K., van Tilburg, T., & Knipscheer, K. C. P. M. (1999). Perceived instrumental support exchanges in relationships between elderly parents and their adult children: Normative and structural explanations. *Journal of Marriage and the Family, 61*, 831–844.

Ingersoll-Dayton, B., Morgan, D., & Antonucci, T. (1997). The effects of positive and negative social exchanges on aging adults. *Journal of Gerontology: Social Sciences, 52B*, S190–S199.

Janevic, M. R., & Connell, C. M. (2001). Racial, ethnic, and cultural differences in the dementia caregiving experience: Recent findings. *The Gerontologist, 41*, 334–347.

Johnson, C. L., & Barer, B. M. (1997). *Life beyond eighty-five years: The aura of survivorship*. New York: Springer Publishing Company.

Lang, F. R., & Baltes, M. M. (1997). Being with people and being alone in late life: Costs and benefits for everyday functioning. *International Journal of Behavioral Development, 21,* 729–746.

Lawton, L., Silverstein, M., & Bengtson, V. (1994). Affection, social contact, and geographic distance between adult children and their parents. *Journal of Marriage and the Family, 56,* 57–68.

McGarry, K., & Schoeni, R. F. (1997). Transfer behavior within the family: Results from the asset and health dynamics study. *Journals of Gerontology, 52B,* 83–92.

Morgan, D. L. (1989). Adjusting to widowhood. *The Gerontologist, 29,* 101–107.

Moss, M. S., Moss, S. Z., & Moles, E. L. (1985). The quality of relationships between elderly parents and their out-of-town children. *Gerontologist, 25,* 134–140.

Newsom, J. T., Rook, K. S., Nishishiba, M., Sorkin, D. H., & Mahan, R. L. (2005). Understanding the relative important of positive and negative social exchanges: Examining specific domains and appraisals. *Journal of Gerontology: Psychological Sciences, 60,* P304–P312.

O'Brien, E. (2005). Medicaid's coverage of nursing home costs: Asset shelter for the wealthy or essential safety net? *Issue brief: Long-term care financing project.* Washington, DC: Georgetown University. http://66.102.1.104/scholar?hl=en &lr=&q=cache:3XeZj3LMGGEJ:ltc.georgetown.edu/pdfs/nursinghomecosts. pdf+author:%22O%27Brien%22+intitle:%22Medicaid%27s+Coverage+ of+Nursing+Home+Costs:+Asset+Shelter+...%22+

Park, D. C., Morrell, R. W., & Shifren, K. (1999). *Processing of medical information in aging patients: Cognitive and human factors perspectives.* Mahwah, NJ: Lawrence Erlbaum Associates Publishers.

Putnam, R. D. (2000). *Bowling alone: The collapse and revival of American community.* New York: Touchstone Books/Simon & Schuster.

Rabig, J., Thomas, W., Kane, R. A., Cutler, L. J., & McAlilly, S. (2006). Radical redesign of nursing homes: Applying the green house concept in Tupelo, Mississippi. *The Gerontologist, 46,* 533–539.

Roberto, K. A. (1999). Making critical health care decisions for older adults: Consensus among family members. *Family Relations, 48,* 167–175.

Roberto, K. A., Weeks, L. E., & Matheis-Kraft, C. (2001). Health care decisions of older adults: Underlying influences, cognitive status, and perceived outcomes. *Journal of Applied Gerontology, 20,* 74–90.

Rook, K. S. (2001). Emotional health and positive versus negative social exchanges: A daily diary analysis. *Applied Developmental Science, 5,* 86–97.

Schnittker, J. (2007). Look (closely) at all the lonely people: Age and the social psychology of social support. *Journal of Aging and Health, 19*, 659–682.

Silverstein, M., & Bengtson, V. L. (1991). Do close parent-child relations reduce the mortality risk of older parents? *Journal of Health and Social Behavior, 32*, 382–395.

Silverstein, M., Conroy, S. J., Wang, H., Giarrusso, R., & Bengtson, V. L. (2002). Reciprocity in parent-child relations over the adult life course. *Journals of Gerontology: Series B: Psychological Sciences & Social Sciences, 57*, S3–S13.

Silverstein, M., Gans, D., & Yang, F. M. (2006). Intergenerational support to aging parents: The role of norms and needs. *Journal of Family Issues, 27*, 1068–1084.

Smith, J., & Goodnow, J. J. (1999). Unasked-for support and unsolicited advice: Age and the quality of social experience. *Psychology and Aging, 14*, 108–121.

Vaux, A. (1988). Social support: Theory, research, and intervention. New York: Praeger.

Vaux, A., & Harrison, D. (1985). Support network characteristics associated with support satisfaction and perceived support. *American Journal of Community Psychology, 13*, 245–268.

Webster, P. S., & Herzog, A. R. (1995). Effects of parental divorce and memories of family problems on relationships between adult children and their parents. *Journal of Gerontology: Social Sciences, 50B*, 24–34.

Zarit, S. H., & Eggebeen, D. J. (2002). Parent-child relationships in adulthood and old age. In M. H. Bornstein (Ed.), *Handbook of parenting* (2nd ed., pp. 135–164). Mahwah , NJ: Erlbaum.

The Cultural Context of Clinical Work with Aging Caregivers

MARTHA CROWTHER AND AUDREY AUSTIN

The population of the United States is growing older and becoming more ethnically diverse. According to Census Bureau projections, the number of persons aged 65 and older will increase from 35 million in the year 2000 to 66 million by 2030 and to 82 million by 2050, a figure accounting for 20.3% of the entire population (U.S. Census Bureau, 2000). This *gerontological explosion* will also occur across groups of minority elders, whose respective population sizes will nearly double by 2050 (U.S. Census Bureau, 2000).

Rates of growth of ethnic minority elderly are expected to exceed those of Whites within the next few decades. Ethnic minority populations are projected to increase from 5.7 million (16.4%) in 2000 to 8.1 million (20.1%) in 2010 and then to 12.9 million (23.6%) in 2020. Between 2004 and 2030 the White population 65 and over is projected to increase by 74% compared with 183% for older minorities, including Hispanics (254%); African Americans (147%); American Indians, Eskimos, and Aleuts (143%); and Asians and Pacific Islanders (208%) (Administration on Aging, 2006). Of note, the population of Hispanic elderly is projected to grow the fastest, from about 2 million in 2000 to over 13 million by 2050. By 2028, older Hispanics are projected to exceed the number of older African Americans (U.S. Census Bureau, 2000).

Approximately 10% of those 65 and older were foreign born. In 2000, 13% of the older population spoke a language other than English at home, compared to 18% for the total population. Of the older adults that spoke a language other than English at home, Indo-European languages other than Spanish were the most prominently used; 14% of older people spoke Asian and Pacific Island languages. Six percent of the older population spoke a language other than English at home and also spoke English very well, compared to 10% for the total population (U.S. Census Bureau, 2004).

Such demographic changes underscore a need to address the role of culture in caregiving. Changes in the ethnic profile of older adults may impact caregiving in a variety of ways, including service utilization and delivery, attitudes, beliefs, values, social support, and expression of mental and physical health symptoms.

CULTURE AND ETHNICITY

Culture encompasses a group's way of life, including the values, beliefs, traditions, language, symbols, and forms of social organization that are meaningful to the group (Aranda, 2001). Factors that influence culture may include gender, geography, socioeconomic status, educational attainment, individual experiences, place of birth, length of residency, and—most importantly for the purposes of this chapter—age and ethnicity. One's cultural perspective is not solely defined by his or her ethnic background; however, ethnicity does provide a cultural context that may guide an individual's worldview. Although heterogeneity exists within ethnic groups, the average characteristics of a given group considered as whole may differ in meaningful ways when compared with the average characteristics of other groups (Zane, Hall, Sue, Young, & Nunez, 2004). Interethnic comparisons are thus presented within this chapter to demonstrate the ways in which differences between the cultural contexts of aging and ethnic minority caregivers may impact the caregiving experience.

Research in the area of interventions for caregivers has focused on identifying and relieving the burden of caregiving. Caregivers commonly shoulder responsibility for helping care recipients to manage multiple activities of daily living. Caregivers most frequently report arranging or providing transportation, completing grocery shopping and housework, and managing finances, as well as helping the care recipient to get in and out of bed and chairs, to get dressed, and to complete personal grooming tasks (National Alliance for Caregiving & AARP, 2004). Although caregivers of varying ages and backgrounds may need to perform similar activities, cultural differences may influence the way caregivers perceive and respond to their responsibilities. These factors will become increasingly important as U.S. population demographics change.

Caregiver reactions, coping strategies, distress levels, acceptance of symptoms, and attitudes toward clinicians and outside help may vary considerably across different cultures ("Culture and Caregiving," 1992). Research has demonstrated differing beliefs, levels of support, and physical and emotional outcomes among caregivers of different ethnic backgrounds. For example, in a recent meta-analysis of 116 empirical studies, Pinquart and Sorenson (2005) examined ethnic differences in caregiver background variables, objective stressors, filial obligation beliefs, psychological and social resources, coping processes, and psychological and physical health. The analysis indicated that ethnic minority caregivers had a lower socioeconomic status, were more likely to receive informal support, provided more care than White caregivers, and had stronger filial obligation beliefs than White caregivers. All ethnic minority groups reported worse physical health than Whites. Comparisons between specific ethnic groups indicated that Asian American caregivers used less formal support than White caregivers. African American caregivers had lower levels of caregiver burden and depression than White caregivers, and Hispanic and Asian American caregivers were more depressed than White caregivers. Other available research suggests that cultural perspectives differ across ethnic groups and may impact caregiver experience in several domains, including service utilization, clinical presentation and interactions with clinicians, and perceptions of the caregiving role.

SERVICE UTILIZATION

Efforts to reduce caregiver burden often include the use of alternative or supplemental services for the care recipient. Nearly half of the caregivers interviewed for the National Alliance for Caregiving and AARP (2004) caregiving study said they had used some type of supportive service to help care for their relatives and friends. Older caregivers were more likely than younger caregivers to seek these outside services, which included requests for financial assistance, formal training, transportation services, support groups, adult day care or recreation programs, meal provision programs, and respite services. Caregivers may benefit from additional clinical and community support for themselves, but may not seek or effectively receive needed help. Because cultural differences may influence caregivers' help-seeking behaviors, clinicians should become knowledgeable regarding cultural factors that may influence caregiver service utilization and service effectiveness. Consideration of culture facilitates understanding of the values, attitudes, and behaviors of caregivers, and it helps clinicians to avoid stereotypes and biases that can undermine clinical efforts. Additionally, culture plays a critical role in the development and delivery of services that are responsive to the needs of the recipient.

Despite the negative emotional effects caregivers may experience, cultural differences may prevent caregivers from seeking psychological help. A survey of older Korean Americans revealed how culturally influenced beliefs may shape individuals' attitudes toward mental health services (Jang, Kim, Hansen, & Chiriboga, 2007). Most participants in the study had a dismissive or negative perception of depression: More than half believed becoming depressed was a normal part of aging, approximately 71% viewed depression as a sign of personal weakness, and approximately 14% reported that having a mentally ill family member brought shame to the whole family. Individuals who had lived in the United States for a longer period were more likely to view mental health services favorably. Perceptions of depression as a weakness or as shameful were associated with negative attitudes toward mental health services. Individuals with higher levels of depressive symptoms also viewed mental health services more negatively. Despite the high level of depressive symptoms found in over a third of the survey sample, only

6.5% of participants reported that they had previously contacted a mental health professional. The researchers note that tolerance or suppression of personal emotions within Asian culture may hinder older Korean Americans from recognizing or admitting that their symptoms reflect a need for care. Such values, along with negative perceptions of psychological difficulty and beliefs regarding shame, may impact Korean American caregivers' service utilization.

Similarly, cultural beliefs may influence Japanese American caregivers' use of support and mental health services. Older adults residing in Japan were more likely to seek day services if the older adult had previous caregiving experiences (Tsukada and Saito, 2006), despite the traditional Japanese cultural norm that care should be provided within a family without outside help. Older people who have experience providing care may recognize that caregiving is a difficult job and might not want to burden others when they need care themselves. There is limited data regarding Japanese American caregivers to determine if this same pattern exists in the United States. Through a case study of a dementia caregiver, Kinoshita and Gallagher-Thompson (2004) demonstrate that some Japanese cultural values—such as willing and graceful acceptance of adversity, a strong sense of family obligation, avoidance of bringing shame to one's family, and an emphasis on personal accountability for responsibilities—may guide caregiving decisions and affect caregiver outcomes. Exclusive reliance on one's own abilities or expected family support may prevent Japanese American caregivers from seeking adult day care, respite care, nursing-home placement, or other formal services for their care recipient, potentially resulting in increased caregiver stress and burden. Additionally, feelings of shame, obligation, or tolerance of negative emotions may prevent these caregivers from seeking psychological or other support for themselves.

Older African Americans generally tend to underutilize mental health services. One study found that 58% of older African Americans with mental disorders were not receiving treatment (Black, Rabins, German, McGuire, & Roca, 1997). Another study found that older African Americans were less likely to use community services than older Whites (Mui & Burnette, 1994). Although some studies have assumed that negative attitudes toward mental health services account for African Americans' lower service utilization, Diala and colleagues (2000) found that African Americans' initial attitudes toward seeking mental health services were comparable to, and in some instances more favorable than, those of Whites. However, certain cultural attitudes may reduce African Americans' desire to seek services. Focus-group discussions have revealed cultural beliefs regarding the need to resolve family concerns within the family and the expectation that African Americans demonstrate strength. These beliefs were reflected in concern about disclosing information outside a trusted circle of family and friends and by an association of psychotherapy with weakness and diminished pride. Additionally, the majority of focus-group participants noted a perception that African Americans were a disadvantaged group who could and would collectively cope with adversity. Older participants were likely to suggest continued endorsement of these cultural beliefs (Thompson, Bazile, & Akbar, 2004). Such beliefs might inhibit older African American caregivers from seeking assistance outside their families to address personal stress or other difficulties.

Hispanic or Latino individuals also underutilize mental health services. Language is one major barrier to mental health service use, particularly among elderly individuals who may have immigrated to the United States. Language differences between minority elderly and nonminority mental health professionals were found to be the top-rated barrier for Hispanic elderly (Biegel, Farkas, & Song, 1997). Cultural values may also influence help-seeking behaviors and service use among this group. Specifically, cultural values related to strong identification with and attachment to family (familism), beliefs that the environment and not individual actions largely determine life's outcomes (fatalism), and stigma associated with psychiatric disorders may prevent Latinos from seeking formal psychological help (Kouyoumdjian, Zamboanga, & Hansen, 2003). These cultural perspectives may decrease elderly Latino caregivers' likelihood of seeking professional support when needed.

CULTURAL MISTRUST

Cultural mistrust may also influence caregivers' help-seeking behaviors and interactions with clinicians. Within the research literature, *cultural mistrust*—defined as the tendency of African Americans to distrust

Whites—has been associated with low expectations about counseling with White therapists, negative attitudes about seeking help from clinics staffed primarily by Whites, fewer self-disclosures with White counselors compared to African American counselors, and higher levels of premature termination from therapy with White counselors in comparison to African American counselors (Alston & Bell, 1996). Though such associations may suggest that matching client and therapist ethnicity might eliminate the effects of cultural mistrust, client-therapist matching on ethnicity may be impractical or impossible in various care settings. Furthermore, an ethnic or racial match is not necessarily the same as a cultural match, which encompasses an understanding of a client's cultural background (Zane et al., 2004). As noted previously, ethnicity is only one component of an individual's culture. Cultural perspectives may differ among individuals of the same ethnicity and clinicians should therefore give greater consideration to these factors than to outward appearance or nominal ethnic or racial categorizations.

Cultural mistrust has often been interpreted as clinical paranoia. Cort (2004) notes that cultural mistrust, when present in African American mental health patients, is believed to be responsible for a disproportionate number of schizophrenia diagnoses of African Americans by White clinicians. Clinicians working with African Americans who exhibit cultural mistrust should acknowledge the possibility that such a reaction may be a legitimate and adaptive method of coping with racism and discrimination (Whaley, 2001). Cultural mistrust may be a challenge to rapport building. Clinicians may increase clients' mistrust and damage rapport if they dismiss clients' cultural beliefs or fail to validate and explore client concerns about racism when warranted. To facilitate rapport and a successful therapeutic relationship, clinicians must be open to learning from clients, and they must be nonjudgmental about each client's cultural perspective, including his or her level of cultural mistrust (Whaley, 2001).

Although cultural mistrust has been commonly defined and conceptualized in the literature as an issue specific to African Americans, issues of trust, particularly with regard to seeking psychological services for oneself or a loved one, are not unique to this group. When working with caregivers of any ethnic background, clinicians must consider how cultural perspectives—stemming from the client's age, ethnicity, or other factors—may influence their level of trust. Furthermore, it is critical that clinicians not assume, when working with African American caregivers or clients of other ethnicities, that cultural mistrust accounts for a client's hesitancy to seek care or for negative encounters with clinicians. Assessment of cultural mistrust along with other possible barriers is necessary in order to eliminate or address potential causes of reluctance in caregivers' utilization of services (Alston & Bell, 1996).

FAMILISM

In the prior section we discussed the impact that cultural values may have on help-seeking behavior and utilization of support services. Cultural values may also impact the ways in which caregivers perceive and react to their caregiving role. Caregiver burden and outcomes may be influenced by familism, a cultural value that is shared by several ethnic minority groups. *Familism* has been defined as strong feelings of loyalty, reciprocity, and solidarity among members of the same family (Crowther, Robinson-Shurgot, Perkins, & Rodriguez, 2006).

Although family affiliation may be important to all cultural and ethnic groups, familism is often contrasted with the sense of individualism thought to characterize "mainstream," predominantly White American culture. Accordingly, adaptation of American culture appears to influence familism levels. Youn, Knight, Jeong, and Benton (1999) found that Korean American caregivers showed significantly lower levels of familism than Korean caregivers and higher levels of familism compared to White American caregivers, suggesting acculturation to American values. Similarly, in a cross-cultural study of familism among caregivers of persons with dementia, Knight and colleagues (2002) found that familism values were significantly lower among White caregivers in comparison to other ethnic groups, and trends in familism appeared to reflect acculturation to Western values. Koreans, first-generation Korean Americans, and first- and second-generation Latinos reported the highest familism levels. Familism values among African Americans were most similar to, but still significantly higher than, familism among White caregivers.

Among caregivers whose cultural values include self-definition in relationship to the family, caregiving may be viewed as a natural extension of family life, as opposed to an interruption of the individual life of the caregiver (Youn et al., 1999). Based on this conceptualization of caregiving, familism has been hypothesized as a protective factor against negative appraisals of the caregiving role and consequent feelings of burden or other poor caregiver outcomes. Available research is not consistent on this point and suggests that familism may have no effect or a negative effect on outcomes among some groups. Familism was found to correlate negatively with burden and negatively, though nonsignificantly, with depression among a sample of Hispanic dementia caregivers residing in the United States (Losada et al., 2006). In contrast, Korean American caregivers, who had higher levels of familism than White caregivers, reported higher levels of burden, depression, and anxiety and less social support than White caregivers, though these differences may have reflected general cultural differences and not been specific to caregiving (Youn et al., 1999). Knight et al. (2002) found that familism was associated with higher burden and depression among Japanese Americans, while no significant relation between familism and emotional distress outcomes was noted among Whites, Latinos, Koreans, Korean Americans, or African Americans.

Despite inconsistencies in the literature, it appears that familism may differentially affect ethnic minority caregivers. Thus, clinicians should consider familism as a cultural value that may potentially influence caregiver burden and outcomes.

INTERACTION BETWEEN MENTAL AND PHYSICAL HEALTH

Often, mental health problems are expressed as physical symptoms among aging and ethnic minority individuals. Older adults may present with physical and cognitive symptoms that mimic or occur comorbidly with physical illness. Although these symptoms are often explored and treated as physical problems, they may reflect an underlying mental health issue (Gallagher-Thompson et al., 2000). Physical symptoms may also co-occur with, mask, or be viewed as a more acceptable expression of psychological difficulty among different ethnic groups as well. Compared to Whites, African American, Asian, and Hispanic individuals may be more likely to express mental distress through physical symptoms (U.S. Department of Health and Human Services, 2001).

Examination of the symptom patterns of Asians has indicated that individuals within this group, particularly those with depressive disorders, tend to present with more somatic complaints than non-Asian clients (Zane et al., 2004). As noted previously, cultural values promoting suppression of personal emotions may inhibit Asian individuals from acknowledging a need for psychological care (Jang et al., 2007). Among individuals who hold such values, addressing physical symptoms may be preferable to openly acknowledging emotional distress. Similarly, cultural stigma associated with mental illness among African Americans may also contribute to greater physical expression of psychological distress. Latinos show a greater tendency to seek a physician's help for psychological problems, possibly because many Latinos view physical symptoms more seriously than problems associated with mental health, are likely to perceive symptoms of depression and anxiety as physical problems, and may desire to avoid cultural stigma associated with seeing a psychologist (Kouyoumdjian et al., 2003).

SPIRITUALITY/RELIGION

The vast majority of research finds that religious involvement is associated with greater well-being and life satisfaction, greater purpose and meaning in life, greater hope and optimism, less anxiety and depression, more stable marriages, and lower rates of substance abuse (Crowther, Parker, Larimore, Achenbaum, & Koenig, 2002; Koenig, McCullogh, & Larson, 2000; Dull & Skokan, 1995). Religious involvement differs across age and ethnic groups. Research has consistently found older adults to rate highest, compared to younger cohorts, on measures of religion and spirituality, with only an occasional exception of reduced attendance at religious services among the oldest old, whose attendance is more likely to be impacted by problems with mobility (Moberg, 2005). National surveys indicate that older adults attach a high value to their religious beliefs and behaviors. This is particularly true of ethnic minority elders, who show a high degree of religious involvement compared to older White Americans (McFadden, 1996).

Participation in spiritual activities or religious behaviors has been found to be helpful in coping with stressful life events and may aid caregivers in dealing with the demands of caregiving. Chang, Noonan, and Tennstedt (1998) found that caregivers who reported using religious or spiritual beliefs to help them handle the caregiving experience had a better quality relationship with their care recipients, which was in turn associated with lower levels of depression and role submersion (i.e., the sense that caregiving had taken over and become all-consuming). Caregivers caring for patients with a variety of disabilities and illnesses frequently report high levels of global religiousness and the use of religious coping strategies (Pearce, 2005).

In a national survey, prayer was the most commonly reported means of coping among caregivers. Although many caregivers across all surveyed ethnic groups reportedly use prayer to help with caregiving stress, African American and Hispanic caregivers were significantly more likely to cope by praying than White or Asian caregivers (National Alliance for Caregiving and AARP, 2004). Religion and spirituality in caregivers may serve as a protective factor against negative psychological outcomes, particularly among African American and Hispanic caregivers. In a study of caregivers of patients with Alzheimer's disease, Morano and King (2005) found that caregivers with higher levels of religiosity reported significantly lower levels of depression. When interethnic comparisons were made, African American caregivers reported the highest level of religiosity and the lowest levels of depression. Ratings of religiosity among Hispanic caregivers were slightly lower than those of African American caregivers, but they were significantly higher than reported religiosity levels among White caregivers. Both the African American and Hispanic caregivers reported lower levels of depression than the White caregivers.

CONCLUSION

The number of older ethnic minorities in the United States is increasing and will continue to grow well into this century. Given this demographic shift, it is imperative that our understanding of the experiences and needs of aging caregivers be considered in the context of the caregivers' culture. A caregiver's cultural perspective—which may include particular views about physical and mental illness, the role of family, and spiritual or religious beliefs—may influence the caregiver's perceptions of and reactions to the caregiving role, utilization of support services, and other aspects of the caregiving experience. Consideration of the cultural context of caregiving can assist health-care professionals in understanding diverse caregiving patterns as well as health and service needs.

To effectively incorporate cultural considerations into our clinical practice, we must go beyond the hierarchical model of health care in working with ethnic minority caregivers. We will need to alter our care paradigm from a vertical model to a horizontal model. The horizontal model ensures a collaborative approach to care with an emphasis on obtaining and maintaining an optimal level of mental and physical health care for the caregiver as well as the care recipient. The collaborative or horizontal model of caregiving includes a consideration of the role of the community in which the caregiver resides.

Health professionals that serve ethnic minority caregivers should consider incorporating community professionals into their work. Community professionals—including lay care providers, civic groups, social groups, and religious institutions—can serve as links between the health professional and the caregiver. In partnership with health-care providers, community professionals can promote strategies to promote healthy behaviors for caregivers, such as increased physical activity and other self-care behaviors. Community professionals typically have personal relationships with the caregivers in their communities and often have greater knowledge of local services that caregivers may need. They are also the persons that may serve as community protectors or gatekeepers. Examples of gatekeepers include social workers, pastors, and health-care providers working within church health ministries. Developing positive relationships with such gatekeepers will facilitate access to the caregiving population and provide opportunities for clinicians to learn about the culture in which the caregiver resides (Wallace, Witucki, Boland, & Tuck, 1998).

While informal community engagement may increase clinicians' knowledge of caregivers' cultural perspectives, there is also a need to increase the amount of regular training available to health professionals across disciplines and to community professionals that focuses on the cultural context of caregiving (Harper, 1990). In addition, there remains a need for updated, clinically applicable research regarding the role of culture in clinical practice. Many caregivers spend significant amounts of money, time, and energy caring for loved ones—sometimes at the expense of their own health and well-being. As recent studies indicate, cultural differences may impact various aspects of the caregiving experience and should thus be considered in clinical practice. With training and community involvement, enhanced awareness of the cultural context of caregiving will enable clinicians working with caregivers to provide the most appropriate and competent care for an aging and increasingly diverse population.

REFERENCES

Administration on Aging. (2006). *A profile of older Americans: 2006.* Washington, DC: Administration on Aging (AoA), U.S. Department of Health and Human Services.

Alston, R., & Bell, T. (1996). Cultural mistrust and the rehabilitation enigma for African Americans. *Journal of Rehabilitation, 62,* 16–20.

Aranda, M. P. (2001). Racial and ethnic factors in dementia and caregiving research in the US. *Aging and Mental Health, 5,* S116–S123.

Biegel, D., Farkas, K., & Song, L. (1997). Barriers to the use of mental health services by African-American and Hispanic elderly persons. *Journal of Gerontological Social Work, 29,* 23–44.

Black, B. S., Rabins, P. V., German, P., McGuire, M., & Roca, R. (1997). Need and unmet need for mental health care among elderly public housing residents. *The Gerontologist, 37,* 717–728.

Chang, B., Noonan, A., & Tennstedt, S. (1998). The role of religion/spirituality in coping with caregiving for disabled elders. *The Gerontologist, 38,* 463–470.

Cort, M. (2004). Cultural mistrust and use of hospice care: Challenges and remedies. *Journal of Palliative Medicine, 7,* 63–71.

Crowther, M., Parker, M., Larimore, W., Achenbaum, A., & Koenig, H. (2002). Rowe and Kahn's model of successful aging revisited: Spirituality the missing construct. *The Gerontologist, 42*(5), 613–620.

Crowther, M., Robinson-Shurgot, G., Perkins, M., & Rodriguez, R. (2006). The social and cultural context of psychotherapy with older adults. In S. H. Qualls & R. G. Knight (Eds.), *Psychotherapy for depression and anxiety* (pp. 179–199). Hoboken, NJ: Wiley.

Culture and Caregiving. (1992). *Aging, 363/364,* 29–31.

Diala, C., Muntaner, C., Walrath, C., Nickerson, K., LaVeist, T., & Leaf, P. (2000). Racial differences in attitudes toward professional mental health care and in the use of services. *American Journal of Orthopsychiatry, 70,* 455–464.

Dull, V. T., & Skokan, L. A. (1995). A cognitive model of religion's influence on health. *Journal of Social Issues, 51*(2), 49–64.

Gallagher-Thompson, D., McKibbin, C., Koonce-Volwiler, D., Menendez, A., Stewart, D., & Thompson, L. (2000). Psychotherapy with older adults. In C. R. Snyder & R. Ingram (Eds.), *Handbook of psychological change: Psychotherapy processes and practices for the 21st century* (pp. 614–637). New York: Wiley.

Harper, M. S. (Ed.). (1990). *Minority aging: Essential curricula content for selected health and allied health professions.* Health Resources and Services Administration, Department of Health and Human Services. DHHS Publication No. HRS (P-DV-90- 4). Washington, DC: Government Printing Office.

Jang, Y., Kim, G., Hansen, L., & Chiriboga, D. (2007). Attitudes of older Korean Americans toward mental health services. *Journal of the American Geriatrics Society, 55,* 616–620.

Kinoshita, L., & Gallagher-Thompson, D. (2004). Japanese American caregivers of individuals with dementia: An examination of Japanese cultural values and dementia caregiving. *Clinical Gerontologist, 27,* 87–102.

Knight, B., Robinson, G., Longmire, C., Chun, M., Nakao, K., & Kim, J. (2002). Cross cultural issues in caregiving for persons with dementia: Do familism values reduce burden and distress? *Ageing International, 27,* 70–94.

Koenig, H. G., McCullogh, M., & Larson, D. B. (2000). *Handbook of Religion and Health.* New York: Oxford University Press.

Kouyoumdjian, H., Zamboanga, B., & Hansen, D. (2003). Barriers to community mental health services for Latinos: Treatment considerations. *Clinical Psychology: Science and Practice, 10*, 394–422.

Losada, A., Shurgot, G., Knight, B., Marquez, M., Montorio, I., Izal, M., & Ruiz, M. (2006). Cross-cultural study comparing the association of familism with burden and depressive symptoms in two samples of Hispanic dementia caregivers. *Aging & Mental Health, 10*, 69–76.

McFadden, S. H. (1996). Religion, spirituality, and aging. In J. E. Birren & K. W. Schaie (Eds.), *Handbook of the psychology of aging: The handbooks of aging* (4th ed., pp. 365–382). San Diego, CA: Academic Press.

Moberg, D. (2005). Research in spirituality, religion, and aging. *Journal of Gerontological Social Work, 45*, 11–40.

Morano, C., & King, D. (2005). Religiosity as a mediator of caregiver well-being: Does ethnicity make a difference? *Journal of Gerontological Social Work, 45*, 69–84.

Mui, A. C., & Burnette, D. (1994). Long-term care service use by frail elders: Is ethnicity a factor? *Gerontologist, 34*, 190–198.

National Alliance for Caregiving & AARP. (2004). *Caregiving in the US.* Washington, DC: National Alliance for Caregiving.

Pearce, M. (2005). A critical review of the forms and value of religious coping among informal caregivers. *Journal of Religion and Health, 44*, 81–118.

Pinquart, M., & Sorensen, S. (2005). Ethnic differences in stressors, resources, and psychological outcomes of family caregiving: A meta-analysis. *The Gerontologist, 45*, 90–106.

Thompson, V., Bazile, A., & Akbar, M. (2004). African Americans' perceptions of psychotherapy and psychotherapists. *Professional Psychology: Research and Practice, 35*, 19–26.

Tsukada, N., & Saito, Y. (2006). Factors that affect older Japanese people's reluctance to use home help care and adult day care services. *Journal of Cross Cultural Gerontology, 21*, 121–137.

U.S. Census Bureau. (2000). *Projections of the total resident population by 5-year age groups, race, and Hispanic origin with special age categories: Middle series, 1999–2000 and 2050–2070.* Retrieved September 23, 2005, from www.census.gov/population/projections/nation/summary/np-t4.a-g.txt

U.S. Census Bureau. (2004). *We the People: Aging in the United States—Census 2000 Special Reports.* Retrieved February 29, 2008, from http://www.census.gov/prod/2004pubs/censr-19.pdf

U.S. Department of Health and Human Services. (2001). *Mental health: Culture, race, and ethnicity—a supplement to mental health: A report of the Surgeon General*. Rockville, MD: U.S. Department of Health and Human Services, Substance Abuse and Mental Health Services Administration, Center for Mental Health Services.

Wallace, D. C., Witucki, J. M., Boland, C. S., & Tuck, I. T. (1998). Cultural context of caregiving with elders. *Journal of Multicultural Nursing and Health*. Retrieved March 9, 2008, from http://www.findarticles.com/p/articles/mi_qa3919/is_199810/ai_n8820605

Whaley, A. (2001). Cultural mistrust: An important psychological construct for diagnosis and treatment of African Americans. *Professional Psychology: Research and Practice, 32,* 555–562.

Youn, G., Knight, B., Jeong, H., & Benton, D. (1999). Differences in familism values and caregiving outcomes among Korean, Korean American, and White American dementia caregivers. *Psychology and Aging, 14,* 355–364.

Zane, N., Hall, G., Sue, S., Young, K., & Nunez, J. (2004). Research on psychotherapy with culturally diverse populations. In M. Lambert (Ed.), *Bergin and Garfield's handbook of psychotherapy and behavior change* (pp. 767–804). New York: Wiley.

4

All in the Family: Providing Care to Chronically Ill and Disabled Older Adults

MARY ANN PARRIS STEPHENS AND MELISSA M. FRANKS

As individuals advance into the later years of life, they become increasingly vulnerable to chronic health problems as well as physical and mental limitations associated with these conditions. In fact, if they live long enough, they will certainly develop one or more chronic illnesses. Moreover, the chances are quite good that they will ultimately need help with performing even simple daily activities, and that they will be cared for by one or more of their family members.

Our chapter aims to illuminate the many ways in which the health status and health-care needs of older adults have profound implications for their families. To set the stage for our chapter, it may be helpful to think as we do that chronic illness is a family problem rather than solely a problem of the afflicted individual. In this chapter, we review chronic illness and disability in late life as well as trends in family caregiving. We focus on adult-daughter caregivers who at midlife are attempting to balance their parent-care responsibilities with the challenges of their mother, wife, and employee roles. We review theoretical and empirical literature that bears on the experiences of women in multiple roles that include parent care. Our review highlights the programmatic research that we and our colleagues have conducted since the early 1990s. We end this chapter with a discussion of social policies that affect women in midlife, including implications of our work on women attempting to balance multiple roles.

CHRONIC ILLNESS IN LATE LIFE AND TRENDS IN FAMILY CAREGIVING

Since the mid-nineteenth century, advances in medicine have drastically altered people's experience of health and illness. During this time period, individuals living in the world's developed countries have witnessed a shift from infectious to chronic diseases as the prime causes of mortality. This shift has resulted in lower infant mortality and fewer deaths early in life, and many more people living into their later years. One consequence of this trend toward greater longevity is the increasing prevalence of chronic health conditions, the onset of disability, and, in some cases, total dependence on others for care.

Chronic conditions such as diabetes, respiratory diseases, cancer, cardiovascular problems, arthritis, hypertension, osteoporosis, and dementia are far more common among older adults than among their younger counterparts. These pathological states are clinically evident and have clear diagnostic classification. Other pathological states are subclinical, such as anemia and chronic inflammation, and are quite common in late life. Although these subclinical conditions may impact health status and may even be precursors of disease, they are not yet considered diseases (Yancik et al., 2007).

Other conditions such as injury from falls, incontinence, and frailty are also commonly associated with aging and, as such, are sometimes referred to as *geriatric syndromes*. The coexistence of pathological and natural factors and the possibility of interactions among them mean that a new diagnosis of any chronic condition is likely to be made in the context of preexisting health problems. These physiological problems and disease states frequently accumulate in late life and complicate older adults' health status and the quality of their lives. Thus, comorbidity has become known as the *ultimate geriatric syndrome* (Yancik et al., 2007).

Although chronic health conditions are physiological in nature, they typically have concomitant behavioral features. Functional limitations (i.e., having difficulty in performing one or more activities of daily living [ADLs]) and functional dependency (i.e., needing help with or being unable to perform such activities) are clear behavioral manifestations of illness. Most research on chronic illness and disability has focused on a single time point in an older adult's life, and, thus, little has been known about the rate at which chronic conditions precipitate functional decline over time. To fill this gap in knowledge, one study followed older adults (average age = 74 years) who were free of disability at baseline and resided in the community. These individuals were reassessed for new health conditions and the onset of dependency over a 3-year period (Wolff, Boult, Boyd, & Anderson, 2005).

After the initial 12 months, 30% of participants reported one or more new chronic conditions. This figure increased to 48% by 24 months, and to 61% by 36 months. After 3 years, the average participant had acquired one new chronic condition, increasing from 2.2 to 3.2 conditions. Osteoporosis, low body mass index, psychiatric disorder, dementia, and Parkinson's disease were the most common new conditions reported. The development of even one new condition was associated with nearly twice the likelihood of dependency onset. By 36 months, 5% reported onset of functional dependency and 2% entered long-term care facilities. This study demonstrated the rapidity with which an accrual of chronic conditions can lead to functional dependency (Wolff et al., 2005).

Although not every chronic disease results in limited functional capacity, and not all functional limitations create dependence on others, functional limitations and dependency are hallmarks of chronic health conditions. Importantly, when illnesses pose sufficient limitations on individuals' abilities to perform essential ADLs and assistance from others is required, the need for caregiving looms large. Thus, chronic illnesses are not only pernicious causes of disability in late life but they often necessitate adjustments in family relationships.

Responsibility for the care of impaired older adults is most often assumed by one family member (Aneshensel, Pearlin, Mullan, Zarit, & Whitlatch, 1995), referred to as the *primary caregiver*. Other family members and friends, however, sometimes provide assistance to both the primary caregiver and to the impaired older adult, and they are referred to as *secondary caregivers*.

There is a well-established hierarchy in determining who will become a *primary* caregiver. The responsibility for care typically falls first to the spouse of the ill older adult. In situations where a spouse assumes primary caregiving responsibilities, adult children often are involved as secondary caregivers. In this way, adult children may assist both of their parents (Bourgeois, Beach, Schulz, & Burgio, 1996). When a spouse is unavailable or unable to assume the role of primary caregiver, adult children are turned to next (Aneshensel et al., 1995).

In the 1980s, over one third (37.4%) of all caregivers in the United States were adult children of the ill person (Stone, Cafferata, & Sangl, 1987). Among daughter caregivers, nearly three quarters assume the role of primary caregiver. Among adult children, daughters were 3 times more likely to assume the role of primary caregiver than sons. Moreover, among the most impaired parents, the disparity between daughters and sons increases such that daughters were 4 times as likely to assume the primary-caregiver role (Stone and Kemper, 1989).

During the 1990s, significant changes emerged in the demography of later-life caregiving in the United States (Wolff & Kasper, 2006). By 1999, the proportion of adult-child primary caregivers increased to 41.3%. During the same decade, the proportion of care recipients receiving help with only instrumental activities of daily living (IADLs) decreased, whereas the proportion receiving help with five or more personal ADLs increased. Consistent with the trend for more adult children to assume the parent-care role and for older adults to be in poorer health, the proportion of caregivers providing help on a daily basis increased substantially between 1989 and 1999, and this change was most notable among adult-child caregivers.

Although men increased slightly in representation among adult-child caregivers during the 1990s, the caregiver role remains highly gendered, with almost three quarters of all adult-child caregivers being women in 1999 (Wolff & Kasper, 2006). The average caregiver in the United States is a woman who is 46 years of age, married, and works outside the home earning an annual income of $35,000. Although men also provide caregiving assistance, female caregivers spend as much as 50% more time providing care than their male counterparts (MetLife Mature Market Institute, 1999).

The parent-support ratio is another index of changing demographic trends in American families. This ratio (number of adults 85 and older per 100 adults aged 50 to 64) provides an estimate of the middle-aged person's support potential for the oldest old. Individuals comprising the middle-aged group are often children of the very old, hence, the term *parent*-support ratio. In 2000, the parent-support ratio in the United States was 10, suggesting that for every 100 midlife adults there were 10 older family members to attend to, a threefold increase from 3 older family members for every 100 midlife adults in 1960. By 2030, this ratio is projected to climb to 16, and to continue to rise to 30 by 2050—when all Baby Boomers themselves will be aged 85 and older (He, Sengupta, Velkoff, & DeBarros, 2005). If these forecasts are correct, the parent-support ratio will triple in only a half-century, and as such, increasing numbers of middle-aged adults are likely to enter the parent-care role.

DAUGHTERS AT MIDLIFE AND THEIR MULTIPLE ROLES

Although the term *midlife* is often used to refer to people somewhere between the ages of 40 and 60, this phase of life is not easily defined by age. Middle adulthood may better be characterized by a constellation of common life events and developments, including biological changes, children leaving home, and becoming a grandparent (Etaugh & Bridges, 2006). For most women, this time in life is one of zest, personal growth, and enjoyment of freedom from childbearing and responsibilities for young children (Mitchell & Helson, 1990). At the same time, however, many women in midlife take on new family roles and responsibilities when aging parents or parents-in-law become ill and need their assistance. Some women and their families are better prepared to manage the demanding tasks of parent care than are others. Addressing the concerns of midlife women caring for their aging parents involves consideration of the stress of their personal situations, the course of their own individual developments, and their interpersonal family dynamics (Qualls, 2002).

Since the early 1980s, a great deal of attention has been paid to midlife women who provide parent care and simultaneously occupy other family and work roles. These women have often been referred to as *women in the middle* (Brody, 1981). This label can refer to the generational position of these women, in that they are between the older generation of their parents and the younger generation of their children. It also can refer to their chronological age, in that these women are in the middle years of the life span (Brody, 1990).

Although awareness of women in the middle began over 25 years ago, the issues and concerns raised at that time appear to be even more applicable to today's women and those who will enter midlife in the near future. The large cohort of babies born in the two decades following World War II (Baby Boomers) is now in its parent-care years. The parents of these individuals are living longer than any generation in history, women in the Boomer cohort are postponing childbearing later into adulthood, and they continue to participate in the paid labor force at record levels. According to census data, one half of American women in their middle years are married and are in the paid labor force and over one third are married and have a child under the age of 18 (United States Bureau of the Census, 2005). Therefore, today's midlife women are more in the middle than ever before (Brody, 2004).

Early research on women in the middle estimated that, in addition to having the roles of mother, wife, and employee, 14% of women between the ages of 40 and 69 also have at least one living parent (Rosenthal, Matthews, & Marshall, 1989). Other research has estimated that 14% of women ages 40 to 64 provide at least 3 hours of assistance per week to a parent, and 4% provide that much assistance to a parent-in-law (Spitze & Logan, 1990). Moreover, the likelihood of being in the role of family caregiver has been shown to increase both with age and across birth cohorts (Moen, Robinson, & Fields, 1994), suggesting that many more women will occupy the parent-care role in the future.

Because so many adult daughters provide parent care, it has been argued that parent care is becoming a *normative* experience in American families, and that these women find themselves increasingly caught between the *competing demands* of their multiple family and work roles (Brody, 1985). This trend also has been widely publicized in the popular media. Such claims initially sparked academic debate about how common it is for women to simultaneously occupy the parent-care, mother, wife, and employee roles (e.g., Boyd & Treas, 1989; Spitze & Logan, 1990). It is generally agreed, however, that even though multiple role configurations that include the parent-care role may not be normative (in the sense of characterizing a majority of middle-aged women), there is an increasingly large number of women who are faced with these multiple role responsibilities, and that this trend is likely to continue into the foreseeable future.

OUR WORK ON ADULT-DAUGHTER CAREGIVERS

We and our colleagues began our work with women in the middle in the early 1990s. In the following sections, we highlight our key findings on the health effects of role constellations that combine parent care with various family and work roles. Before doing so, however, we first describe the sociological perspectives on multiple roles that guided our own theoretical framework.

The *competing demands hypothesis* evolved to explain the negative impact that caregiving often has on caregivers' psychological and physical well-being. This perspective argues that multiple role responsibilities create demands on these women that compete for their time and energy. The competing demands hypothesis rests on similar assumptions to those of the scarcity hypothesis, which assumes that individuals have limited personal resources, and that social organizations and role partners demand all of these resources (Goode, 1960). Thus, an individual's total role obligations are thought to be overly demanding, making role conflict inevitable.

The scarcity hypothesis has been challenged by the expansion hypothesis, which emphasizes the energy gains, rather than the energy expenditures, accrued by individuals with multiple roles (Marks, 1977). This energy-expansion perspective predicts positive consequences due to the enhancement of such personal resources as mastery, self-esteem, identity, and social and material gains from various roles. Moreover, when resources are scarce in one role, it is assumed that resources are likely to be available from other roles to compensate. Indeed, a growing literature has shown that the more roles occupied (most often those of mother, wife, and employee), the better sense of well-being women experience (e.g., Waldron & Jacobs, 1989).

Although the scarcity and expansion perspectives make different predictions about the effects of multiple roles, both are limited in that they focus on the number of roles occupied, rather than on the quality of experiences that transpire within roles. Both perspectives, with their emphasis on quantity, predict a net gain or a net loss of resources, regardless of role experiences. In contrast, perspectives that emphasize the quality of role experiences assert that two similar roles could create different cost–benefit ratios within and across these roles. The role-quality perspective asserts that both problems and rewards experienced within a role should be considered (Barnett & Baruch, 1985).

Drawing from prior work emphasizing role quality over role occupancy, our research with adult-daughter caregivers has been largely driven by two opposing questions: Do the roles that these women occupy in addition to the parent-care role have deleterious effects on their well-being (as the competing demands perspective assumes)? Or do these additional roles benefit their well-being (as the expansion perspective assumes)? To address these questions, we conducted a series of studies in which we conceptualized the parent-care role as an important family role that women experience as a part of their larger family and work lives.

PARENT CARE IN THE CONTEXT OF OTHER FAMILY ROLES

At the time we began our work, issues of role quality had been largely overlooked in research on family caregiving. Caregiving research typically focused on the problems associated with parent care and had given little attention to the positive aspects of care provision. Moreover, this work tended to examine the caregiver role in isolation from other roles.

When other roles were considered, they often were not given equal weight to that of the caregiver role. In our studies of family roles, we focused on women who not only occupied the role of caregiver to a parent or parent-in-law (i.e., primary family member who provided ADL assistance), but who also occupied the roles of mother to children at home and wife.

Evidence for the Competing Demands Hypothesis

Guided by the competing demands hypothesis, we set out to identify sources of stress and conflict in women's family roles, as well as the effects of these problems on women's psychological well-being. In the parent-care role, women most often report stressors such as the interpersonal conflict they experience when the parent criticizes or complains or is unresponsive, uncooperative, or demanding. As with the parent-care role, these women experience stress in each of their additional roles as mothers and wives. In the mother role, the stressors most often mentioned are the heavy demands or responsibilities for children, arguments with children, uncertainty about child-rearing practices, and the financial burdens of raising a family. Lack of companionship and emotional support from the husband and poor communication or conflict about the children are the stressors most often mentioned in the wife role. Consistent with the competing demands hypothesis, stress in these other family roles detracts from women's well-being beyond the negative effects of stress in the parent-care role (Stephens, Franks, & Townsend, 1994).

In addition to more global aspects of well-being, our work further reveals that stress in these family roles has the potential to erode women's sense of mastery. Women who experience more stress in the parent-care, mother, and wife roles also feel less confidence and competence to fulfill their responsibilities in each role domain (Franks & Stephens, 1992). Moreover, as stress increases in parent-care and mother roles over time, women's feelings of role-specific mastery continues to decline (Norton, Gupta, Stephens, Martire, & Townsend, 2005).

Our work has examined the effects of combining women's roles as mother and wife with their parent-care responsibilities (Stephens & Townsend, 1997). Our aims have been to investigate whether the stress experienced in these additional family roles might exacerbate (i.e., increase) the negative effects of parent-care stress on well-being (competing demands hypothesis); and whether the rewards experienced in these additional roles might buffer (i.e., decrease) the stress effects of parent care (expansion hypothesis). We found clear evidence to support the stress-exacerbation prediction in the mother role. Parent-care stress relates to poorer well-being among women whose mother roles are highly stressful; but for women whose mother roles are less stressful, parent-care stress is unrelated to their well-being. In contrast, the rewards of being a mother do not appear to buffer the harmful effects of parent-care stress on well-being. Experiences in the wife role, however, neither exacerbate nor buffer the effects of parent-care stress.

Our research team has also investigated the possibility that the experiences associated with any given role may not necessarily be confined to that role domain. Rather, because the boundaries between roles are sometimes ambiguous, it is likely that experiences in one role will *spill over* and color experiences in another. Role spillover is thought to be bidirectional in that experiences in one role have the potential to influence experiences in a second role, and vice versa.

In our work on role spillover, we have investigated ways in which parent care and marriage might affect one another (Stephens & Franks, 1995). Consistent with competing demands, we conceptualized negative spillover as the pressures on time and energy in one role that influence the quality of experiences in the other role as well as psychological interference between the roles. The type of negative spillover between the parent-care and wife roles most frequently encountered by women is the limited time available for the husband because of caregiving responsibilities. Regarding negative spillover in the other direction, very few women indicate that their marriage interferes with their parent-care responsibilities.

Evidence for the Expansion Hypothesis

Our work has been strongly influenced by assumptions of role-quality perspectives, in addition to those of the expansion hypothesis. Specifically, we have assumed that, in order to understand women's psychological well-being, it is crucial to consider the positive aspects of their multiple roles, as well as the more problematic aspects. Thus, we initially identified the rewarding and satisfying features of the parent-care, mother, and wife roles.

Frequent rewards in parent care result from the satisfaction taken from knowing that their parent is well-cared for, that this role fulfills a family obligation, and that they spend more time with their parent as a result of the needed assistance. As with their parent-care role, women experience many rewards as mothers and wives. As mothers, women most often find as rewarding the meaning and purpose children bring to their lives, as well as feeling needed and loved by their children. Rewards derived from being a wife most often include the husband being a good father and provider and the husband lending support and providing companionship (Stephens et al., 1994).

As predicted by the expansion hypothesis, rewards in each of these family roles contribute to psychological well-being regardless of the amount of stress occurring in each role. Moreover, an increase in reward-ing experiences in the parent-care, mother, and wife roles over time tends to be accompanied by an increased sense of mastery in these roles. In fact, when increases in rewards and increases in stress are considered simultaneously, only role rewards relate to changes in mastery (Norton et al., 2005).

We also have considered ways in which these roles might benefit one another. Consistent with the role expansion hypothesis, we conceptu-alized positive spillover as involving feelings of attachment, mastery, and self-esteem in one role that influence the quality of experiences in the other role. The spillover of self-esteem from one role to another is the most frequent type of positive spillover occurring in both direc-tions. In contrast to the relative absence of negative spillover from the wife role to parent care, many women indicate that their marriage helps to bolster their parent-care experiences (Stephens & Franks, 1995).

Social support from the husband is yet another resource from being married that helps to offset the stress of parent care (Franks & Stephens, 1996). Women frequently receive instrumental assistance from their husbands that affords them additional time and energy to care for the parent. Moreover, some husbands provide care directly to the ill parent as a way to support their caregiving wives.

PARENT CARE IN THE CONTEXT OF PAID EMPLOYMENT

Because the past several decades have witnessed increasingly large numbers of midlife women in the workforce, gerontologists have speculated about the impact of this trend. In particular, concerns have been raised about how employment will affect women's involvement in family caregiving and the long-term care of frail older adults. National data estimate that approximately half of adult children who assume the parent-care role are also employed full or part time (Wolff & Kasper, 2006).

Life-course research shows that employed women are likely to continue participation in the workforce, regardless of their caregiving responsibilities (Moen et al., 1994). Employed women who make the transition into family caregiving typically experience a decline in physical and mental health. Although physical limitations often attenuate with time, psychological distress accumulates over the course of care. Despite these increases in distress, however, women generally do not make changes in caregiving arrangements (Pavalko & Woodbury, 2000).

Much attention has been given to the health effects of employment for women (regardless of their caregiving status). Compared to those who are not employed, employed women tend to be less psychologically distressed, have better physical health, and have higher self-esteem (e.g., Ross & Mirowsky, 1995). The literature on later-life caregiving has also shown the benefits of employment for caregivers. Employed caregivers tend to experience better well-being than those who are not employed (Giele, Mutschler, & Orodenker, 1987; Miller, 1989; Skaff & Pearlin, 1992; Stoller & Pugliesi, 1989).

Because these studies of employed caregivers focused only on the occupancy of the employment role, they did not offer insight into the characteristics of women's work experiences that might be responsible for these effects. Our research team set out to fill this gap in the literature by investigating features of women's employment and work lives that seemed to protect them from the harmful consequences of parent-care stress. As with our studies of caregivers' other family roles, our research on employed caregivers was guided largely by the competing demands and expansion hypotheses. That is, we were open to the possibility that occupying the dual roles of parent-care provider and employee could have both detrimental and beneficial effects on women's well-being.

Evidence for the Competing Demands Hypothesis

Studies of employed caregivers have consistently shown that the demands of parent care and employment frequently interfere with one another (e.g., Aneshensel et al., 1995; Gignac, Kelloway, & Gottlieb, 1996; Neal, Chapman, Ingersoll-Dayton, & Emlen, 1993), as the competing demands hypothesis predicts. Approximately half of employed primary caregivers report that they experience work conflict in terms of rearranging work schedules, working fewer hours, or taking time off without pay (Wolff & Kasper, 2006).

Our studies of adult-daughter caregivers—all of whom were employed, married, and had children at home—have reported similar findings. When considering their other roles (mother, wife, and employee), the largest proportion of women identify the employee role as the one that conflicts most with parent care (Stephens, Townsend, Martire, & Druley, 2001).

Even though many of the women in our studies have been employed in managerial or professional occupations, they spend an average of 3 hours per day assisting with caregiving tasks (Stephens et al., 2001). These women indicate that, because of the responsibilities in these two roles, substantial conflict occurs. As the competing demands hypothesis predicts, women emphasize that there is not enough time and energy to do everything, the two roles are emotionally draining, and both roles pose considerable demands on them.

In addition to investigating the conflict that often occurs at the intersection of parent care and employment, we have been interested in ways the expenditure of resources in one role might spill over to affect the other role (Stephens, Franks, & Atienza, 1997). We considered the possibility that not only may caregiving interfere with work, but work may interfere with caregiving. Being exhausted and unable to concentrate at work and having work disrupted are the interferences from parent care that women report most often. Likewise, employment frequently interferes with the amount of time and attention that women can devote to parent care. Regardless of the source of the spillover, however, we have strong evidence that the more one role interferes with functioning in another, the more likely it is that women's well-being will suffer.

Our work also suggests that the stress of parent care and employment exert their deleterious effects on well-being through the incompatible pressures of these roles (Stephens et al., 1997). Thus, the proliferation of stressful experiences across roles appears to be one means by which stress that is specific to a given role has consequences for more global aspects of well-being. Our interrole conflict and role spillover findings are consistent with the most basic assumptions of the competing demands hypothesis—namely, that the demands of multiple roles are necessarily incompatible and can have harmful effects on well-being.

In addition to our focus on the incompatible demands of work and parent care, we have examined the possibility that the social environment of the workplace might bear on women's abilities to juggle parent care and employment. Working caregivers often state that their supervisors and coworkers are sometimes insensitive about attempts to balance parent care and work, or they fail to understand the difficulties of providing parent care (Atienza & Stephens, 2000). Women who encounter more of such problematic interactions with their work associates also experience poorer well-being, even after considering the number of hours they work per week and the stress they experience in parent care and employment. In contrast, emotionally supportive interactions with work associates about juggling the responsibilities of parent care and work do not seem to relate to women's well-being.

Evidence for the Expansion Hypothesis

In addition to the resources expended in parent care and employment, our studies of employed-daughter caregivers examined the resources gained from holding these dual roles, a key assumption of the expansion hypothesis. We found that, as with family roles, positive experiences in the caregiver role often spill over to affect employment and vice versa (Stephens et al., 1997). Being in a good mood in one role because of rewarding experiences in the other role occurs frequently for these women. They indicate that the feelings of confidence and accomplishment they gain in one role have benefits for their other role. Although the majority of women indicate experiencing positive spillover in both directions, only spillover from the employment role to parent care relates to better well-being.

A key goal of our research team has been to identify characteristics of employment that might moderate the deleterious health effects of parent-care stress. In addition to the expansion perspective, the literature on work and women's health helped to guide this endeavor. Our studies have identified two factors that seem to function as buffers to the stress of parent care—satisfying and full-time employment.

As with the more general literature on women's health (e.g., Barnett & Marshall, 1992), our research has found buffering effects of rewarding employment for adult-daughter caregivers (Stephens & Townsend, 1997). Among women with less rewarding work, parent-care stress is likely to erode well-being, whereas among women with very rewarding work, parent-care stress is unlikely to be related to well-being. It is possible that women with satisfying employment are more effective in distracting themselves at work from the demands of parent care. Additionally, they may be better able to regain from work such personal resources as self-esteem and mastery that are often eroded by the stress of parent care, as predicted by the expansion hypothesis.

Research on women's health has also shown that full-time employment is particularly beneficial. Working full time is associated with better well-being than is part-time employment (e.g., Wethington & Kessler, 1989). Moreover, caregivers who work more than 20 hours per week experience less stress from caregiving than those who work fewer hours (Enright & Friss, 1987).

Consistent with these findings, our research has shown that among daughter caregivers who work part-time, as the stress of their parent-care responsibilities increases, their well-being declines (Martire, Stephens, & Atienza, 1997). In contrast, among those working full time, there is no association between caregiving stress and well-being. These associations emerge even after considering work stress, the degree of the ill parents' impairment, hours of care provided, and hours of formal (paid) caregiving assistance received.

Time spent at work has the potential to provide women with much-needed respite or distraction from the responsibilities of caregiving (Brody, 1990). Thus, the stress-buffering effects of full-time employment may be due in part to the greater amount of time away from caregiving that working full time affords. The advantage of full-time work may also stem from the greater financial, social, and psychological resources it provides over part-time work.

CONCLUSIONS AND IMPLICATIONS

We believe that one of the important contributions of our initial research has been to demonstrate our most basic premise, that adult-daughter caregivers not only find their parent-care responsibilities to be stressful, but that they also find them to be rewarding. These women do indeed report both types of experiences in their caregiving roles. Notably, rewards from parent care and from other family roles are reported more often than stressors. Findings from our work on women's family roles provide evidence for both the competing demands hypothesis and for the expansion hypothesis. Moreover, our findings underscore the value of considering the quality of role experiences beyond the mere number of family roles occupied to more fully understand the health effects of women's parent-care responsibilities.

Our review of empirical literature on combining parent care and employment strongly suggests that this dual-role configuration is not necessarily detrimental to the health of midlife women, as the competing demands hypothesis would suggest. Like many other demanding roles, parent care and employment have the potential to interfere with each other in ways that are harmful to well-being. It is clear, however, that positive experiences in each role, especially in employment, may serve to offset the negative aspects of the other. Most notably, being employed in full-time work that is highly rewarding is likely to buffer the health of adult daughters against the stress of providing care to an ill parent, as the expansion hypothesis would suggest. Thus, this chapter's review of the parent-care and employment literature, including our own contributions, should help allay expressed (and implied) concerns that holding these two roles would be wholly problematic for the well-being of adult daughters (Martire & Stephens, 2003).

In addition to concerns that have been raised about the effects of parent care and employment on women's well-being and their availability to provide parent care, concerns have also been raised about the impact that later-life caregiving might have on the midlife workforce and ultimately on productivity. Employees who are providing care to ill family members cost U.S. employers $29 billion annually, which translates into an annual cost of $1,142 per employee. Costs are, in part, a result of decreased productivity, increased turnover rate, and the loss of between 5 and 12 days of work annually. Other sources of these costs stem from the fact that employed caregivers have more stress-related illnesses, utilize health plans to a greater degree, and ultimately add cost for the employer to provide health-care benefits (United States Department of Health and Human Services, Administration on Aging, 2003).

After we had begun our program of research in the early 1990s, a number of societal and organizational policy developments have taken place. The U.S. government enacted the Family Medical Leave Act (FMLA), which assures workers that they can return to jobs after a leave of up to 12 weeks to care for family members with serious health conditions. This act guarantees, however, only unpaid leave and generally applies to workers in larger organizations. Other employer benefits that could assist women attempting to balance their parent-care and work roles include flexible work hours, paid sick leave, and vacation days.

Emerging research aimed at evaluating the impact of these legislated and employer-initiated programs reveals some beneficial outcomes for caregivers and employers alike. Women whose employment provides flexible hours, unpaid family leave, and paid sick or vacation days are more likely to remain employed and maintain work hours after assuming the caregiver role than are women whose employers provide fewer benefits (Pavalko & Henderson, 2006). In addition, caregivers are more satisfied with their jobs if their places of employment provide more of these benefits and value the integration of employees' work and family lives (Sahibzada, Hammer, Neal, & Kuang, 2005).

Although employed caregivers who have workplace benefits are likely to remain in the workforce and be satisfied with their work, some research shows that the impact on their well-being stemming from access to these benefits is negligible (Pavalko & Henderson, 2006). Other research shows that women caregivers whose employers offer flexible work arrangements have only marginally better well-being than caregivers without such arrangements (Chesley & Moen, 2006). It is possible that even if such employer benefits do not directly impact women's well-being, their effects may be indirect. If such resources allow women caregivers to remain in the labor force and enjoy satisfying work, our research indicates that women's well-being will ultimately be enhanced.

Research on employed caregivers, including our own, has focused most often on women in professional, managerial, or administrative support occupations. Much less is known about the effects of juggling parent care and employment for adult daughters who are in occupations that offer less pay, fewer (or no) fringe benefits, little flexibility in work schedules, or few opportunities for career advancement. This issue is important given that caregivers with lower socioeconomic status have poorer well-being (e.g., Meshefedjian, McCusker, Bellavance, & Baumgarten, 1998).

Our chapter's review focused separately on the evidence for the competing demands and expansion perspectives, but problematic and positive role experiences are likely to coexist for any given woman. A caregiver is likely to be affected by both the stressful and rewarding aspects of combining her family and work roles. Indeed, our own research as well as the broader literature on balancing work and family responsibilities shows that the effects of occupying multiple roles depend heavily on the quality of experiences that transpire within and across these roles.

Findings from our studies provide abundant evidence that the lives of these women cannot be easily captured by either the competing demands or the expansion hypothesis alone. We find the strongest support for competing demands when we focus only on the problems and stressors encountered in the parent-care role and in other family and work roles.

Likewise, we find the strongest support for the expansion hypothesis when we focus exclusively on the satisfying and rewarding aspects of role experiences.

A far more complex picture emerges when we consider problematic and rewarding role experiences simultaneously. Our studies have amply demonstrated that positive experiences in one role have the potential to offset the effects of negative experiences in another role. This pattern of findings is not entirely consistent with either the competing demands or with the expansion perspectives.

Based on the accumulated findings, we have become convinced that the two questions that guided our original work in this area are more complementary to one another than opposing. Moreover, it is our contention that the processes governing the ways in which multiple roles affect well-being are more complicated than the ones proposed by either role theory. Thus, our research strongly suggests the need for a more comprehensive theoretical framework for understanding the lives of women who are in the middle of parent-care and other roles.

REFERENCES

Aneshensel, C. S., Pearlin, L. I., Mullan, J. T., Zarit, S. H., & Whitlatch, C. J. (1995). *Profiles in caregiving: The unexpected career.* San Diego: Academic Press.

Atienza, A. A., & Stephens, M. A. P. (2000). Social interactions at work and the well-being of daughters involved in parent care. *Journal of Applied Gerontology, 19,* 243–263.

Barnett, R. C., & Baruch, G. (1985). Women's involvement in multiple roles and psychological distress. *Journal of Personality and Social Psychology, 49,* 135–145.

Barnett, R. C., & Marshall, N. L. (1992). Worker and mother roles, spillover effects and psychological distress. *Women and Health, 18,* 9–40.

Bourgeois, M. S., Beach, S., Schulz, R., & Burgio, L. D. (1996). When primary and secondary caregivers disagree: Predictors and psychosocial consequences. *Psychology and Aging, 11*(3), 527–537.

Boyd, S. L., & Treas, J. (1989). Family care of the frail elderly: A new look at "women in the middle." *Women's Studies Quarterly, 1 & 2,* 66–74.

Brody, E. M. (1981). "Women in the middle" and family help to older people. *The Gerontologist, 21,* 471–480.

Brody, E. M. (1985). Parent care as a normative family stress. *The Gerontologist, 25,* 19–29.

Brody, E. M. (1990). *Women in the middle: Their parent-care years.* New York: Springer.

Brody, E. M. (2004). *Women in the middle: Their parent care years* (2nd ed.) New York: Springer.

Chesley, N., & Moen, P. (2006). When workers care: Dual-earner couples' caregiving strategies, benefit use, and psychological well-being. *American Behavioral Scientist, 49,* 1248–1269.

Enright, R. B., & Friss, L. (1987). *Employed caregivers of brain-impaired adults.* San Francisco: Family Survival Project.

Etaugh, C. A., & Bridges, J. S. (2006). Midlife transitions. In J.Worell & C. D. Goodheart (Eds.), *Handbook of girls' and womens' psychological health* (pp. 359–367). New York: Oxford University.

Franks, M. M., & Stephens, M. A. P. (1992). Multiple roles of middle generation caregivers: Contextual effects and psychological mechanisms. *Journal of Gerontology: Social Sciences, 47,* 123–129.

Franks, M. M., & Stephens, M. A. P. (1996). Social support in the context of caregiving: Husbands' provision of support to wives involved in parent care. *Journals of Gerontology: Psychological Sciences, 51B,* 43–52.

Giele, J. Z., Mutschler, P. H., & Orodenker, S. Z. (1987). *Stress and burdens of caregiving for the frail elderly* (Working Paper No. 36). Waltham, MA: Brandeis University.

Gignac, M. A. M., Kelloway, E. K., & Gottlieb, B. H. (1996). The impact of caregiving on employment: A mediational model of work-family conflict. *Canadian Journal on Aging, 15,* 525–542.

Goode, W. J. (1960). A theory of role strain. *American Sociological Review, 25,* 483–496.

He, W., Sengupta, M., Velkoff, V. A., & DeBarros, K. A. (2005). *65+ in the United States: 2005.* Retrieved June 7, 2006, from http://www.census.gov/prod/2006pubs/p23-209.pdf

Marks, S. R. (1977). Multiple roles and role strain: Some notes on human energy, time and commitment. *American Sociological Review, 42,* 921–936.

Martire, L. M., & Stephens, M. A. P. (2003). Juggling parent care and employment responsibilities: The dilemmas of adult daughter caregivers in the work force. *Sex Roles: A Journal of Research, 48,* 167–173.

Martire, L. M., Stephens, M. A. P., & Atienza, A. A. (1997). The interplay of work and caregiving: Relationships between role satisfaction, role involvement, and caregivers' well-being. *Journal of Gerontology: Social Sciences, 52B,* S279–S289.

Meshefedjian, G., McCusker, J., Bellavance, F., & Baumgarten, M. (1998). Factors associated with symptoms of depression among informal caregivers of demented elders in the community. *The Gerontologist, 38,* 247–253.

MetLife Mature Market Institute, National Alliance for Caregiving, & The National Center on Women and Aging. (1999, November). *The Metlife juggling act study: Balancing caregiving with work and the costs involved.* Retrieved June 28, 2006, from http://www.metlife.com/WPSAssets/12949500261100547 900V1FJuggling%20Study%20-111004.pdf.

Miller, B. (1989). Adult children's perceptions of caregiver stress and satisfaction. *Journal of Applied Gerontology, 8,* 275–293.

Mitchell, V., & Helson, R. (1990). Women's prime of life: Is it the 50s? *Psychology of Women Quarterly, 14,* 451–470.

Moen, P., Robinson, J., & Fields, V. (1994). Women's work and caregiving roles: A life course approach. *Journal of Gerontology, 49,* 176–186.

Neal, M. B., Chapman, N. J., Ingersoll-Dayton, B., & Emlen, A. C. (1993). *Balancing work and caregiving for children, adults, and elders.* Newbury Park, CA: Sage.

Norton, T. R., Gupta, A., Stephens, M. A. P., Martire, L. M., & Townsend, A. L. (2005). Stress, rewards, and change in the centrality of women's family and work roles: Mastery as a mediator. *Sex Roles, 52,* 325–335.

Pavalko, E. K., & Henderson, K. A. (2006). Combining care work and paid work: Do workplace policies make a difference? *Research on Aging, 28,* 359–374.

Pavalko, E. K., & Woodbury, S. (2000). Social roles as process: Caregiving careers and women's health. *Journal of Health and Social Behavior, 41,* 91–105.

Qualls, S. H. (2002). Women in the middle: Caretaking issues in therapy. In F. K. Trotman & C. M. Brody (Eds.), *Psychotherapy and counseling with older women: Cross-cultural, family, and end-of-life issues* (pp. 87–103). New York: Springer.

Rosenthal, C. J., Matthews, S. H., & Marshall, V. W. (1989). Is parent care normative? The experiences of a sample of middle-aged women. *Research on Aging, 11,* 224–260.

Ross, C. E., & Mirowsky, M. (1995). Does employment affect health? *Journal of Health and Social Behavior, 36,* 230–243.

Sahibzada, K., Hammer, L. B., Neal, M. B., & Kuang, D. C. (2005). The moderating effects of work-family role combinations and work-family organizational culture on the relationship between family-friendly workplace supports and job satisfaction. *Journal of Family Issues, 26*, 820–839.

Skaff, M. M., & Pearlin, L. I. (1992). Caregiving: Role engulfment and the loss of self. *The Gerontologist, 32*, 656–664.

Spitze, G., & Logan, J. (1990). More evidence on women (and men) in the middle. *Research on Aging, 12*, 182–198.

Stephens, M. A. P., & Franks, M. M. (1995). Spillover between daughters' roles as caregiver and wife: Interference or enhancement? *Journal of Gerontology: Psychological Sciences, 50B*, 9–17.

Stephens, M. A. P., Franks, M. M., & Atienza, A. A. (1997). Where two roles intersect: Spillover between parent care and employment. *Psychology and Aging, 12*, 30–37.

Stephens, M. A. P., Franks, M. M., & Townsend, A. L. (1994). Stress and rewards in women's multiple roles: The case of women in the middle. *Psychology and Aging, 9*, 45–52.

Stephens, M. A. P., & Townsend, A. L. (1997). Stress of parent care: Positive and negative effects of women's other roles. *Psychology and Aging, 12*, 376–386.

Stephens, M. A. P., Townsend, A. L., Martire, L. M., & Druley, J. A. (2001). Balancing parent care with other roles: Interrole conflict of adult daughter caregivers. *Journal of Gerontology: Psychological Sciences, 56B*, P24–P34.

Stoller, E. P., & Pugliesi, K. L. (1989). The transition to the caregiving role. *Research on Aging, 11*, 312–330.

Stone, R. I., Cafferata, G. L., & Sangl, J. (1987). Caregivers of the frail elderly: A national profile. *The Gerontologist, 27*, 616–626.

Stone, R. I., & Kemper, P. (1989). Spouses and children of disabled elders: How large a constituency for long-term care reform? *Milbank Quarterly, 67*, 485–506.

United States Bureau of the Census, 2005. (n.d.). *America's families and living arrangements: 2005*. Retrieved June 23, 2006, from http://www.census.gov/population/socdemo/hh-fam/cps2005.html.

United States Department of Health and Human Services, Administration on Aging. (2003, August 27). *National family caregiver support program*. Retrieved June 7, 2006, from http://www.aoa.gov/press/fact/pdf/ss_nfcsp.pdf.

Waldron, I., & Jacobs, J. A. (1989). Effects of multiple roles on women's health: Evidence from a national longitudinal study. *Women and Health, 15*, 3–19.

Wethington, E., & Kessler, R. C. (1989). Employment, parental responsibility, and psychological distress: A longitudinal study of married women. *Journal of Family Issues, 10,* 527–546.

Wolff, J. L., Boult, C., Boyd, C., & Anderson, G. (2005). Newly reported chronic conditions and onset of functional dependency. *Journal of the American Geriatrics Society, 53,* 851–855.

Wolff, J. L., & Kasper, J. D. (2006). Caregivers of frail elders: Updating a national profile. *The Gerontologist, 46,* 344–356.

Yancik, R., Ershler, W., Satariano, W., Hazzard, W., Cohen, H. J., & Ferrucci, L. (2007). Report of the National Institute on Aging Task Force on Comorbidity. *Journal of Gerontology: Medical Sciences, 62A,* 275–280.

5

Impact of Dementia Caregiving: Risks, Strains, and Growth

WEILING LIU AND DOLORES GALLAGHER-THOMPSON

There are many things to consider when discussing dementia caregiving; this chapter will focus on the positive and negative impacts of it. We will begin by providing some background information on dementia and Alzheimer's disease. Cultural factors to consider when working with various ethnic caregivers will also be addressed. Risk associated with caregiving and positive aspects of caregiving will be discussed. Finally, recommendations and implications for clinicians will be provided.

ALZHEIMER'S DISEASE AND RELATED DEMENTIAS

The number of individuals who will suffer from Alzheimer's disease or related dementias in the United States is expected to increase dramatically over the next half century (Ory, Hoffman, Yee, Tennstedt, & Schulz, 1999). The diseases causing dementia are some of the most important challenges facing Western medicine (Feldman & O'Brien, 1999). Alzheimer's disease (AD), the most common cause of dementia, affects over 4 million people in the United States, and it is estimated to account for over half of all cases of dementia. The prevalence of AD will be greater among minority elderly people than among their Caucasian/White counterparts (U.S. Census Bureau, 2000). AD mainly affects those over the age of 60 and the prevalence of AD is estimated to double every 5 years beyond the age of 65 (U.S. Department of Health and Human Services: National Institute of Health and National Institute on Aging, 2005).

The prevalence trends translate into a huge impact on people with the disease, their families and friends, and caregivers. Most AD and related dementia caregivers are family members caring for their relatives (U.S. Department of Health and Human Services: National Institute of Health and National Institute on Aging, 2005). Eighty-seven percent of AD caregivers are mostly cared for by members of their family (Alzheimer's Association and National Alliance for Caregiving, 2004). Dementia caregivers are primarily female (73%) with an average age of 48 years, caring for persons whose average age is 78 (Ory et al., 1999). During their years of AD caregiving, spouses, relatives, and friends experience emotional, physical, and financial stress. Caucasians comprise 43% of all dementia caregivers while African Americans, Latinos, and Asians comprise 27%, 19%, and 10%, respectively. These numbers may reflect the current demographic make-up of the United States as a whole and the role of a family caregiver.

Caregivers expend time, energy, and emotional and financial resources to meet caregiving demands. Care recipients rely heavily upon caregivers with difficult daily tasks. Two-thirds of dementia caregivers help with one or more Activities of Daily Living (ADLs), such as getting out of beds and chairs, getting dressed, incontinence, bathing, and feeding. Additionally, they provide assistance with Instrumental Activities of Daily Living (IADLs), such as medication management, shopping, housework, preparing meals, transportation, arranging or supervising services, and managing finances. Dementia caregivers commonly commit 40 or more hours per week to caregiving compared to nondementia caregivers.

Caregivers watch their relative become more and more forgetful, frustrated, and confused. Eventually, the person with AD does not even recognize his or her nearest and dearest relatives and friends. When caregivers were asked to report their emotional stress on a 5-point Likert scale (5 = great deal of emotional stress), 41% of dementia caregivers rate their stress as a 4 or 5 (Alzheimer's Association and National Alliance for Caregiving, 2004).

With the heavy burden, stress, and sacrifices involved in caring for someone with dementia, it is not surprising that caregivers express a number of unmet needs for information and support. The burden associated with caring for an impaired relative has been associated with several risk factors that encompass physical, social, psychological, and financial domains (Ory et al., 1999; Schulz et al., 1997; Schulz & Williamson, 1997). In terms of psychological outcomes, caregivers have been shown to experience elevated levels of depression (Atienza, Collins, & King, 2001; Draper, Poulos, Poulos, & Ehrlich, 1996; Gallagher, Rose, Rivera, Lovett, & Thompson, 1989; Pinquart & Sorensen, 2003a, b, 2004; Russo, Vitaliano, Brewer, Katon, & Becker, 1995).

Social support is one of several variables that have been demonstrated to have a buffering effect against depression. Increased social support has been linked to greater well-being (Atienza et al., 2001; Cohen, Sherrod, & Clark, 1986; Cohen & Wills, 1985; Lepore, 1992). Additionally, those who have greater support from their spouses and families have lower risk for depression (Atienza et al., 2001; Hooker, Monahan, Bowman, Frazier, & Shifren, 1998; Li, Seltzer, & Greenberg, 1997).

Positive aspects of caregiving have also been identified as having a positive correlation with better health of the caregiver (Cohen, Gold, & Shulman, 1994; Cohen, Colantonio, & Vernich, 2002; Kramer, 1997; Pearlin, Mullan, Semple, & Skaff, 1990). Caregivers who reported more positive feelings were less likely to report depression (Boerner, Schulz, & Horowitz, 2004; Cohen et al., 1994, 2002; Roff et al., 2004). In addition, caregivers who describe more positive aspects of caregiving might be buffered from negative consequences (e.g., depression, increased risk of mortality) (Schulz & Beach, 1999).

DEFINITION OF TERMS

Dementia

The literal meaning of *dementia* is a state of being out of or deprived of one's mind (Weiner, 2003). Today, the term is used to describe a range of impairments of cognitive abilities sufficient to interfere with self-maintenance, work, or social relationships (Weiner, 2003). Dementia is characterized by cognitive and behavioral disturbances, and despite the main symptom of memory loss, other areas of functioning are affected. Other areas of impairment or change include attention, orientation, language, mood, personality, judgment, and visual spatial performance. *The Diagnostic and Statistical Manual of Mental Disorders–IV–Text Revision* (DSM-IV-TR) states that the essential diagnostic features of dementia are the development of various cognitive impairments that include memory impairment and at least one of the following: *aphasia*: loss of expressive and/or receptive language; *apraxia*: impairment in performing voluntary movements; *agnosia*: inability to interpret sensory stimuli, or disturbance in executive functioning (higher order intellectual functioning such as planning and inhibition) (American Psychiatric Association, 2000). The symptoms cannot be due to other medical or psychiatric illnesses. A diagnosis of dementia also requires significant impairments in social or occupational functioning.

Caregiving

Caregiving is a term that does not have a clear definition because the definition is dependent on the context in which it is used. For instance, caregiving is defined as assisting in the identification, prevention, or treatment of an illness or disability (Dictionary.com, 2004). However, in another context it is defined as attending to the needs of a child or dependent adult (Dictionary.com, 2004). The latter definition is closer to the context this chapter will address. Caregiving generally reflects extraordinary care and exceeds the bounds of what is typically considered normative for others (e.g., preparing meals, housekeeping) (Schulz & Quittner, 1998). As mentioned in the previous section, dementia-caregiver responsibilities include help with one or more ADLs, such as getting out of beds and chairs, getting dressed, incontinence, bathing, and feeding. Additionally, they provide assistance with IADLs, such as medication management, shopping, housework, preparing meals, transportation, arranging or supervising services, and managing finances.

Other than assisting in ADLs and IADLs, caregiving includes providing emotional support, personal care, and case management. In comparison, caregivers of nondementia care recipients are not as heavily involved with ADLs and IADLs and do not expend as much time in caregiving (Alzheimer's Association and National Alliance for Caregiving, 2004). Another large difference in caregiving for an individual with dementia is that the caregiver must face psychological and social adjustments (National Alliance for Caregiving and American Association for Retired Persons, 2004). As the illness progresses, the caregiver must confront not only the fact that their relative no longer is able to recognize him/her, but also the emotional lability, violent outbursts, and increase in medical crises. As a result, the caregiving is often overstressed and disruption in daily routine increases. Additionally, the caregiving takes over one's life and the caregiver gradually loses support from family and friends (Alzheimer's Association and National Alliance for Caregiving, 2004; Andren & Elmstahl, 2005; Brummett et al., 2006).

Caregivers

Caregivers of individuals with dementia are mainly adult children, relatives, or spouses of the care recipient (National Alliance for Caregiving and American Association for Retired Persons, 2004; Niederehe & Fruge, 1984; Strawbridge, Wallhagen, Shema, & Kaplan, 1997; Zarit, Reever, & Bach-Peterson, 1980). Additionally, most caregivers are women (National Alliance for Caregiving and American Association for Retired Persons, 2004; U.S. Department of Health and Human Services: National Institute of Health and National Institute on Aging, 2005). The typical female caregiver has had at least some college experience and spends an average of 20 or more hours per week providing unpaid care to someone 50 years or older (National Alliance for Caregiving and American Association for Retired Persons, 2004). A majority of caregivers are married and most have managed work with caregiving responsibilities at some point during their role as a caregiver. Female dementia caregivers are more likely to provide care at a high level of burden, which includes providing care on average 87 hours a week and assisting with six IADLs and five ADLs (National Alliance for Caregiving and American Association for Retired Persons, 2004). The research literature postulates that female caregivers may be psychologically more vulnerable (Atienza et al., 2001;

Draper et al., 1996; Tennstedt, Crawford, & McKinlay, 1993), but it is not surprising given their caregiving situations.

The number of individuals aged 65 and over is rapidly increasing in the United States because the Baby Boomer generation is entering older age. By the year 2050, the total U.S. population age of 65 and older will double while the number of people aged 85 and older is expected to triple (U.S. Census Bureau, 2000). Not only is the elder population growing but the ethnic minority population is also increasing. Hispanics/Latinos now constitute the largest population of an ethnic minority group living in the United States (Bernstein & Bergman, 2003), based on numbers alone. But among the different racial/ethnic groups, Asians had the highest rate of growth at nearly 64% from 1980 to 2000, compared to 31% overall growth of the Hispanic population during the same years (Bernstein & Bergman, 2003). In comparison, the Black/African Americans and White/Caucasians have a low projected growth rate (Angel & Hogan, 2004).

The scholarly literature documents the disparities in health status, health services utilization, and health-care access among American racial and ethnic minorities (LaVeist, 2004). Additionally, racial and ethnic minorities have a worse health profile and less access to health care compared with Whites and African Americans. Factors in each ethnic group create health risks, including social risks (i.e., acculturation, poorer quality medical care, exposure to discrimination or racism, social support, socioeconomic status) that have been associated with health as a variant by race (LaVeist & Wallace, 2000; Yeo & Gallagher-Thompson, 2006). Additionally, there may be characteristics of the culture of a racial/ethnic group that can influence health/illness behaviors.

Cultural Factors

Acculturation is an important concept and is considered to be an important part of cross-cultural psychology. A general framework that links what is known as cultural and psychological acculturation was presented (Berry, 2003). *Cultural acculturation* is "change that is indirect (not cultural, but 'ecological'), can be delayed (because internal adjustments presumably of a cultural and psychological character take time), and can be reactive (i.e., rejecting the cultural influence and changing toward a more traditional way of life rather than inevitably toward greater similarity with the dominant culture)" (Berry, 2003, p. 19). *Psychological acculturation* refers to "changes in an individual who is a participant in a culture-contact situation—a person who is being influenced directly by the external cultural and by the changing culture of which the individual is a member" (Berry, 2003, p. 20). These concepts of acculturation are ways to help explain why some members of a certain ethnic group show symptoms or problems while others do not. For instance, Chinese Americans view dementia as "a form of normal aging, a form of mental illness, a source of shame, the result of fate, retribution for the sins of the family or of one's ancestors, or imbalance between the body complementary forms of energy (*yin and yang*)" (Wang et al., 2006, p. 177). Because of these views, barriers to care have emerged and they include not knowing about AD at the early stage of the disease, strong stigma attached to AD, lack of family and community support, and negative interactions with health services providers (Wang et al., 2006).

The level of acculturation of an individual may also affect perceptions of, and responses to, caregiving. For example, ethnic and cultural factors influence caregiver stress appraisal and coping responses (Aranda & Knight, 1997). Results from the literature have shown that ethnicity and culture can influence whether cognitive impairment or physical impairment is perceived as being stressful between Blacks and Whites (Aranda & Knight, 1997). This model is a widely used sociocultural model of stress and coping for caregivers. Recently, there has been an increase in interest in how different cultural and ethnic groups cope with the role of caregiver for a family member with dementia (Adams, Aranda, Kemp, & Takagi, 2002). Cultural differences have been found in psychological responses to stress, individual coping styles, and variables associated with utilization of services (Gallagher-Thompson et al., 2007). Ethnicity significantly affects how a family member views a disease and how one approaches the role of providing care for a relative with dementia (Gallagher-Thompson et al., 2003).

RISKS ASSOCIATED WITH CAREGIVING

Physical Risks

Family caregivers perform an important service for their relatives but they do so at a considerable cost to themselves. Studies have concluded that acute stressful situations are associated with adverse immune changes in humans (Kiecolt-Glaser, Glaser, Gravenstein, Malarkey, & Sheridan, 1996; Schleifer, Keller, & Stein, 1985). Additionally, those who are undergoing large-scale stressful changes in their lives such as divorce or separation and bereavement (Kiecolt-Glaser et al., 1996; Stein, Keller, & Schleifer, 1985) display lower immunologic strength. There is a consensus that caring for an elderly individual with a disability is burdensome and stressful to many family members (Schulz, O'Brien, Bookwala, & Fleissner, 1995). In studies assessing caregiver physical health, caregivers consistently report decreased overall health and increased health problems and this also contributes to psychiatric morbidity in the form of increased depression (Schulz et al., 1995; Vitaliano, Scanlan, Krenz, Schwartz, & Marcovina, 1996).

Researchers have also suggested that the combination of prolonged distress and physical demands of caregiving may compromise caregivers' physiological functioning and increase their risk for health problems (Kiecolt-Glaser et al., 1996; Schulz et al., 1997). Some studies have shown that caregivers are less likely to engage in preventive health behaviors and exhibit greater cardiovascular reactivity (Lee, Colditz, Berkman, & Kawachi, 2003; Mausbach, Patterson, Rabinowitz, Grant, & Schulz, 2007). Specifically, female caregivers who provided more than 8 hours of care per week for a disabled or ill spouse were twice as likely to have coronary heart disease (Lee et al., 2003). The reasons for increased coronary heart disease may have been due to the fact that these caregivers also had elevated blood pressure, increased risk for hypertensions, and poorer immune functioning. Some researchers found that caregivers were higher than noncaregivers for prevalence of chronic illnesses and medications (Haley, Levine, Brown, Berry, & Hughes, 1987; Kiecolt-Glaser, Dura, Speicher, Trask, & Glaser, 1991).

Caregivers have poorer immune responses than noncaregivers, but this is not due to nutrition, sleep, or other health issues (Kiecolt-Glaser et al., 1996). Caregiving has also been associated with increased mortality risk. Schulz and Beach found that participants who were providing care and experiencing caregiver strain had mortality risks that were 63% higher than noncaregiving controls (1999). More specifically, after controlling for sociodemographic factors, baseline prevalence, and subclinical disease, they found that caregivers who provided support to their spouses and reported caregiving strain were 63% more likely to die within 4 years. This is consistent to other studies showing that strained caregivers compared with age- and sex-matched noncaregiving controls have significantly higher levels of depressive symptoms and anxiety and lower levels of perceived health (Schulz et al., 1997). Additionally, they are much less likely to have time to rest when sick, time to exercise, or to get adequate rest.

In regards to physical risks, very little is known about ethnically diverse caregivers. Many Asian Indian elders have Type II Diabetes Mellitus, which is usually associated with hyperinsulinemia, coronary vascular disease, and stroke—all assumed to be associated with a form of dementia (Periyakoil, 2006). In the general caregiving literature, chronic stress among dementia caregivers is commonly reported. However, not much is known about how physical risks differ among cultural and ethnic groups.

Financial Risks

The economic issues associated with caregiving can be burdensome, especially for Alzheimer's disease or related dementia caregivers since on average they spend $324 per month, compared to nondementia caregivers who spend an average of $124 per month. AD caregivers spend a lot out-of-pocket, even when the person with dementia is not the caregiver's dependent for tax purposes (Alzheimer's Association and National Alliance for Caregiving, 2004). Many caregivers are making significant financial sacrifices, both in out-of-pocket expenses and reduced earnings, to provide care. For instance, six out of ten caregivers say that they had to make some work-related adjustments in order to help the person they care for (National Alliance for Caregiving and American Association for Retired Persons, 2004). More than half of working caregivers say that as a result of their caregiving responsibilities they had to go to work late, leave early, or take time off during the day to provide care. Dementia caregivers report greater need to take less demanding jobs, take early retirement, lose job benefits, or give up work entirely than other caregivers (Ory et al., 1999). With these hardships, providing financial care can be difficult since considering the cost by the primary caregiver along with other informal assistance can average about $18,256 per year (National Alliance for Caregiving and American Association for Retired Persons, 2004). Generally, older minorities were in more severe poverty (defined as 100% below the poverty threshold) than the older, non-Hispanic Whites (Proctor & Dalaker, 2002). Specifically, 25% of Hispanic females and 18% of Hispanic males were poor. Additionally, elderly Black women and men had high poverty status (26% and 16%, respectively) (Proctor & Dalaker, 2002). Given the scarce amount of information of financial status of ethnic minorities, it is assumed from the information available that there is an increased financial strain in ethnic minorities than their non-Hispanic White counterparts.

Social Risks

Family relationships change when AD or related dementias emerge and intense caregiving occurs regardless of living arrangements (Spitznagel, Tremont, Davis, & Foster, 2006). A greater percentage of dementia caregivers reported having less time for other relatives and friends and perceived other members of the family as not doing their fair share (Ory et al., 1999). Additionally, dementia caregivers report having to give up pleasurable personal activities and report a higher degree of family conflict. Increased family conflict is common among dementia caregivers (Vitaliano, et al. 1996).

Dementia spouse caregivers report a higher incidence of marital conflict and decreased incidence of positive interactions for the couples (Narayan, Lewis, Tornatore, Hepburn, & Corcoran-Perry, 2001; Pruchno, Kleban, Michaels, & Dempsey, 1990). A concern as a couple ages is if one person develops dementia. Additionally, worries include burdening your partner with taking on the role of caregiver. As an individual with dementia gradually deteriorates ultimately, so does the relationship (Stephens & Qualls, 2007). The emotional and social relationship is what is lost. Partners of people with dementia recall once the diagnosis of dementia was provided, that was the loneliest moment (Stephens & Qualls, 2007). It is important to work with these couples and educate the partner of the new role along with renegotiating the relationship, such as the issue of intimacy. This is another aspect of dementia caregiving that should be considered when working with a caregiver and care recipient.

Social support plays a large role in certain ethnic groups. For African American families, the kin and nonkin are part of the social support network and they are willing to provide care to dependent elders (Dilworth-Anderson, Gibson, & Detry Burke, 2006). Filial piety plays a role in Chinese families (Wang et al., 2006). Nuclear and extended-family systems are emphasized in Asian Indian families and Cuban American families (Argüelles & Argüelles, 2006; Periyakoil, 2006). These are a few examples of how social roles play a part in caregiving. Often, minority caregivers of loved ones with dementia are nonspouses, in comparison to their White caregiving counterparts who are more often the spouse (Adams et al., 2002).

Psychological Risks

Depression, one of the major mental health problems in the United States (American Psychiatric Association, 2000), is a serious risk factor for dementia caregivers. Depression in its various forms, such as insomnia, fatigue, anxiety, stress, and headache, is one of the most common disturbances seen by physicians (Tabora & Flaskerud, 1994). It varies in severity from mild mood swings (e.g., dysthymia) to severe depression (e.g., major or manic depression). According to the DSM-IV-TR (American Psychiatric Association, 2000) a diagnosis of Major Depressive Disorder requires the presence of at least five symptoms for a minimum period of 2 weeks. These symptoms include persistent depressed mood (e.g., feelings of sadness or emptiness), helplessness or hopelessness, diminished interest in pleasurable activities, sleep disturbance, appetite and weight change, psychomotor agitation or retardation, diminished ability to think or concentrate, inappropriate feelings of guilt, and frequent suicidal thoughts.

According to the DSM-IV-TR, the prevalence rates of Major Depressive Disorder in adults are 1 in 20, with one person in ten having a depressive episode at least once in his or her life. More than twice as many women are currently being treated for depression than men (American Psychiatric Association, 2000). Given the fact that most dementia caregivers are currently women, it is not surprising to find that they are susceptible to depression. In fact, studies have found prevalence rates of depressive disorders as high as 50% (Gallagher-Thompson, Rose, Rivera, Lovett, & Thompson, 1989; Thompson, Spira, Depp, McGee, & Gallagher-Thompson, 2006), with a range from about 25% to about 80% in one study (Alspaugh, Stephens, Townsend, Zarit, & Greene, 1999).

General agreement within the literature states caregiving for a demented family member is associated with increased dysphoria, particularly for spouses (Dura, Stukenberg, & Kiecolt-Glaser, 1991). Stress, defined either as the objective or subjective experience of individuals, has been consistently linked to depression (Alspaugh et al., 1999; Pearlin et al., 1990). Objective primary stressors such as the relative's problem behaviors (e.g., wandering) have been related to caregivers' psychological distress, especially depression (Adams, 2007; Alspaugh et al., 1999; Pinquart & Sorensen, 2003a, b; Schulz et al., 1995; Wagner, Logsdon, Pearson, & Teri, 1997; Zarit et al., 1980). Prior work has also demonstrated that subjective primary stressors such as feeling overloaded by caregiving responsibilities and feelings of being captive in the caregiving role have been associated to depressive symptomatology and increases in depressive symptoms over time (Aneshensel, Pearlin, Mullan, Zarit, & Whitlach, 1995; Eisdorfer et al., 2003; Kiecolt-Glaser et al., 1991; Schulz et al., 1995; Vitaliano et al., 1996).

Mixed samples of dementia caregivers (e.g., spouse and adult children combined) report current disorder rates ranging from 14% to as high as 60% (Brummett et al., 2006; Dura et al., 1991; Gallagher et al., 1989; Pagel, Becker, & Coppel, 1985; Pinquart & Sorensen, 2004; Strawbridge et al., 1997). Factors that contribute to depression include behavior problems among the care recipient, the caregiver's appraisal of their caregiving skills, isolation, family disharmony, lack of support, and disruption in other roles and activities (Dura et al., 1991; Eisdorfer et al., 2003; Gallagher-Thompson & Coon, 2007; Ory et al., 1999; Stephens, Norris, Kinney, Ritchie, & Grotz, 1988).

Understanding depression among caregivers is important, as the onset of depression is not only harmful to the caregivers but also may affect their continued ability to provide care for the care recipient or other family members (Mok, Lai, Wong, & Wan, 2007). Depression in the caregiver may also lead to depression in the relative with dementia, resulting in furthering the level of impaired functioning beyond that associated with the disease itself (Eisdorfer et al., 2003; Gitlin et al., 2003).

Caregiving has also been associated with increased prevalence of anxiety disorders (Dura et al., 1991; Gallagher et al., 1989; Russo et al., 1995). Dementia caregivers were 10 times more likely to meet criteria for an anxiety disorder compared to nondementia caregivers (Dura et al., 1991). One in three caregivers reported significant anxiety symptomatology (Vitaliano, Russo, Young, Teri, & Maiuro, 1991).

In addition to depression and anxiety, caregivers have reported significant problems with controlling and frequency of angry emotions and hostility (Gallagher et al., 1989; Pagel et al., 1985; Vitaliano et al., 1991). Forty percent of caregivers had difficulty with healthy expression of angry emotions, such as shouting or losing control of their temper (Gallagher et al., 1989). Regardless of having these negative emotions, caregivers also have difficulty expressing them in a constructive manner.

Very little is known about psychological risks experienced by ethnic caregivers. There have been a few studies investigating the effectiveness of interventions in decreasing depressive symptoms and distress in ethnic groups besides those that have investigated Latino and Chinese female dementia caregivers (Gallagher-Thompson et al., 2003, 2007). Differences in psychological and physiological responses to caregiving stress were examined in Hispanic and non-Hispanic White women through salivary cortisol collection (Gallagher-Thompson et al., 2006). Results showed that caregivers had higher cortisol levels than noncaregivers, with variation among the caregivers but no difference in the noncaregivers among ethnic groups. Specifically, Hispanic caregivers had higher cortisol levels than non-Hispanic White caregivers, suggesting higher levels of stress overall in their lives. High cortisol is associated with risk for diseases and so one should consider that Hispanic caregivers may be in need of interventions to reduce overall day-to-day stress—in addition to caregiving-specific stress, such as transportation issues, problems on the job, and/or economic issues that make it difficult for them to use services such as respite care, which tends to be costly (Gallagher-Thompson et al., 2006).

In addition, Hispanic caregivers may benefit from interventions targeted at health maintenance as a way of reducing the potentially negative impact of dysregulated cortisol.

Past research has clearly documented the negative consequences of caregiving, including depression, poor perceived health, and increased risk of mortality (Schulz & Beach, 1999; Schulz et al., 1995). Aside from the negative aspects of caregiving, recently there has been a growing body of literature focusing on the positive aspects of caregiving (PAC).

POSITIVE ASPECTS OF CAREGIVING

Caregiving can also be a positive experience, as noted in research on PAC, alternatively labeled *caregiver gain*, *caregiver rewards*, and *caregiver satisfaction* (Boerner et al., 2004; Cohen et al., 1994; Kramer, 1997; Lawton, Kleban, Moss, Rovine, & Glicksman, 1989; Lawton, Moss, Kleban, Glicksman, & Rovine, 1991; Narayan et al., 2001). The majority of PAC research has focused on Caucasian and/or African American dementia caregivers (Andren & Elmstahl, 2005; Boerner et al., 2004; Cohen et al., 1994, 2002; Habermann & Davis, 2005; Kramer, 1997; Lawton et al., 1989, 1991; Murphy, Bobele, Gill, Solorzano, & Lewis, 2006; Narayan et al., 2001; Roff et al., 2004; Tarlow et al., 2004). The focus on these two ethnic populations may be due to a variety of reasons (e.g., access to care/resources, utilization of services, cultural beliefs). However, the positive perception of caregiving may be influenced by culture and we recommend seeking other ethnic groups that may emphasize community versus agency. The focus on more positive psychological functioning is raised because the field needs to think about caregiving experiences and outcomes to include positive aspects of caregiving and positive indicators of well-being. A caregiver with a positive outlook on caregiving may experience less stress and physical ailments, possibly allowing a provider to be hopeful. The caregiver may be more cooperative with a provider and follow-through may increase in regards to instructions from a provider. The lack of attention to the positive dimensions of caregiving may skew perceptions of the caregiving experience and limits our ability to enhance the theory of caregiver adaptation and quality of care.

Clinicians may not be aware of the positive perspective on caregiving and focus on coping skills and stress management rather than facilitating the positive psychological factors. At least four reasons are highlighted for exploring the positive psychological factors: caregivers want to talk about them, these will be an important determinant of quality of care provided to the care recipient, clinicians will be assisted in knowing what works most effectively, and the need to enhance the theory in this area (Kramer, 1997). The task of providing care to a disabled family member often places a burden on the caregiver, but it can also involve rewarding components, enabling the caregiver to feel useful, important, and competent (Boerner et al., 2004; Cohen et al., 2002; Kramer, 1997). PAC may also reduce the stresses of caregiving and improve outcomes for caregivers (Kinney & Stephens, 1989; Murphy et al., 2006). Some positive aspects might be protective factors against the increased risk of mortality from caregiving (Cohen et al., 2002). When caregivers felt positively about what they were doing, they were less likely to report depression, poor heath, or feelings of burden.

Positive aspects of caregiving would mediate between the demands of the role and the well-being of the individual (Tarlow et al., 2004). Tarlow and colleagues defined positive aspects of caregiving as both the caregiver's appraisal of the situation and their ability to adapt to the stressors of the role. They found that most participants in their multisite study perceived satisfying experiences in their role as dementia caregivers.

Various positive themes in caregiving have been researched, such as the meaning attributed to the caregiving and the reciprocity in the relationship between the caregiver and care recipient (Noonan & Tennstedt, 1997). Habermann and Davis focused on African American and White dementia caregivers and found that the majority could identify only one aspect of satisfaction (2005). Specifically, "knowing that he is getting good care," "I'm the only relative," and "It helps the family." In order to better appreciate the caregiver experience it will also be important to understand how these aspects of caregiving relate to the negative consequences such as burden and depression. For clinicians, this suggests encouraging an increase in positive affect (i.e., feelings such as gratitude, forgiveness, and the like) while at the same working on decreasing negative feelings such as depression, anxiety, and guilt.

SOCIAL SUPPORT

A consistent finding in the gerontology literature is that those providing informal care to an ill or disabled older adult are vulnerable to the experience of burden and psychological distress (Atienza et al., 2001; Schulz, Visintainer, & Williamson, 1990). Daily stressors have been shown to diminish psychological or emotional well-being as experienced in the natural environment (Dura, Stukenberg, & Kiecolt-Glaser, 1990). Perceived social support can reduce the detrimental effects of stress on psychological well-being (Brummett et al., 2006; Cohen & Wills, 1985). Evidence consistently supports an inverse relationship between support ratings and caregiver distress (Thompson, Futterman, Gallagher-Thompson, Rose, & Lovett, 1993; Vitaliano et al., 1991).

Friends provide and facilitate both emotional support and social integration (Thompson et al., 1993). Social integration has been defined as, "a sense of belonging based on engaging in social and recreational activities with other people who share common interests outside the caregiving role" (Thompson et al., 1993, p. S246). Based on this definition, social support and well-being are important in decreasing caregiver burden and in reducing interpersonal tensions between the caregiver and care recipient. Haley, Levine, Brown, and Bartolucci reported that "caregivers with larger numbers of friends and close relationships and higher levels of social activities with friends" (1987, p. 329) were more satisfied with their lives. Women reporting higher perceived social support had less psychological distress and less conflict with others as compared to men (Lepore, 1992).

Throughout the caregiving experience, not only will there be adverse psychological reactions to functioning limitations, but there will also be an important disruption in an individual's social support system (Newsom & Schulz, 1996; Schulz & Martire, 2004). This is mainly due to the fact that the caregiver is spending many hours in the day taking care of the care recipient and does not have time for him or herself or to spend with others. Such changes will undoubtedly have critical consequences for psychological well-being (Cohen et al., 1986). Such disruptions in the support system may take the form of actual reductions in the social support network or just perceived loss of social support, but the psychological consequences are likely to be significant in either case (Cohen & Wills, 1985). Therefore, it is important to consider the process through which social support has a beneficial effect on well-being.

INTERVENTION RESEARCH WITH FAMILY CAREGIVERS

There is a dearth of controlled empirical intervention research to improve caregivers' psychological well-being that focuses on ethnically and culturally diverse family caregivers. However, there have been recent efforts to address this situation. Two large-scale, well-controlled, multisite, multiethnic, and multicomponent studies were completed under the auspices of Resources for Enhancing Alzheimer's Caregiver Health (REACH) projects (Belle et al., 2006; Wisniewski et al., 2003). These are the first large-scale studies that focused recruitment on three specific ethnic and racial groups: Whites/Caucasians, Blacks/African Americans, and Hispanics/Latinos; close to 2,000 different caregivers enrolled in these two studies. Through carefully designed, tailored, and well-executed interventions, caregiver stress was reduced/mitigated (Schulz et al., 2003a, b). A comprehensive review of empirically based interventions for distressed family caregivers was conducted by Gallagher-Thompson and Coon (2007). They found that, in general, psychoeducational studies that focused on teaching caregivers specific cognitive, behavioral, and communication skills were by far the most effective and exist in sufficient number to be classified as meeting strict American Psychological Association criteria for being evidence based. Review of the relatively small number of psychotherapy studies indicated that cognitive-behavioral therapy can be considered evidence based for reducing caregiver distress. Finally, multicomponent interventions, such as those of Mittelman (2004) and the REACH II project (Belle et al., 2006) also met criteria for this classification. In addition, other interventions for which there were insufficient studies to reach evidence-based criteria were reviewed by Gallagher-Thompson and Coon (2007). Clinicians are encouraged to consider the broad range of interventions available at present for working effectively with a distressed dementia family caregiver—including those that have been carefully researched with ethnically and culturally diverse caregivers.

CONCLUSION

Taken as a whole, the literature suggests that the relationships among social support, positive aspects of caregiving, and caregiver psychological health should be examined with greater specificity. This is an important area of research given that caregivers' abilities to persevere in their roles while maintaining their own health may be influenced by their psychological well-being. Additionally, social support and positive aspects of caregiving may present a buffering effect for caregiver well-being. There have been studies that have documented the buffering effects of social support only and positive aspects of caregiving only for caregiver well-being, but not the two combined (Cohen & Wills, 1985; Krause & Markides, 1990; Lepore, 1992). In addition, identifying positive aspects of caregiving and various forms of social support may be predictive of both positive and negative psychological well-being and may implicate characteristics that help the caregiver's and care recipient's well-being.

Unfortunately, as seen from the studies cited in the previous discussion, there are various problems with the existing literature and a clear image of the effects of social support and positive aspects of caregiving in caregiver mood has not emerged. Many studies do not include caregiver resources as a potential factor influencing caregiver well-being (Schulz et al., 1995).

The lack of research on social support and positive aspects of caregiving needs to be addressed with studies that have adequate sample sizes, incorporate multiethnic samples, address the complexity naturally occurring in the caregiving process, and identify both correlates and predictors of caregiver well-being. Specifically, in developing a predictive profile of caregiver well-being, it will be important to identify caregiver resources (e.g., social support, positive aspects of caregiving), understudied factors that may play a significant role in explaining individual differences in response to caregiving.

For the practicing clinician, the existing literature directs you to think in terms of strengths (as well as the weaknesses) that a particular caregiver can draw upon. The emerging field of *positive psychology*—as applied to issues of middle age and later life by Hill (2005)—has, in our opinion, much to offer to researchers and clinicians who work with family caregivers. For example, interventions can focus on the benefits of caregiving along with an emphasis on social support and other mechanisms to help reduce depression in caregivers. Positive resources may be identified within the social network or within the individual. Cultural views of social support require us to broaden the focus from nuclear family to include also fictive kin, extended relatives, friends, and others, thus leading toward family therapy for cultural populations who are considered more "family oriented" versus self-help groups. Positive psychology approaches to individual intervention may focus on how to maintain a healthy lifestyle while taking care of someone else. Whether individual or family level of focus, a caregiver's particular strengths (as well as their weaknesses) are an important focus for intervention.

REFERENCES

Adams, B., Aranda, M., Kemp, B., & Takagi, K. (2002). Ethnic and gender differences in distress among Anglo American, African American, Japanese American and Mexican American spousal caregivers of persons with dementia. *Journal of Clinical Geropsychology, 8*(4), 279–301.

Adams, K. B. (2007). Specific effects of caring for a spouse with dementia: Differences in depressive symptoms between caregiver and non-caregiver spouses. *International Psychogeriatrics,* 1–13.

Alspaugh, M. E., Stephens, M. A., Townsend, A. L., Zarit, S. H., & Greene, R. (1999). Longitudinal patterns of risk for depression in dementia caregivers: Objective and subjective primary stress as predictors. *Psychology and Aging, 14*(1), 34–43.

Alzheimer's Association and National Alliance for Caregiving. (2004). *Families care: Alzheimer's caregiving in the United States 2004.* Washington, DC: National Alliance for Caregiving.

American Psychiatric Association. (2000). *Diagnostic and statistical manual of mental disorders* (4th ed., text revision). Washington, DC: Author.

Andren, S., & Elmstahl, S. (2005). Family caregivers' subjective experiences of satisfaction in dementia care: Aspects of burden, subjective health and sense of coherence. *Scand J Caring Sci, 19*(2), 157–168.

Aneshensel, C. S., Pearlin, L. I., Mullan, J. T., Zarit, S., & Whitlach, C. J. (1995). *Profiles in caregiving: The unexpected career.* San Diego: Academic Press.

Angel, J. L., & Hogan, D. P. (2004). Population aging and diversity in a new era. In K. E. Whitfield (Ed.), *Closing the gap* (pp. 1–12). Washington, DC: Gerontological Society of America.

Aranda, M., & Knight, B. G. (1997). The influence of ethnicity and culture on the caregiver stress and coping process: A sociocultural review and analysis. *The Gerontologist, 37*(3), 342–354.

Argüelles, T., & Argüelles, S. (2006). Working with Cuban American families. In G. Yeo & D. Gallagher-Thompson (Eds.), *Ethnicity and the dementias* (2nd ed., pp. 311–326). New York: Routledge/Taylor and Francis.

Atienza, A. A., Collins, R., & King, A. C. (2001). The mediating effects of situational control on social support and mood following a stressor: A prospective study of dementia caregivers in their natural environments. *Journals of Gerontology Series B: Psychological Sciences and Social Sciences, 56*(3), S129–S139.

Belle, S. H., Burgio, L., Burns, R., Coon, D., Czaja, S. J., Gallagher-Thompson, D., et al. (2006). Enhancing the quality of life of dementia caregivers from different ethnic or racial groups: A randomized, controlled trial. *Annals of Internal Medicine, 145*(10), 727–738.

Bernstein, R., & Bergman, M. (2003). Hispanic population reaches all-time high of 38.8 million, new Census Bureau estimates show *(CB03–100).* Washington, DC: U.S. Census Bureau Public Information Office.

Berry, J. W. (2003). Conceptual approaches to acculturation. In K. M. Chun, P. B. Organista, & G. Marín (Eds.), *Acculturation: Advances in theory, measurement, and applied research* (pp. 17–37). Washington, DC: American Psychological Association.

Boerner, K., Schulz, R., & Horowitz, A. (2004). Positive aspects of caregiving and adaptation to bereavement. *Psychology and Aging, 19*(4), 668–675.

Brummett, B. H., Babyak, M. A., Siegler, I. C., Vitaliano, P. P., Ballard, E. L., Gwyther, L. P., et al. (2006). Associations among perceptions of social support, negative affect, and quality of sleep in caregivers and noncaregivers. *Health Psychology, 25*(2), 220–225.

Cohen, C., Gold, D. P., & Shulman, K. (1994). Positive aspects in caregiving: An overlooked variable in research. *Canadian Journal on Aging, 13*(3), 378–391.

Cohen, C. A., Colantonio, A., & Vernich, L. (2002). Positive aspects of caregiving: Rounding out the caregiver experience. *International Journal of Geriatric Psychiatry, 17*(2), 184–188.

Cohen, S., Sherrod, D. R., & Clark, M. S. (1986). Social skills and the stress-protective role of social support. *Journal of Personality and Social Psychology, 50*(5), 963–973.

Cohen, S., & Wills, T. A. (1985). Stress, social support, and the buffering hypothesis. *Psychological Bulletin, 98*(2), 310–357.

Dictionary.com. (2004). http://www.dictionary.com. Retrieved August 1, 2006.

Dilworth-Anderson, P., Gibson, B. E., & Detry Burke, J. (2006). Working with African American families. In G. Yeo & D. Gallagher-Thompson (Eds.), *Ethnicity and the dementias* (2nd ed., pp. 127–144). New York: Routledge/Taylor and Francis.

Draper, B. M., Poulos, R. G., Poulos, C. J., & Ehrlich, F. (1996). Risk factors for stress in elderly caregivers. *International Journal of Geriatric Psychiatry, 11*(3), 227–231.

Dura, J. R., Stukenberg, K. W., & Kiecolt-Glaser, J. K. (1990). Chronic stress and depressive disorders in older adults. *Journal of Abnormal Psychology, 99*(3), 284–290.

Dura, J. R., Stukenberg, K. W., & Kiecolt-Glaser, J. K. (1991). Anxiety and depressive disorders in adult children caring for demented parents. *Psychology and Aging, 6*(3), 467–473.

Eisdorfer, C., Czaja, S. J., Loewenstein, D. A., Rubert, M. P., Arguelles, S., Mitrani, V. B., et al. (2003). The effect of a family therapy and technology-based intervention on caregiver depression. *Gerontologist, 43*(4), 521–531.

Feldman, H. H., & O'Brien, J. T. (1999). Differentiation of common dementias. In G. K. Wilcok, R. S. Bucks, & K. Rockwood (Eds.), *Diagnosis and management of dementia: A manual for memory disorder teams* (pp. 231–251). New York: Oxford University Press.

Gallagher, D., Rose, J., Rivera, P., Lovett, S., & Thompson, L. W. (1989). Prevalence of depression in family caregivers. *Gerontologist, 29*(4), 449–456.

Gallagher-Thompson, D., & Coon, D. W. (2007). Evidence-based psychological treatments for distress in family caregivers of older adults. *Psychology and Aging, 22*(1), 37–51.

Gallagher-Thompson, D., Coon, D. W., Solano, N., Ambler, C., Rabinowitz, Y., & Thompson, L. W. (2003). Change in indices of distress among Latino and Anglo female caregivers of elderly relatives with dementia: Site-specific results from the REACH national collaborative study. *Gerontologist, 43*(4), 580–591.

Gallagher-Thompson, D., Gray, H. L., Tang, P. C., Pu, C. Y., Leung, L. Y., Wang, P. C., et al. (2007). Impact of in-home behavioral management versus telephone support to reduce depressive symptoms and perceived stress in Chinese caregivers: Results of a pilot study. *American Journal of Geriatric Psychiatry, 15*(5), 425–434.

Gallagher-Thompson, D., Rose, J., Rivera, P., Lovett, S., & Thompson, L. W. (1989). Prevalence of depression in family caregivers. *The Gerontologist, 29*, 449–456.

Gallagher-Thompson, D., Shurgot, G. R., Rider, K., Gray, H. L., McKibbin, C., Kraemer, H., et al. (2006). Ethnicity, stress, and cortisol function in Hispanic and non-Hispanic White women: A preliminary study of family dementia caregivers and noncaregivers. *American Journal of Geriatric Psychiatry, 14*(4), 334–342.

Gitlin, L. N., Belle, S. H., Burgio, L. D., Czaja, S. J., Mahoney, D., Gallagher-Thompson, D., et al. (2003). Effect of multicomponent interventions on caregiver burden and depression: The REACH multisite initiative at 6-month follow-up. *Psychology and Aging, 18*(3), 361–374.

Habermann, B., & Davis, L. L. (2005). Caring for family with Alzheimer's disease and Parkinson's disease: Needs, challenges and satisfaction. *Journal of Gerontological Nursing, 31*(6), 49–54.

Haley, W. E., Levine, E. G., Brown, S. L., & Bartolucci, A. A. (1987). Stress, appraisal, coping, and social support as predictors of adaptational outcome among dementia caregivers. *Psychology and Aging, 2*(4), 323–330.

Haley, W. E., Levine, E. G., Brown, S. L., Berry, J. W., & Hughes, G. H. (1987). Psychological, social, and health consequences of caring for a relative with senile dementia. *Journal of the American Geriatrics Society, 35*(5), 405–411.

Hooker, K., Monahan, D. J., Bowman, S. R., Frazier, L. D., & Shifren, K. (1998). Personality counts for a lot: Predictors of mental and physical health of spouse caregivers in two disease groups. *Journals of Gerontology Series B: Psychological Sciences and Social Sciences, 53*(2), P73–85.

Kiecolt-Glaser, J. K., Dura, J. R., Speicher, C. E., Trask, O. J., & Glaser, R. (1991). Spousal caregivers of dementia victims: Longitudinal changes in immunity and health. *Psychosomatic Medicine, 53*(4), 345–362.

Kiecolt-Glaser, J. K., Glaser, R., Gravenstein, S., Malarkey, W. B. & Sheridan, J. (1996). Chronic stress alters the immune response to influenza virus vaccine in older adults. *Proceedings of the National Academy of Sciences, USA, 93*, 3043–3047.

Kinney, J. M., & Stephens, M. A. (1989). Hassles and uplifts of giving care to a family member with dementia. *Psychology and Aging, 4*(4), 402–408.

Kramer, B. J. (1997). Gain in the caregiving experience: Where are we? What next? *Gerontologist, 37*(2), 218–232.

Krause, N., & Markides, K. (1990). Measuring social support among older adults. *International Journal of Aging and Human Development, 30*(1), 37–53.

LaVeist, T. A. (2004). Conceptualizing racial and ethnic disparities in access, utilization, and quality of care. In K. E.Whitfield (Ed.), *Closing the gap* (pp. 87–93). Washington, DC: Gerontological Society of America.

LaVeist, T. A., & Wallace, J. (2000). Health risk and inequitable distribution of liquor stores in African American neighborhoods. *Social Science & Medicine, 51*(4), 613–617.

Lawton, M. P., Kleban, M. H., Moss, M., Rovine, M., & Glicksman, A. (1989). Measuring caregiving appraisal. *Journal of Gerontology, 44*(3), 61–71.

Lawton, M. P., Moss, M., Kleban, M. H., Glicksman, A., & Rovine, M. (1991). A two-factor model of caregiving appraisal and psychological well-being. *Journal of Gerontology, 46*(4), 181–189.

Lee, S., Colditz, G. A., Berkman, L. F., & Kawachi, I. (2003). Caregiving and risk of coronary heart disease in U.S. women: A prospective study. *American Journal of Preventive Medicine, 24*(2), 113–119.

Lepore, S. J. (1992). Social conflict, social support, and psychological distress: Evidence of cross-domain buffering effects. *Journal of Personality and Social Psychology, 63*(5), 857–867.

Li, L. W., Seltzer, M. M., & Greenberg, J. S. (1997). Social support and depressive symptoms: Differential patterns in wife and daughter caregivers. *Journals of Gerontology Series B: Psychological Sciences and Social Sciences, 52*(4), S200–S211.

Mausbach, B. T., Patterson, T. L., Rabinowitz, Y. G., Grant, I., & Schulz, R. (2007). Depression and distress predict time to cardiovascular disease in dementia caregivers. *Health Psychology, 26*(5), 539–544.

Mittelman, M., Roth, D., Coon, D., & Haley, W. (2004, May). Sustained benefit of supportive intervention for depressive symptoms in caregivers of patients with Alzheimer's disease. *American Journal of Psychiatry, 161*(5), 850–856.

Mok, E., Lai, C. K., Wong, F. L., & Wan, P. (2007). Living with early-stage dementia: The perspective of older Chinese people. *Journal of Advanced Nursing, 59*(6), 591–600.

Murphy, M. R., Bobele, M., Gill, S., Solorzano, B., & Lewis, S. L. (2006). Is there more to caregiving than burden? *Journal of the American Geriatrics Society, 54*(Supplement 4), S86.

Narayan, S., Lewis, M., Tornatore, J., Hepburn, K., & Corcoran-Perry, S. (2001). Subjective responses to caregiving for a spouse with dementia. *Journal of Gerontological Nursing, 27*(3), 19–28.

National Alliance for Caregiving and American Association for Retired Persons. (2004). *Caregiving in the U.S.* Retrieved April 1, 2008 from http://www.caregiving.org/data/04finalreport.pdf.

Newsom, J. T., & Schulz, R. (1996). Social support as a mediator in the relation between functional status and quality of life in older adults. *Psychology and Aging, 11*(1), 34–44.

Niederehe, G., & Fruge, E. (1984). Dementia and family dynamics: Clinical research issues. *Journal of Geriatric Psychiatry, 17*(1), 21–60.

Noonan, A. E., & Tennstedt, S. L. (1997). Meaning in caregiving and its contribution to caregiver well-being. *Gerontologist, 37*(6), 785–794.

Ory, M. G., Hoffman, R. R., III, Yee, J. L., Tennstedt, S., & Schulz, R. (1999). Prevalence and impact of caregiving: A detailed comparison between dementia and nondementia caregivers. *Gerontologist, 39*(2), 177–185.

Pagel, M. D., Becker, J., & Coppel, D. B. (1985). Loss of control, self-blame, and depression: An investigation of spouse caregivers of Alzheimer's disease patients. *Journal of Abnormal Psychology, 94*(2), 169–182.

Pearlin, L. I., Mullan, J. T., Semple, S. J., & Skaff, M. M. (1990). Caregiving and the stress process: An overview of concepts and their measures. *Gerontologist, 30*(5), 583–594.

Periyakoil, V. S. (2006). Working with Asian Indian American families. In G. Yeo & D. Gallagher-Thompson (Eds.), *Ethnicity and the dementias* (2nd ed.). New York: Routledge/Taylor and Francis.

Pinquart, M., & Sorensen, S. (2003a). Associations of stressors and uplifts of caregiving with caregiver burden and depressive mood: A meta-analysis. *Journals of Gerontology Series B: Psychological Sciences and Social Sciences, 58*(2), 112–128.

Pinquart, M., & Sorensen, S. (2003b). Differences between caregivers and noncaregivers in psychological health and physical health: A meta-analysis. *Psychology and Aging, 18*(2), 250–267.

Pinquart, M., & Sorensen, S. (2004). Associations of caregiver stressors and uplifts with subjective well-being and depressive mood: A meta-analytic comparison. *Aging and Mental Health, 8*(5), 438–449.

Proctor, B. D., & Dalaker, J. (2002). Poverty in the United States: 2001. Current population reports, P60–219. U.S. Bureau of the Census. Washington, DC: U.S. Government Printing Office.

Pruchno, R. A., Kleban, M. H., Michaels, J. E., & Dempsey, N. P. (1990). Mental and physical health of caregiving spouses: Development of a causal model. *Journal of Gerontology, 45*(5), P192–P199.

Roff, L. L., Burgio, L. D., Gitlin, L., Nichols, L., Chaplin, W., & Hardin, J. M. (2004). Positive aspects of Alzheimer's caregiving: The role of race. *Journals of Gerontology Series B: Psychological Sciences and Social Sciences, 59*(4), 185–190.

Russo, J., Vitaliano, P. P., Brewer, D. D., Katon, W., & Becker, J. (1995). Psychiatric disorders in spouse caregivers of care recipients with Alzheimer's disease and matched controls: A diathesis-stress model of psychopathology. *Journal of Abnormal Psychology, 104*(1), 197–204.

Schleifer, S. J., Keller, S. E., & Stein, M. (1985). Stress effects on immunity. *Psychiatric Journal of the University of Ottawa, 10*(3), 125–131.

Schulz, R., & Beach, S. R. (1999). Caregiving as a risk factor for mortality: The Caregiver Health Effects Study. *Journal of the American Medical Association, 282*(23), 2215–2219.

Schulz, R., Belle, S. H., Czaja, S. J., Gitlin, L. N., Wisniewski, S. R., & Ory, M. G. (2003). Introduction to the special section on Resources for Enhancing Alzheimer's Caregiver Health (REACH). *Psychology and Aging, 18*(3), 357–360.

Schulz, R., Burgio, L., Burns, R., Eisdorfer, C., Gallagher-Thompson, D., Gitlin, L. N., et al. (2003). Resources for Enhancing Alzheimer's Caregiver Health (REACH): Overview, site-specific outcomes, and future directions. *Gerontologist, 43*(4), 514–520.

Schulz, R., & Martire, L. M. (2004). Family caregiving of persons with dementia: Prevalence, health effects, and support strategies. *American Journal of Geriatric Psychiatry, 12*(3), 240–249.

Schulz, R., Newsom, J., Mittelmark, M., Burton, L., Hirsch, C., & Jackson, S. (1997). Health effects of caregiving: The caregiver health effects study: An ancillary study of the Cardiovascular Health Study. *Annals of Behavioral Medicine, 19*(2), 110–116.

Schulz, R., O'Brien, A. T., Bookwala, J., & Fleissner, K. (1995). Psychiatric and physical morbidity effects of dementia caregiving: Prevalence, correlates, and causes. *Gerontologist, 35*(6), 771–791.

Schulz, R., & Quittner, A. L. (1998). Caregiving through the life-span: Overview and future directions. *Health Psychology, 17*(2), 107–111.

Schulz, R., Visintainer, P., & Williamson, G. M. (1990). Psychiatric and physical morbidity effects of caregiving. *Journal Gerontology, 45*(5), 181–191.

Schulz, R., & Williamson, G. M. (1997). The measurement of caregiver outcomes in Alzheimer disease research. *Alzheimer Disease and Associated Disorders, 11*(Suppl 6), 117–124.

Spitznagel, M. B., Tremont, G., Davis, J. D., & Foster, S. M. (2006). Psychosocial predictors of dementia caregiver desire to institutionalize: Caregiver, care recipient, and family relationship factors. *Journal of Geriatric Psychiatry and Neurology, 19*(1), 16–20.

Stein, M., Keller, S. E., & Schleifer, S. J. (1985). Stress and immunomodulation: The role of depression and neuroendocrine function. *Journal of Immunology, 135*(2 Suppl), 827s–833s.

Stephens, M. A., Norris, V. K., Kinney, J. M., Ritchie, S. W., & Grotz, R. C. (1988). Stressful situations in caregiving: Relations between caregiver coping and well-being. *Psychology and Aging, 3*(2), 208–209.

Stephens, M. A., & Qualls, S. H. (2007). Therapy to help aging couples cope with dementia. *Generations, 31*(3), 54–56.

Strawbridge, W. J., Wallhagen, M. I., Shema, S. J., & Kaplan, G. A. (1997). New burdens or more of the same? Comparing grandparent, spouse, and adult-child caregivers. *Gerontologist, 37*(4), 505–510.

Tabora, B., & Flaskerud, J. H. (1994). Depression among Chinese Americans: A review of the literature. *Issues in Mental Health Nursing, 15*(6), 569–584.

Tarlow, B. J., Wisniewski, S. R., Belle, S. H., Rubert, M., Ory, M. G., & Gallagher-Thompson, D. (2004). Positive aspects of caregiving: Contributions of the REACH project to the development of new measures for Alzheimer's caregiving. *Research on Aging, 26*(4), 429–453.

Tennstedt, S. L., Crawford, S., & McKinlay, J. B. (1993). Determining the pattern of community care: Is co-residence more important than caregiver relationship? *Journal of Gerontology, 48*(2), S74–S83.

Thompson, E. H., Jr., Futterman, A. M., Gallagher-Thompson, D., Rose, J. M., & Lovett, S. B. (1993). Social support and caregiving burden in family caregivers of frail elders. *Journal of Gerontology, 48*(5), S245–S254.

Thompson, L. W., Spira, A. P., Depp, C. A., McGee, J. S., & Gallagher-Thompson, D. (2006). The geriatric caregiver. In M. E. Agronin & G. J. Maletta (Eds.). *Principles and practice of geriatric psychiatry* (pp. 37–46). Philadelphia, PA: Lippincott Williams & Wilkins.

U.S. Census Bureau. (2000). *The elderly population.* Retrieved August 1, 2006, from http://www.census.gov/population/www/pop-profile/elderpop.html.

U.S. Department of Health and Human Services: National Institute of Health and National Institute on Aging. (2005). *Progress report on Alzheimer's disease 2004–2005* (NIH Publication Number: 05-5724).

Vitaliano, P. P., Russo, J., Young, H. M., Teri, L., & Maiuro, R. D. (1991). Predictors of burden in spouse caregivers of individuals with Alzheimer's disease. *Psychology and Aging, 6*(3), 392–402.

Vitaliano, P. P., Scanlan, J. M., Krenz, C., Schwartz, R. S., & Marcovina, S. M. (1996). Psychological distress, caregiving, and metabolic variables. *Journals of Gerontology Series B: Psychological Sciences and Social Sciences, 51*(5), P290–P299.

Wagner, A. W., Logsdon, R. G., Pearson, J. L., & Teri, L. (1997). Caregiver expressed emotion and depression in Alzheimer's disease. *Aging and Mental Health, 1*(2), 132–139.

Wang, P. C., Tong, H. Q., Liu, W., Long, L. Y. L., Yau, E., & Gallagher-Thompson, D. (2006). Dementia caregiving in Chinese American families. In G. Yeo & D. Gallagher-Thompson (Eds.), *Ethnicity and the dementias* (2nd ed., pp. 173–188). New York: Routledge/Taylor and Francis.

Weiner, M. F. (2003). Clinical diagnosis of cognitive dysfunction and dementing illness. In M. F. Weiner & A. M. Lipton (Eds.), *The dementias: Diagnosis, treatment, and research* (pp. 1–48). Washington, DC: American Psychiatric Publishing.

Wisniewski, S. R., Belle, S. H., Coon, D. W., Marcus, S. M., Ory, M. G., Burgio, L. D., et al. (2003). The Resources for Enhancing Alzheimer's Caregiver Health (REACH): Project design and baseline characteristics. *Psychology and Aging, 18*(3), 375–384.

Yeo, G., & Gallagher-Thompson, D. (Eds.). (2006). *Ethnicity and the dementias* (2nd ed.). New York: Routledge/Taylor and Francis.

Zarit, S. H., Reever, K. E., & Bach-Peterson, J. (1980). Relatives of the impaired elderly: Correlates of feelings of burden. *Gerontologist, 20*(6), 649–655.

6

Assessment and Intervention with Family Caregivers

JUDY ZARIT

W orking with family caregivers can be both productive for the client and rewarding for the therapist. Often, caregivers are capable and successful individuals who are overwhelmed with a new and complex situation. A wife who has raised children, for example, has had experience as a caregiver, but she may not know how to draw on that experience in this novel situation with her husband who is in the early stages of Alzheimer's disease. An adult child who may be quite adept at running an office or managing her own household may have difficulty transferring those skills to the problems of her aging and ailing mother. Sometimes caregivers will also present with the whole range of personality disorders and/or problems, which will complicate therapy and force a reassessment of goals and methods. Given that there is always at least a dyad involved in therapy, there are nearly infinite combinations of caregivers, patients, and problems that are possible. Consequently, careful assessment must be done initially, and periodic review of those results will ensure that therapy is proceeding toward achievable goals. Once the nature and scope of the problem have been determined, those data can be used to begin attacking the memory and/or behavior problems systematically. It goes without saying that no intervention is possible without a strong, supportive working alliance between therapist and caregiver, and that emotional support is a prerequisite for any successful therapy.

This chapter provides a brief discussion of assessment and treatment as it has been developed in my private practice over the past 2 decades. The areas that will be covered include identifying the client, having the client identify the problem, structured evaluations of different aspects of the problem, the problem-solving method, and the role of support in treatment. Often, the process of evaluating the problem can be therapeutic in itself, as it may be the first time that the caregiver has an opportunity to tell the story in its entirety, and of course, solutions may be generated in the process. For a more complete description of these topics, you may wish to refer to *Mental Disorders in Older Adults, Second Edition* (Zarit & Zarit, 2007).

ASSESSMENT

Who Are You Seeing Today?

One of the challenges of working with older adults is determining where in the family system you will intervene. Unlike the traditional therapy client, who presents with a fairly discrete issue or symptoms (e.g. relationship issues, depression), the older patient is likely to have been referred either by a physician or under pressure from family members. You may find yourself working with the dementia patient, the caregiver, the older couple, a mother and daughter, or any other combination of individuals concerned with the impaired older adult. The first step in assessment, then, will be to determine who will participate in the therapy. To some extent this will also depend on what the client is asking for. An example may clarify this point.

The identified patient here is Abigail, an 82-year-old woman, with her daughter, Sue, taking on the caregiver role. While the therapy is focused on Abigail's depression, attention is also being given to Sue's caregiving issues. In this way, she is the second identified patient. For the purposes of this chapter, I refer to Abigail as the *patient* (since she has a cognitive disorder) and Sue as the *client*.

Another presentation that is quite common is to see the caregiver without ever meeting the dementia patient. In this situation, caregiver stress

Abigail was referred for a neuropsychological evaluation by her primary care physician. She is a retired nurse, who had been the primary babysitter for her grandchildren for about 10 years after she retired from nursing, now living at home with her husband. She was accompanied by the elder of her two children, a daughter named Sue. Sue described her mother's increasing memory problems over the past several years, although Abigail seemed surprised with each example and was able to rationalize each problem presented. Testing showed Abigail to be in the moderate stages of a vascular dementia and to have a moderate depression. She was still independent in her activities of daily living (ADLs) and was still driving, although she went out less and less. When feedback on the testing was given to Abigail and Sue, Sue requested further sessions to help her mother with her depression. Sue accompanied her mother to the therapy, in part so that she could remind her mother of what was being recommended. Abigail's husband was described as very difficult, their relationship as distant, and she had no interest in having him involved in her therapy.

is usually the presenting problem, although it may be only indirectly presented. Another example will help present these dynamics.

Who Is the Primary Caregiver?

This is the person who will most likely be your client. By definition, the *primary caregiver* is the person who has taken on the responsibility of care for the patient. This can be a spouse, a significant other, a child, a sibling, or anyone else who has stepped into the role of being responsible. Most often, when there is a spouse, he or she will feel that it is a part of the marital relationship to provide care. However, there are many instances when a spouse may be ill-suited to take on this responsibility, such as poor health, a long-standing contentious relationship, or simply an unwillingness to make sacrifices. In a recent case, the eldest and youngest brothers (minus the one in the middle) brought their father in

Leslie came into therapy after a three-year relationship ended disastrously. She was 45 years old and had never been married. She had a career she enjoyed and many friends, but she was devastated by the relationship's end. In the course of initial assessment, she mentioned that her mother was in the moderate stages of dementia, living alone in the family home, but increasingly needing help during the day. Over several years, Leslie continued to deal with her own interpersonal problems, but she also spent time solving a variety of caregiving problems relating to her mother. She obtained in-home help, eventually round the clock, and when her mother was no longer able to be safe at home, found a long-term care facility for her, where she continues to visit her. The caregiving issues have been many and varied, and will be used to illustrate several points later on in this chapter.

for an assessment. The father had been recently separated from his second wife of 20 years. They had about 10 good years of marriage, then slow and steady deterioration over the last 10 years. It is unclear whether the wife understood that her husband was cognitively impaired, but her children had stepped in to protect her when the situation had become too stressful for her. Now his sons were belatedly coming to understand their father's problem. In another case, an assessment was requested by a woman who had been dating a widower for a number of years. She had noticed his declining ability to perform ADLs and had become concerned. Later, his son and daughter, both of whom lived out of town, were involved by telephone to help set up a support network. In this situation, the companion was the only local caregiver, and her role was limited to obtaining whatever supports he might need to remain independent as long as possible.

Today's Problem

When people come to a clinical setting for an evaluation, there has usually been a triggering event. It is safe to assume that they have spent time thinking about the problem and how they want to present the information so that the clinician will understand why they are concerned. Rather than take over the interview, it is best to allow the client to tell the story in his or her own fashion first. Later on you can go back over a structured interview and pick up any important information that has not been provided. Typical entry points are coping with the memory and behavior problems, the patient's medical problems, legal problems (such as capacity for decision making), financial problems, and questions about the appropriateness of the amount of care provided in the living situation. You will want to assess all of these, but the order can be determined by the presenting problem as the client sees it.

History of the Problem

You will want to get a history of the patient's problem, whether it is a dementia or other disability. This includes onset, course, duration, and severity of symptoms. Additionally, it is important to ascertain the effects that the problem has had on the caregiver. For example, has the caregiver had to stop working to care for the patient? When the caregiver has been referred by a physician, it is advisable to have medical records sent prior to the first meeting. You will save valuable time by reading the physician's notes, but they must be read as only one interpretation of the situation, and it is vital that the client and/or patient tell the story in his or her own words as well. In today's medical system, individuals often see multiple specialists in addition to their own primary care physicians, and there may not be optimal coordination of care. You may find it helpful to obtain the specialists' records as well.

Assessment of the Identified Patient

Three main areas must be evaluated: a medically oriented history, a history of memory and behavior problems and the caregiver's reaction to them, and an assessment of social supports. One of the challenges of working with this population is the need to familiarize yourself with the more common (and sometimes uncommon) medical problems of aging. A partial list includes dementia in all of its various presentations, cardiovascular disease, diabetes, arthritis, respiratory diseases, and sensory impairments (hearing and vision). Additionally, your clients will teach you about the treatments that have been given and the positive and negative effects of those treatments. Over time, you will be able to identify the sequelae to different types of surgery and medications, simply by asking your clients about their experiences and listening carefully to their answers. As the client provides this information, you are also assessing the client's ability to participate in the current treatment and identifying his or her limitations. The outline in Table 6.1 may be useful in structuring your interview.

Table 6.1 Initial Interview

- ❏ Presenting Problem
- ❏ Cognitive Symptoms
- ❏ Functional Problems (falls, gait, incontinence)
- ❏ Problems with vision
- ❏ Problems with hearing
- ❏ Born & raised? (where)
- ❏ Education
- ❏ Vocation (and retirement)
- ❏ Married/Single/Divorced/Widowed
- ❏ Children
- ❏ Current living situation
- ❏ Family Medical and psychiatric history
    - ❏ Father
    - ❏ Mother
    - ❏ Siblings
- ❏ Family history of cognitive disorder/dementia
- ❏ Personal medical history
- ❏ Neurological history (imaging or prior testing)
- ❏ Current Medications
- ❏ Drug & Alcohol:
    - ❏ Alcohol
    - ❏ Tobacco
    - ❏ Caffeine
    - ❏ Other substances (including OTC)

Reviewing these areas can help identify areas where additional information may be needed from other sources, such as a request for medical records from the physician.

Next, it is important to use a structured form to assess the frequency of different memory and behavior problems. If the caregiver is present in the initial interview, we may send the form home with him or her to return by mail or at the first testing session. Alternatively, if the caregiver is not present, we may discuss it with him or her by telephone and send the form to him or her with a return envelope. If testing is to be done following the initial interview, the caregiver can fill out the form in the waiting room while the patient is being tested.

The form in Table 6.2 contains many of the more common problems.

The Memory and Behavior Problem Checklist (Zarit & Zarit, 1990) can be used in a variety of ways. Initially, it may provide information about which problems are occurring most frequently and which are most distressing to the caregiver. Later it can be used to assess the effectiveness of the interventions.

Living Situation

Next, it is important to assess the living situation. Where and with whom does the patient live? What resources are available there? How good is the match between the living situation and the patient's problems? For example, Abigail is living in her home with her husband. He is domineering and denies that she has any problems. He expects his meals on time and expects Abigail to take care of the home as she always has. Sue and her brother are in daily contact by telephone and in person, but they are beginning to have concerns for their mother's safety, both at home and when she is driving. In Leslie's case, her mother initially was living at home with a part-time aide provided by the Area Agency on Aging.

Evaluate the Family System

We continue to experiment with methods to best assess who is providing care and how to strengthen the social support available for the dementia

Table 6.2 Memory and Behavior Problem Checklist

Memory & Behavior Problem Checklist	0 = Never occurred	1 = Has occurred, not past week	2 = 1 or 2 times past week	3 = 3 to 6 times past week	4 = Daily or more often
Instructions: Put a check (√) in the box that indicates the frequency of the problem. Please answer all the items.					
Verbal					
1. Repetitive questions					
2. Mixes past and present					
3. Talks aggressively					
4. Talks constantly					
5. Talks little or not at all					
6. Dwells on the past					
Actions					
7. Loses, misplaces or hides things					
8. Engages in dangerous behavior					
9. Easily tearful					
10. Problems eating					
11. Incontinence					

Memory			
12. Wanders or gets lost			
13. Does not recognize familiar people			
14. Forgets what day it is			
15. Unable to occupy self			
16. Follows you around			
Psychological			
17. Suspicious or accusative			
18. Inactive			
19. Appears sad or depressed			
20. Becomes angry			
21. Sees/hears things that are not there			
22. Relives situations from the past			
Agitation			
23. Restless or agitated			
24. Uncooperative			
25. Strikes out			
26. Wakes you at night			
27. Interrupts you when you are busy			

Adapted from Zarit & Zaarit, 1990.

patient. Basically, you are trying to determine whether the patient is receiving help with any of the usual ADLs, and if so, who is providing that assistance. This is a quick way of assessing the caregiver burden and can also be used therapeutically when one caregiver is providing all of the help.

It can be extremely helpful to develop a family Caregiving Genogram. Table 6.3 provides an example of one variation. We have filled it in to illustrate the example of Leslie and her brother, Brad.

While filling in the genogram, you will also be assessing how well the caregiver understands the problems. It also will address the issue of how much support there is and whether or not there is conflict.

Leslie, who lives near her mother, is the primary caregiver. Her brother, Brad, lives a thousand miles away and visits a few times a year. He does not take responsibility, but he is likely to swoop in on a visit with criticism of how Leslie is handling things. When Leslie filled out the genogram with her therapist, she discovered that her mother's day-to-day needs were all being met by either the nursing-home staff or herself. Brad's contribution was the occasional phone call or visit. She could understand, then, that he could not appreciate the stress she feels when he is not really carrying the burden with her. She was then able to understand that his criticism might be coming from his not really understanding and perhaps not being able to emotionally deal with their mother's decline.

Leslie had been through about 5 years of caring for her mother at home. During that time she had to respond to emergency calls from her mother and, later, from the paid caregivers. Her mother lived about 45 minutes away, and she made many middle-of-the-night trips during those years to take her mother to the emergency room or otherwise deal with the problems. These are what we call *primary stressors*, when the caregiver must do something to resolve an issue. Leslie was fortunate to have an understanding employer, but she still experienced stress when she had to leave work or miss work altogether when she was dealing with her mother's crises. Her brother's lack of support and criticism of Leslie's solutions also contribute to her stress. These last two are more complex because Leslie cannot really *do* anything about them, but she must resolve the conflict internally.

Table 6.3 Caregiving Genogram

CAREGIVING Assistance Given	GENOGRAM	Patient	Leslie	Brad	Nursing Home Staff			
Personal Care	Dressing				✓			
	Grooming				✓			
	Pills				✓			
	Bathing				✓			
	Elimination				✓			
Household Care	Meals				✓			
	Housekeeping				✓			
	Maintenance		✓					
	Repairs		✓					
	Shopping		✓					
Money	Bills		✓					
	Banking		✓					
Communication	Phone		✓					
	Writing		✓					
Activities	Driving		✓					
	Staying alone				✓			
	Walking				✓			
	Conversation		✓	✓	✓			

One of the misperceptions that many people have is that nursing-home placement is the end of the problems for a caregiver. In reality, the nature of the burden changes, but it may not really decrease. Leslie thinks about her mother's comfort and care as much as always, and she is always aware of the quality of care that she is receiving. Consequently, she now puts energy into developing good relationships with key staff members at the nursing home. She also chose to have her mother in the nursing facility in her mother's community, which is still 45 minutes away. The difference is that when there is a crisis, such as a fall, she does not have to go there immediately, but she is confident that the staff can handle it.

Assess the Caregiver's Reaction

One of the most interesting aspects of caregiver stress is the extreme variability with which individuals handle problems. Many years ago, a family presented at a VA clinic with dysfunction in a multigenerational family. Parents, children, and grandparents were living under one roof for economic reasons. The main conflict presented was between the parents and grandparents around issues with the adolescent children. During sessions, it became apparent that the grandmother was quite demented. In fact, she was incontinent during one visit. The family response was to very matter-of-factly take care of her, with no real upset or comment. Many people believe that incontinence is the problem that will most frequently lead to institutionalization, but in this family it was clearly not a problem at all.

The most common responses to stress are anxiety and depression. These can be measured using the Beck inventories or any other instrument that you are comfortable with. Symptoms of anxiety and depression should also be explored during the interview, along with suicidal or homicidal ideation. When the caregiver is also elderly, evaluating the mental status of the client is appropriate as well.

Caregiver stress can certainly lead to health problems. You will want to assess the medical problems of the caregiver, as well as health behaviors, such as appetite, sleep disorders, and drug and alcohol use. Part of therapy may be working on the cognitive barriers that the caregiver has erected that prevent him or her from obtaining care for him or herself. One caregiver was told that he had spinal stenosis so severe that if he was in the slightest accident he would become a quadrapalegic. His wife was in the late stages of Alzheimer's disease and he refused to have the surgery until after she died.

INTERVENTION

Caregivers typically seek help when there has been a crisis or when they are overwhelmed. As mentioned previously, therapy may be with individuals, marital partners, or with family members. The treatment is essentially the same, but it is adapted to the treatment modality. If the group is large, it may be advisable to enlist another therapist. In that case, one therapist focuses on the content of the session, while the other attends to the process to ensure that all present are engaged and involved in the process.

One of the functions of therapy is to organize the client's experience by those problems that can be solved and those that cannot. For example, it may not be possible to teach a patient to remember her daughter's name or to not ask repetitive questions. But it may be possible to find a better way to respond to those situations. Very often caregivers have become so emotionally affected by what has happened to their loved ones that they are not able to either clearly identify the problems or come up with solutions. Collaboratively developing a method of dealing with problems provides a framework that allows caregivers to see the situation as manageable rather than impossible.

I tend to think of treatment as having three components: information, problem solving, and support. All are equally important, and each will be differentially important to different families or clients. Part of the assessment process will have been to determine where the family's strengths and weaknesses are. If they are just beginning to learn about the problem, information may be the most important component of treatment. If they have a good knowledge base, but are overwhelmed with day-to-day problems, learning how to use a systematic problem-solving method will be most helpful. And if they are just plain overwhelmed, emotional and social support may be the most important intervention.

INFORMATION

There has been a glut of information about Alzheimer's in the popular press, much of it filled with inaccuracies and poorly interpreted correlations. The first priority in therapy is to provide accurate information about the patient. This may involve simply explaining the medical records in everyday language, or it could mean referral to a neuropsychologist, and then incorporating those results with the medical records to help the client understand the facts as they are known. This will require familiarizing yourself with the literature on the etiology, course, and treatment of the dementias, which are beyond the scope of this chapter. Again, a good starting point would be *Mental Disorders in Older Adults, Second Edition* (Zarit & Zarit, 2007).

THE PROBLEM-SOLVING METHOD

The problem-solving method consists of three basic steps: generate a list of problem behaviors, brainstorm possible solutions, use trial and error to evaluate the solutions, and repeat until you have dealt with problems or the caregiver is able to execute the strategy without your assistance.

Generate a List of Problem Behaviors

The assessment process will provide much of the data that you will be using to begin to intervene. Given that most caregivers are referred during periods of high stress, it is important to attack the problem that the caregiver perceives as the most important first. To determine where to start, go over the Memory and Behavior Problem Checklist with the client. Create a hierarchy from most to least stressful. If the caregiver is not able to provide a very detailed list, it may be helpful to use a Daily Problem Guide for a week or more to collect current data. It could look like Table 6.4.

Sue identified repetitive questions and multiple telephone calls from her mother, Abigail, as the most problematic behavior. She was not sure how often her mother called and was frustrated that answering her question did not prevent the next call. For a week she filled out the Daily

Table 6.4 Problem List

Time of Day	Problem	What Went Before	What Happened After

Problem Guide and was able to identify that her mother was always anxious when she called and relieved when she hung up. Sue then realized that Abigail was calling her out of anxiety, not for the information. However, the repeated interruptions during her working day were a problem. By analyzing the problem, Sue and her therapist were able to search for solutions to the anxiety that was underlying the repetitive questions and phone calls.

Generate Solutions

Solutions are only valuable if they directly address the problem at hand. The solution must also be practical and available. Whenever possible, it is advisable to use existing resources. In the previous example, Sue came up with three possible solutions:

1. Remind Abigail that she had just called.
2. Tell her that she already knows the answer.
3. Set up a notepad by the telephone and ask Abigail to write down the answer, then when she calls again, Sue can ask her to check her notepad for the answer.

Trial and Error

It is important to systematically go through the solution list, as some solutions may be more effective than expected, while others that the caregiver may prefer may not be as effective. I always say to my clients that failure is to be expected, and that a failed experiment can generate new solutions. This helps prevent the caregiver from becoming discouraged early on and not completing the process.

Using the solutions that Sue produced, the next step is to look at the pros and cons of each solution.

1. Remind Abigail that she had just called.

Pro	Con
Reality. This is the first thought Sue has when her mother calls.	Abigail gets upset when she is told that she has called a few minutes earlier.

2. Tell her that she already knows the answer.

Pro	Con
This also feels true since she just told her the answer.	Abigail gets even more upset because she has no memory of knowing the answer.

3. Set up a notepad by the telephone and ask Abigail to write down the answer, then when she calls again, Sue can ask her to check her notepad for the answer.

Pro	Con
Sue feels that she is teaching Abigail something, and she feels hopeful that Abigail may eventually learn to refer to the notepad.	It does not directly answer the question, and Abigail may never learn to use the notepad.

There are no perfect solutions, but Sue decided that she felt better when she went through solution number 3 because she was not just repeating the same thing over and over again, and her mother did not seem to get as agitated. Sue realized that when she either just repeated her answer or reminded her mother that she had just called with that question, her aggravation was coming through in her voice, which made her mother even more anxious. Some caregivers are able to continue answering the questions calmly, without considering the repetitive questions to be a significant problem. The important thing to remember is that each family situation is different and the solution must match the problem as it is presented. One reason that this work is so rewarding for therapists is the opportunity for creativity and imagination in crafting novel solutions to complicated problems.

Providing Support

One of the most important findings in the early research on caregiver burden was that the frequency and kind of behavior problems was a poor predictor of burden and distress (e.g., Zarit, Todd, & Zarit, 1986). Having communication from family or friends that provided both understanding and emotional support was the most important factor in reducing the sense of burden. The therapist will be providing some support, as part of the therapeutic alliance, and should also be indentifying and strengthening the support network available to the client.

A family meeting, inviting as many people in the network as possible, can be a powerful intervention and can begin shifting the support role from the therapist to the family, friends, and other resources that have been identified. Referring to the Caregiving Genogram can provide a structure or agenda for this meeting. The goal is to spread out the caregiving demands so that no one person is overburdened. It is often very difficult for caregivers to ask directly for this help, but sometimes there is someone in the network who is good at organizing or who will take on a leadership role. Depending on the family structure and dynamics, this can be a very easy and enjoyable process or it can be extremely tricky. It is wise to have some sense of how the family works together and makes decisions before conducting the meeting. For a more complete discussion of this type of intervention, please refer to *Mental Disorders in Older Adults, Second Edition* (Zarit & Zarit, 2007).

A variety of support groups are available, particularly for Alzheimer caregivers. Interacting with people who are sharing similar experiences can be valuable. A good support group will offer accurate information about the disease and the current state of medical knowledge. The group will provide a forum for an exchange of problems and solutions. Members will be supportive of one another, and there will be a sense that those in the group share a unique emotional understanding of caregiving. Group process is very complex and, as a consequence, a professionally led support group is preferable. In the absence of a professional leader, the person with the strongest personality will prevail, and the results can be quite toxic.

CONCLUSIONS

This chapter has touched on some of the important clinical issues involved in assessment and treatment of family caregivers dealing with an impaired older adult. A careful assessment, both of the older patient and of the family members who are able and willing to provide assistance, is the foundation of any treatment plan. The instruments provided can be a good starting point in your evaluation. The intervention plan provided consists of the basics of any effective behavioral problem-solving program: providing information, teaching problem solving, and organizing the support system. These are likely to be familiar skills, but they take on some different dimensions in the context of the complex issues of cognitive impairment and aging. I hope that you will find that working with caregiving families is a creative and dynamic process, which you will find both challenging and rewarding.

REFERENCES

Zarit, S. H., Todd, P. A., & Zarit, J. M. (1986). Subjective burden of husbands and wives as caregivers: A longitudinal study. *The Gerontologist, 26,* 260–270.

Zarit, S. H., & Zarit, J. M. (1990). *The memory and behavior problems checklist and the burden interview.* University Park, PA: Penn State University Gerontology Center.

Zarit, S. H. & Zarit, J. M. (2007). *Mental disorders in older adults* (2nd ed.) New York: Guilford.

Empirically Supported Treatment for Family Caregivers

Steven H. Zarit, PhD

Caring for a family member with dementia or another late-life disability is a challenging and often stressful process. As other chapters in this volume have observed, family caregivers are at increased risk of mental health problems, physical illness, and mortality compared to people the same age who are not caregivers. This is a high price to pay, although some caregivers take on the task willingly and without complaint. In this situation, the clinical specialist in geropsychology can make a valuable contribution by drawing upon a wide range of clinical skills that have proven efficacy in helping caregivers manage the stressors in their lives, thereby reducing the threat to their health and emotional well-being.

This chapter reviews a growing body of evidence on treatments and other interventions for family caregivers. Several comprehensive meta-analyses have been published in recent years (e.g., Gallagher-Thompson & Coon, 2007; Pinquart & Sorensen, 2006; Sörensen, Pinquart, & Duberstein, 2002). These reviews provide useful descriptive and quantitative information on the effects of interventions. Rather than cover the same material, I have decided to highlight those clinical approaches that appear the most promising. My goal is to build toward an empirically validated tool kit for clinicians for reducing stress on caregivers. The information presented here will be followed in subsequent chapters by more detailed discussions of promising clinical techniques.

The chapter is divided into three sections. First, as a foundation, I examine some of the goals and assumptions about clinical interventions with caregivers. Second, I provide a brief overview of the most frequent clinical components of caregiver interventions. Finally, I turn to the findings from specific empirical studies, examining approaches that have support and discussing some of the problems in the research literature that need to be taken into account in interpreting the findings.

A FRAMEWORK FOR CLINICAL INTERVENTION WITH CAREGIVERS

How we view a problem determines whether or not we see the possibility for change. With all the negative expectations that surround old age, it is particularly important to examine basic concepts that guide clinical interventions with caregivers. These concepts address the goals for treatment and the underlying theory for why and how clinical interventions with older people and specifically with caregivers can be effective. I address four points: (a) minimum intervention; (b) caregiving stress as a multidimensional process; (c) modifiable aspects of the stress process; and (d) the diversity of caregivers and the caregiving context.

The Principle of Minimum Intervention

Robert L. Kahn, one of the pioneers in clinical geropsychology, introduced the concept of *minimum intervention* (Kahn, 1975), which he viewed as the guiding principle for treatment with older people, including caregivers. Kahn defined minimum intervention as treatment that disrupts the older person's life as little as possible. According to Kahn, older people maintain a delicate balance between independence and dependence. Viewing their older clients as needy and vulnerable, clinicians and caregivers alike can overreact and try to do too much. Being overprotective, however, undermines the person's independence, leading to what Kahn (1975) called *excess disability*—that is, more disability than would be expected based on the older person's underlying diseases and impairments. Excess disabilities develop both for psychological and for physical reasons. If someone is struggling to dress himself, for example, and a caregiver helps at the first sign of difficulty, that older person may lose the sense of being able to do that activity himself, and he may also lose the flexibility needed to be able to do so.

Excess disabilities can develop in home settings, but Kahn (Kahn & Zarit, 1974) believed they were much more likely to occur in institutional settings. In nursing homes and other care facilities, staff are more likely to take over activities such as dressing that the person can still do, either out of concern for the difficulty that resident might be having with a task or for efficiency to get everyone dressed, bathed, fed, or toileted by a certain time. This scenario was illustrated in Margret Baltes's (1994) landmark observational studies in nursing homes. Baltes and her colleagues found that nursing-home staff reinforced dependent behavior in residents and actively discouraged independent actions, a process likely to lead to increasing disability and dependence. Of course, another feature of institutional life is that almost all decision making is taken away from the resident. People cannot decide such basic issues as whether and with whom to share a room, when or what to eat, when to get up and go to bed, and so on.

In order to support independence and quality of life, Kahn (1975) argued that clinicians should strive to help people stay in their own homes, whenever possible. He suggested that placement often involves an overreaction to a situation that could be treated in a more focused and less disruptive manner. For example, a clinician is concerned that an older person might not be able to manage shopping and/or meal preparation and as a result may not be receiving adequate nutrition at home. Placement could address the problem, but an alternative approach consistent with minimum intervention would be to arrange for a shopping service or to arrange for prepared meals to be brought in. Similarly, a clinician might determine that a caregiver was burned out and recommend placement, but another strategy consistent with minimum intervention would be to arrange for respite services that would directly treat the caregiver's emotional distress. Rather than assuming that the answer is 24-hour care for the patient (a maximal intervention), the clinician would identify services such as adult day services (ADS) that give the caregiver a break and allow him/her to continue. Technological advances such as those discussed by Blechman in this volume (Chapter 14) can also be helpful to caregivers. Of course, some caregivers would not want that and may have reached a point of wanting to turn all the care over to someone else. I am not advocating that we discourage caregivers from placement. Instead, I am proposing that we provide caregivers with options that allow them to make choices consistent with their own values. In many situations, family caregivers want to continue providing help in the home and will do so with the right support.

Caregiving Stress as a Multidimensional Process

A critical perspective for working with family caregivers is to view the stress that they experience as a multidimensional process. Many people talk about caregiving stress or burden as if it is a unitary entity. As shown in Table 7.1, however, caregiving stress is made up of several distinct components (Aneshensel, Pearlin, Mullen, Zarit, & Whitlatch, 1995). At the first level of stressors are the older person's disabilities and resulting care demands placed on the family. These stressors are sometimes called *primary* because they derive directly from the person's disease or injury. Primary stressors include assisting with activities of daily living, managing memory and behavior problems, and providing supervision.

At a second level are the appraisals or meanings that caregivers give to these stressors. Consistent with both stress theory (Lazarus & Folkman, 1984; Pearlin, Mullen, Semple, & Skaff, 1990) and cognitive therapy (e.g., Beck, Rush, Shaw, & Emery, 1979), the impact that events have depends on caregivers' interpretation of them. Some caregivers, for example, are upset when a patient asks the same question over and over again, while other caregivers shrug such behavior off. The difference is due to the meanings they attribute to the behavior as well as their view of their resources for managing it. Similar to the cognitive processes seen

Table 7.1 Dimensions of Caregiving Stress

Primary Stressors	• Help for Activities of Daily Living • Managing Memory, Emotional and Behavior Problems • Supervision
Appraisals (Subjective Meanings and Stressfulness of Events)	• Stressfulness of Memory and Behavior Problems • Role Overload • Role Captivity • Loss of the Person
Secondary Stressors ("Spillover")	• Work—caregiving Conflict • Family Conflict • Financial Strain • Loss of Self
Outcomes	• Perceived Burden • Emotional well-being: Depression, anger, anxiety, positive emotions • Health

in depression, caregivers may feel hopeless, helpless, and overwhelmed by specific behaviors. The problem is only partly due to the behavior. The caregiver's appraisal of the behavior and his/her resources for managing it also contribute to experiencing the behavior as stressful.

Caregivers' subjective experience of stressors can also be measured at a global level. Relevant dimensions include the caregiver's feelings of loss of the person and of valued aspects of the relationship, as well as feelings of overload (Aneshensel et al., 1995; Pearlin et al., 1990).

The third level of stressors, which are called *secondary*, represent the spillover into other areas of the caregiver's life. The time and effort involved in providing care may interfere with work or family life or place a strain on family finances. Caregivers may become so absorbed in the role that they lose sense of other parts of their identity (Pearlin et al., 1990).

The final dimension is caregiver *outcomes*—that is, the cumulative effects of the stress process. The most frequently measured outcomes are burden and depression (Sörensen et al., 2002). Other important outcomes include anger, changes in the caregiver's health, and institutional placement.

For clinicians, the value of a multidimensional view of caregiving stress is that it leads to targeting treatment to the aspects of caregiving that are most troubling to a particular caregiver. Not every caregiver has the same set of problems, and not every caregiver finds the same problem to be stressful. If a caregiver is managing a problem such as incontinence with little or no distress, there is no point to target it for treatment. Consistent with minimum intervention, treatment can address those specific problems that are difficult or challenging for the caregiver.

Modifiable Aspects of the Stress Process

One assumption that is common among health-care providers is that, because an elder's underlying illness cannot be cured, there is little that can be done to help caregivers. By viewing the stress on caregivers as an unfolding multidimensional process, however, it is possible to identify treatable aspects of the situation. Although the underlying disease cannot be reversed, caregivers may be able to use more effective strategies for managing common stressors such as behavior problems as well as identifying when their beliefs might lead them to overreact to their relative. This type of skill training is a critical component of caregiver interventions, as will be seen. In addition, it is possible to introduce new resources into the situation. As in other stress situations, increasing the emotional support caregivers receive helps them manage more effectively. At another level, resources that provide relief or respite, whether from family or paid help, give caregivers a needed break and effectively reduce the amount of exposure to stressors.

The goal of interventions with caregivers, then, is to identify and address treatable components of the stress process. The possible targets for intervention, however, will vary from one caregiver to the next, which necessitates a flexible and varying approach to treatment.

The Diversity of Caregivers and the Caregiving Context

Although we often talk about caregivers as if they were a single group, they actually differ considerably from one another in several important ways. One difference is the type of relationship between the primary caregiver and the care recipient. Data from national surveys show that a spouse is most likely to take on the caregiving role (Wolff & Kasper, 2006). As shown in Figure 7.1, 38% of caregivers are spouses, compared to 31% who are daughters or daughters-in-law. A small number of sons (11% of all caregivers) take on the primary care role. Finally, there is a highly diverse "other" group that includes siblings, grandchildren, other relatives, and nonkin. The type of kin relationship between caregiver and care recipient carries different meanings and expectations. Spouses are more likely to make a complete, open-ended commitment to care than are adult children. Conversely, adult children may use respite services more readily than spouse caregivers (Zarit, Stephens, Townsend, Greene, & Leitsch, 1999). Apart from the normative expectations that accompany type of kin relationship, the quality of the past relationship will affect the caregiver's commitment and response to stress.

The structure of the caregiver's support network also can vary considerably. Some caregivers have a large network of kin and nonkin, and others may rely on only one or two people. Beyond size, however, support networks vary in their willingness and ability to help.

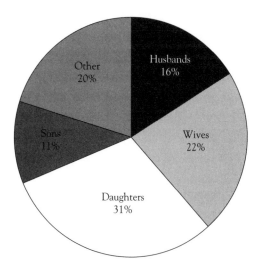

Figure 7.1   Primary Caregivers to Disabled Elders
Source: Wolff & Kasper, 2006

Another way that caregivers differ from one another is in their social and economic resources. Caregivers who are well-off financially have more options to pay for respite care. Conversely, people at the low end of the income scale can often take advantage of Medicaid-waiver and other programs designed to make services affordable. Ironically, people in the middle often struggle the most with the financial pressures of providing care.

Finally, the ethnic and racial background of the family will be associated with beliefs and expectations about care (see Chapter 2 by Crowther and Austin). As in any other clinical situation, understanding the culture of the family is an important step in providing an effective intervention.

CORE FEATURES OF CAREGIVER INTERVENTIONS

Before turning to specific research findings, I want to provide an overview of the types of interventions that have generally been used and some important steps that have frequently been omitted. Although there is considerable variation from one program to the next, most treatments have incorporated to varying degrees a core set of therapeutic strategies, as shown in Table 7.2.

Table 7.2 Core Features of Caregiver Interventions

- Assessment—clarifying what aspects of caregiving are stressful
- Clarification of goals
- Education about the disease/disability and its effects on behavior
- Problem solving
  - For behavior problems
  - For management of other stressors
- Supportive Interventions
  - Support of the therapist
  - Family meeting
  - Use of respite services

The beginning point of a caregiver intervention is an assessment, which identifies and targets aspects of caregiving that are stressful to the particular caregiver. Assessment has been used in most research protocols only to obtain baseline information and not to formulate an individualized treatment plan. One of the weaknesses in this approach is the assumption that all caregivers have the same problems. The most effective treatments in the literature are multidimensional programs that can respond more flexibly to the issues that are problematic for a particular caregiver (Sörensen et al., 2002; Pinquart & Sorensen, 2006).

A related issue is that the clinician and caregiver need to have a conversation about goals. It has become standard in psychotherapy to begin treatment by discussing with clients how treatment will proceed and why it will be helpful. Although many research interventions with caregivers present an overview of the treatment protocol, not much emphasis has been given to examining goals in a collaborative way or reaching an agreement about the direction of treatment. Caregivers may not understand the clinician's goals or may have a different set of expectations about what they hope to accomplish. A common discrepancy in goals occurs when the therapist tries to focus on the caregiver's problems, but the caregiver expects that treatment should help the care receiver. Many caregivers seek help in the hope that there will be something that can be done for their relative, a goal that needs to be reformulated tactfully to focus on those elements of the situation that can be changed.

Most treatment protocols have an educational component. Educating caregivers about their relative's illness and its effects on behavior can help them view these problems in a new light. In dementia care, for example, caregivers should understand that the patient's problems are due to an underlying brain disease and that problems remembering are not due to willfulness or a lack of effort, and they are not being done just to annoy the caregiver. Many treatment protocols also teach caregivers how to use behavioral management approaches for the patient's problem behavior. In some cases, cognitive and behavioral strategies are used to help change the caregiver's own behavior and emotions.

Finally, most treatments include supportive elements. Although often not mentioned explicitly, the supportive relationship of the therapist and caregiver can be a very important part of treatment. As in any other therapeutic situation, a supportive relationship can help caregivers take the steps to change old habits and risk trying something new. In group treatments, support comes through the understanding of people who are experiencing a similar situation. Treatment can also be used to increase the support of family and friends or help link caregivers to formal services programs. Although many community programs have conceptualized the process of linking caregivers to services as a straightforward matter, caregivers often perceive barriers to getting help. Some of these barriers are real and practical, and some involve the caregiver's own misapprehensions about services. Using cognitive-behavioral and other psychotherapeutic skills to address these barriers can make the difference between a successful and unsuccessful outcome (Zarit & Zarit, 2007).

EMPIRICALLY SUPPORTED TREATMENT

I now turn to specific empirical studies that demonstrate the efficacy of interventions with caregivers. Studies have been grouped into four categories: (1) Multidimensional interventions; (2) Behavioral treatment: (3) Group interventions; and (4) Respite services. For each area, I identify treatment components that appear the most promising, as well as discuss some of the methodological considerations that are important for understanding the strengths and limitations of the current research literature.

Multidimensional Interventions

Several of the most promising treatments have addressed multiple dimensions of the stress process (Pinquart & Sörensen, 2006; Gallagher-Thompson & Coon, 2007). These protocols include most or all of the core treatment processes previously described.

In an early study, my colleagues and I compared three treatment conditions for caregivers of people with dementia: a protocol that combined individual with a family meeting, a structured support group, and a wait-list control (Whitlatch, Zarit, & von Eye, 1991). In the individual and family counseling, caregivers learned about dementia and its effects on behavior. They were also taught to apply a behavioral problem-solving approach, identifying antecedents and consequences of the patient's problem behaviors and then generating solutions that could reduce the occurrence of the behavior by changing the exposure to triggering events or reinforcement. The most innovative feature of the treatment was the use of a family meeting. We viewed families as the most likely source of increased help and support to the caregiver. The meetings were structured to first provide information about the disease so that everyone shared a similar perspective and then to identify assistance that would be helpful to the caregiver.

In contrast to individual and family counseling, the support group used the interactions among participants to achieve its therapeutic goals. Caregivers in the groups shared information about the disease and generated suggestions for managing problem behaviors. These interventions are described in detail in Zarit, Orr, and Zarit (1985) and in Zarit and Zarit (2007).

The results showed that caregivers who received the individual and family treatment had the best outcomes in terms of subjective burden and emotional distress.

An important consideration is that the analysis of outcomes did not follow a traditional statistical approach of comparing mean differences across groups. We found in our initial examination of the results that many caregivers had low scores on the primary outcome measures of subjective burden and emotional distress (Whitlatch et al., 1991). Although faced with challenging situations, they were not necessarily depressed or feeling high levels of burden. As a result, this portion of the sample could not improve with treatment, at least on these measures. To address this problem, we used an approach that took into account participants' initial scores and specified an individualized result that represented a successful or unsuccessful outcome (von Eye & Brandstädter, 1988). Participants with initial high levels of burden or distress had a successful outcome if their scores decreased with treatment. By contrast, those with initially low scores had a successful outcome if they did not worsen. The results showed that people in individual and family counseling had higher rates of successful outcomes than the other two groups—that is, more people with initially high scores decreased and more people with initially low scores remained unchanged, compared to the other conditions. Ducharme and her colleagues (Ducharme et al., 2005) used a similar statistical approach in a study of a psychoeducational group and found comparable results. The treatment condition that emphasized changing appraisals and learning new coping strategies had higher rates of successful outcomes than two control conditions.

A question that could be raised about these findings is why did caregivers who did not report burden or emotional distress seek help? There are probably two answers. First, most caregivers in the study were experiencing care-related stressors, and while these problems troubled them, they had not resulted in feelings of burden or depression. In other words, these were caregivers who might be considered at risk for burden or depression, but who were not currently feeling burdened or depressed. Another way to look at that situation is that the caregivers have sought help for care-related problems, but the dependent measures used in the study do not match the problems they have. The treatment may still be of use if it helps them manage care-related stressors more effectively. Second, some caregivers may have sought help because they knew their situation would become more stressful in the future, and they wanted to be prepared. Treatment in both those instances could prevent a downward spiral, a finding consistent with the results of the Whitlatch et al. study.

Unfortunately, most studies in the literature have continued to blur this distinction between care-related stressors, which are a problem for most caregivers, and the outcome measures used to determine if a treatment is successful. The problem originates in how caregivers are recruited into these studies. Eligibility criteria are that participants are caregivers and not that they necessarily have the problem or problems that are targeted as outcomes by the intervention. The effect of including people in a treatment study who cannot improve on the outcome measures is to reduce the possibility of detecting significant change for the sample as a whole (i.e., a reduction in statistical power). One reason that many of the treatment studies in the literature have not had positive findings, particularly for global outcomes such as depression or burden, is that a portion of the sample does not have these problems in the first place (see Zarit & Femia, 2008, for a review). Again, some of these studies may have had positive effects in reducing important care-related problems that brought caregivers into treatment in the first place, but they were not able to show change on more traditional outcome measures such as depression.

Some studies have been able to overcome this dilemma. One strategy, of course, is to enroll only those caregivers who meet a minimum threshold on planned outcome measures. If the goal is to treat depression among caregivers, for example, the procedure should be to enroll only caregivers who are depressed. Studies that have taken this approach have generally reported positive findings (e.g., Belle et al., 2006; Lopez, Crespo, & Zarit, 2007). Another approach is to target the risk factors, such as behavior problems, that are problematic for many caregivers, rather than focusing on more global outcomes such as burden or depression. As we see in the following section, many interventions have been successful in reducing behavior problems and/or decreasing caregivers' stress in reaction to them.

Other studies have had positive outcomes without using these strategies. In these cases, the treatment may have been powerful enough to overcome the limitations of the sampling procedure used, or the sample may have included enough people at baseline who had problems such as depression so that significant change could be detected. Two such studies that included family counseling as part of the treatment reported positive outcomes for burden and depression, one conducted by Marriott and her colleagues in Britain (Marriott, Donaldson, Tarrier & Burns, 2000) and the New York University (NYU) studies conducted by Mittelman and her colleagues (Mittelman et al., 1995; Mittelman, Ferris, Shulman, Steinberg, & Levin, 1996). The NYU studies found that depression and burden were lower after 1 year for the treatment group, compared to a control condition where caregivers received referrals to community agencies. They also found long-term benefits—specifically, that caregivers in the treatment condition had lower depression after 3 years and lower appraisals of care stressors than the controls, and they also kept their relative at home for a longer period of time (Mittelman, Roth, Coon & Haley, 2004).

Several features of the NYU studies may have contributed to these positive outcomes. First, the family component was emphasized and there were up to four family meetings during the course of active treatment. Second, after completing the active period of treatment, caregivers participated in a maintenance program. They were encouraged to attend support groups and also could call upon their counselor if they encountered problems they could not handle. Third, the counselor could obtain assistance from consulting psychiatrists for management of behavior problems, if needed. A full description of the treatment program can be found in Mittelman, Epstein, and Peirzchalla (2002).

Another multidimensional trial that had positive outcomes was the REACH II project (Belle et al., 2006). The first REACH study was a large-scale, multisite trial of 6 types of interventions for caregivers. Results were largely negative, although there were indications that some subgroups of caregivers may have benefited differentially from specific treatments (Gitlin et al., 2003). The disappointing outcomes were in part due to the low baseline scores of many participants, as well as assigning people to a treatment (e.g., behavior management) without consideration of whether or not they needed that type of assistance (Zarit & Femia, 2008). REACH II was designed to address these problems. Caregivers were included in the study only if they reported some initial care-related distress, thereby reducing the baseline problem. Treatment was also flexible, such that more time was spent addressing problems a particular caregiver had, rather than following a fixed treatment protocol, as had been done in the first REACH project. The length of treatment was also extended to include 12 in-home, 6 telephone, and 2 check-in appointments. Caregivers in the treatment condition improved more in quality of life and had lower rates of clinical depression than a minimal-contact control group. These results indicate that the type of flexible treatment approach that a competent clinician would use effectively reduces depression and improves quality of life. It is also noteworthy that the REACH II study was effective with minority populations.

Behavioral Interventions

Several studies have examined the effects of training caregivers to use specific behavioral interventions. In contrast to multidimensional treatments, these programs focus primarily on behavioral techniques for managing specific, targeted behaviors. Outcomes are assessed both for the care receiver and the caregiver.

The most promising behavioral research has been conducted by Teri and her associates (McCurry, Gibbons, Logsdon, Vitiello, & Teri, 2005; Teri, Logsdon, Uomoto, & McCurry, 1997; Teri et al., 2003). In a landmark study, Teri and her colleagues (1997) evaluated the effects of treatment on depressive symptoms among people with dementia. Eligibility for this study included the presence of clinically significant symptoms of depression among the people with dementia. In other words, participants had to have the problem targeted by the treatment. Persons with dementia and comorbid depression and their caregivers were randomly assigned to one of four treatment conditions. The first condition applied Lewinsohn's (Lewinsohn, Biglan, & Zeiss, 1976) pleasant-events strategy for treatment of depression. Caregivers learned to identify activities the person with dementia could do that he/she enjoyed and then developed a plan to increase the frequency of engagement in those activities. The second condition was a modified version of the behavioral problem-solving approach used by Whitlatch and colleagues (1991). In that condition, caregivers identified antecedents and consequences of the patient's depressive behaviors, and then they developed and implemented strategies designed to reduce those behaviors. The third condition was a typical care control group, in which caregivers received advice and support from an experienced counselor. The fourth condition was a wait-list control group.

The results indicated that people with dementia in the two behavioral conditions, pleasant activities and problem solving, had reduced depressive behaviors immediately after completing treatment and at follow up, compared to the other groups. Caregivers in those two conditions also had lower depression and subjective burden. This study is noteworthy for its focus on a specific problem, depressive behaviors, as well as for demonstrating that reducing depressive behaviors in the patient is associated with improvements among caregivers.

A second study (Teri et al., 2003) again focused on comorbid depression among dementia patients. Patients and their caregivers were randomly assigned either to a treatment condition that trained caregivers to implement an exercise program for their relative and also taught them problem-solving techniques or to a usual care group. The results showed that caregivers in the treatment group were able to implement regular exercise for their relative. As a result, the dementia patients improved in their physical functioning and had lower depression. These gains were maintained for 24 months after completion of treatment, an outcome far more positive than the medications currently used to treat Alzheimer's disease.

The final study focused on a problem that can be quite distressing to caregivers—sleep disturbance (McCurry et al., 2005). In this study, caregivers of persons with dementia who were assigned to the treatment group received instruction in setting up a sleep-hygiene program for their relative, and they were also trained in behavioral management procedures. Sleep-hygiene procedures addressed stimuli likely to be associated with sleep or with insomnia, such as caffeine intake, daytime napping, and whether or not the bedtime routine was restful. A control group received only printed information about sleep hygiene. The results showed that people with dementia in the treatment group had fewer nighttime awakenings and more total hours of sleep, as well as decreased depression, compared to people in the control group. Gains were found both immediately posttreatment and at a 6-month follow up.

Group Interventions

Support groups for caregivers have been very popular for many years. Group treatment offers considerable opportunity for creative interventions, and the groups can help reduce caregivers' social isolation. Participants can share information with one another about the disease, coping strategies, and local resources, and they also gain the special kind of support that comes from someone who is going through the same experience. Despite these possibilities, it has been difficult to demonstrate empirical evidence of the efficacy of support groups (e.g., Haley, Brown & Levine, 1987; Whitlatch et al., 1991).

Some recent group interventions have demonstrated more positive findings. A characteristic of these groups is that instead of attempting to address a full range of care issues, or let the agenda be shaped by participants, the intervention is clearly focused on a limited set of outcomes. Coon and his colleagues (2003) compared two psychoeducational classes for caregivers of people with dementia. The first group focused on teaching caregivers anger-management skills and the second taught them strategies for managing depressive feelings. Both classes resulted in significant reductions of anger and depression, compared to a wait-list control group. Self-efficacy was also found to increase in both groups and mediated the treatment outcomes.

Using stress theory as a guide, Hébert and colleagues (2003) used a group intervention to teach cognitive and behavior coping strategies. The results showed that appraisals of the stress associated with memory and behavior problems was lower among participants in the treatment group, compared to caregivers assigned to a traditional support group. Measures of emotional distress and burden, however, did not change with treatment.

One limitation of many treatment studies is that they measure outcomes immediately after completion of treatment. In interventions that emphasize skill-building techniques, however, benefits might emerge slowly as caregivers gain more experience in applying the techniques that they learned. As an example of delayed benefits, Ostwald and her colleagues (1999) used a typical broad-scope psychoeducational group for caregivers that included providing information, teaching management skills, and helping build family support. There were no immediate posttreatment differences in outcome between the treatment group and a wait-list control. By 2 months later, however, burden and depression were significantly lower among caregivers in the treatment group, compared to the control group.

The Effects of Respite Services

A major goal of many psychosocial interventions is to increase caregivers' use of formal paid help, particularly respite services. Respite—which includes adult day services (ADS, also called adult day care), overnight respite, and brief institutional stays—provides relief from the exposure to care-related stressors and demands. As a result, caregivers should experience decreased emotional distress and burden when receiving respite.

Two important questions must be asked about this approach: Are these interventions successful in increasing service use, and does increased service use lead to reductions in caregivers' emotional distress, burden, or other outcomes? Large trials of care management, in which the goal of the intervention is to increase service use, have found that it is possible to increase how much paid help caregivers receive compared to control conditions (e.g., Lawton, Brody, & Saperstein, 1989; Newcomer, Fox, & Harrington, 2001). These studies, however, have not demonstrated that respite leads to reduced distress or other positive outcomes.

An examination of these trials suggests that while more caregivers receiving care management used paid respite services, the amount of service use remained low. To test whether adequate amounts of respite might have more positive outcomes, my colleagues and I studied caregivers who were enrolling a relative with dementia in an adult day service (ADS) program in a state (New Jersey) where a subsidy program made it possible for people to use adequate amounts of service (Zarit, Stephens, Townsend, & Greene, 1998). Since it is not possible to assign people randomly to an ADS program, we used a control group recruited from another state where day care for people with dementia was largely unavailable at the time of our study. We found that caregivers who used ADS regularly for 3 months or more had decreased feelings of overload and role captivity and decreased depression compared to the control group.

One limitation of these findings is that there is considerable attrition among users of ADS programs. In our study, 30% of participants were no longer using day care by 3 months (Zarit et al, 1999). In some cases, attrition was due to worsening in the patient's health. Many caregivers waited to use day care until late in their relative's dementia, when he/she was quite frail. At that point in the disease, health problems often decreased functioning even further and led to institutionalization. Other caregivers, particularly spouses of the person with dementia, appeared to use day care as a bridge to placement. Still others appeared unable to tolerate turning the care over to a paid provider. These caregivers took their relative out of day care, resuming full-time care at home. Follow up indicated that many of these caregivers continued to provide care at home 1 and 2 years later, even though their relative's dementia was quite advanced.

To address the problem of attrition, Reever and her colleagues (2004) designed a program called ADS-plus. This approach provides an individualized care-management program for caregivers using ADS, including counseling to identify the caregiver's concerns and needs, referral to other appropriate services, and follow up. Compared to a usual-care ADS program, participants in ADS-plus attended day care longer and were less likely to be placed in a nursing home. Caregivers in ADS-plus experienced significantly less depression over time and developed more confidence in managing problem behaviors (Gitlin, Reever, Dennis, Mathieu, & Hauck, 2006). These results replicate an earlier program in the Netherlands that provided systematic support to the caregiver of people with dementia using day care (Dröes, Meiland, Schmitz, & van Tillburg, 2006).

CONCLUSIONS

The main conclusion from this review is that there is a growing body of empirical literature that demonstrates that many interventions with caregivers are effective. Family-focused interventions and those that train caregivers in behavior management have had the best outcomes. Respite services such as adult day care are also helpful when provided in sufficient amounts and with attention to caregivers' needs. In addition to the specific clinical techniques used, the difference between successful and unsuccessful trials often is the approach taken to design of the study and measurement of outcomes. Those approaches, such as identifying the risk factors and outcomes unique to each caregiver and selecting interventions appropriate for them, are precisely what a good clinician would do. Treatment of caregivers is, in effect, an area of research where findings from controlled trials have affirmed sound clinical practices.

Of course, much remains to be learned, particularly for subgroups of caregivers. Do we, for example, need different approaches with spouses compared to other relatives, or with minority populations? Another issue is if the approaches that have generally been effective with caregivers of people with primarily Alzheimer's disease and vascular dementia can be effective with other disorders such as fronto-temporal dementia or Lewy Body Dementia, where behavior problems can be quite prominent and persistent. Clinicians, however, can address these situations by drawing upon a strong foundation of promising and empirically validated approaches. These interventions can help caregivers manage the complex demands in their lives, while contributing to the quality of life of the people receiving care.

REFERENCES

Aneshensel, C., Pearlin, L. I., Mullan, J. T., Zarit, S. H., & Whitlatch, C. J. (1995). *Profiles in caregiving: The unexpected career.* New York: Academic Press.

Baltes, M. M. (1994). Aging well and institutional living: A paradox? In R. P. Abeles, H. C. Gift, & M. G. Ory (Eds.), *Aging and quality of life* (pp. 185–201). New York: Springer.

Beck, A. T., Rush, A. J., Shaw, B. F., & Emery, G. (1979). *Cognitive therapy of depression.* New York: Guilford.

Belle, S. H., Burgio, L., Burns, R., Coons, D., Czaja, S. J., Gallagher-Thompson, D., et al. (2006). Enhancing the quality of life of dementia caregivers from different ethnic or racial groups. *Annals of Internal Medicine, 145,* 727–738.

Coon, D. W., Thompson, L., Steffen, A., Sorocco, K., & Gallagher-Thompson, D. (2003). Anger and depression management: Psychoeducational skill training intervention for women caregivers of a relative with dementia. *The Gerontologist, 43*(5), 678–689.

Dröes, R. M., Meiland, F. J. M., Schmitz, M. J., & van Tilberg, W. (2006). Effect of the Meeting Centres Support Program on informal carers of people with dementia: Results from a multi-centre study. *Aging and Mental Health, 10*(2), 112–124.

Ducharme, F., Lévesque, L., Lachance, L., Giroux, F., Legault, A., & Préville, M. (2005). "Taking Care of Myself": Efficacy of an intervention programme for caregivers of a relative with dementia living in a long-term care setting. *Dementia, 4*(1), 23–47.

Gallagher-Thompson, D., & Coon, D. W. (2007). Evidence-based psychological treatments for distress in family caregivers of older adults. *Psychology and Aging, 22,* 37–51.

Gitlin, L. N., Belle, S. H., Burgio, L. D., Czaja, S. J., Mahoney, D., Gallagher-Thompson, D., et al. (2003). Effect of multicomponent interventions on caregiver burden and depression: The REACH multisite initiative at 6-month follow-up. *Psychology and Aging, 18*(3), 361–374.

Gitlin, L. N., Reever, K., Dennis, M. P., Mathieu, E., & Hauck, W. W. (2006). Enhancing quality of life of families who use adult day services: Short- and long-term effects of the Adult Day Services Plus Program. *The Gerontologist, 46*(5), 630–639.

Haley, W. E., Brown, S. L., & Levine, E. G. (1987). Experimental evaluation of the effectiveness of group intervention for dementia caregivers. *The Gerontologist, 27*(3), 376–382.

Hébert, R., Lévesque, L., Vézina, J., Lavoie, J.-P., Ducharme, F., Gendron, C., et al. (2003). Efficacy of a psychoeducative group program for caregivers of demented persons living at home: A randomized controlled trial. *Journal of Gerontology: Social Sciences, 58B*(1), S58–S67.

Kahn, R. L. (1975). The mental health system and the future aged. *Gerontologist, 15*(1, pt. 2), 24–31.

Kahn, R. L., & Zarit, S. H. (1974). The evaluation of mental health programs for the aged. In P. O. Davidson, F. W. Clark, & L. A. Hamerlynck (Eds.), *Evaluation of behavioral programs* (pp. 223–252). Champaign, IL: The Research Press.

Lawton, M. P., Brody, E., & Saperstein, A. R. (1989). A controlled study of respite services for caregivers of Alzheimer's patients. *Gerontologist, 29*, 8–16.

Lazarus, R. S., & Folkman, S. (1984). *Stress, appraisal, and coping.* New York: Springer.

Lewinsohn, P. M., Biglan, A., & Zeiss, A. M. (1976). Behavioral treatment of depression. In P. O. Davidson (Ed.), *The behavioral management of anxiety, depression and pain* (pp. 91–146). New York: Brunner/Mazel.

Lopez, J., Crespo, M., & Zarit, S. H. (2007). Assessment of the efficacy of a stress management program for informal caregivers of dependent older person. *The Gerontologist, 47*, 205–214

Marriott, A., Donaldson, C., Tarrier, N., & Burns, A. (2000). Effectiveness of cognitive-behavioral family intervention in reducing the burden of care in carers of patients with Alzheimer's disease. *British Journal of Psychiatry, 176*, 557–562.

McCurry, S. M., Gibbons, L. E., Logsdon, R. G., Vitiello, M. V., & Teri, L. (2005). Nighttime insomnia treatment and education for Alzheimer's disease: A randomized controlled trial. *Journal of the American Geriatric Society, 53*(5), 793–802.

Mittelman, M. A., Epstein, C., & Peirzchalla, A. (2002). *Counseling in the Alzheimer's caregiver: A resource for health care professionals*. Chicago: American Medical Association.

Mittelman, M. S., Ferris, S. H., Shulman, E., Steinberg, G., Ambinder, A., Mackell, J., & Cohen, J. (1995). A comprehensive support program: Effect on depression in spouse-caregivers of AD patients. *Gerontologist, 35*, 792–802.

Mittelman, M. S., Ferris, S. H., Shulman, E., Steinberg, G., & Levin, B. (1996). A family intervention to delay nursing home placement of patients with Alzheimer disease: A randomized controlled trial. *Journal of the American Medical Association, 276*(21), 1725–1731.

Mittelman, M. S., Roth, D. L., Coon, D. W., & Haley, W. E. (2004). Sustained benefit of supportive intervention for depressive symptoms in caregivers of patients with Alzheimer's disease. *American Journal of Psychiatry, 161*(5), 850–856.

Newcomer, R. J., Fox, P. J., & Harrington, C. A. (2001). Health and long-term care for people with Alzheimer's disease and related dementias: Policy research issues. *Aging and Mental Health, 5* (suppl), S124–S137.

Ostwald, S. K., Hepburn, K. W., Caron, W., Burns, T., & Mantell, R. (1999). Reducing caregiver burden: A randomized psychoeducational intervention for caregivers of persons with dementia. *The Gerontologist, 39*(3), 299–309.

Pearlin, L. I., Mullan, J. T., Semple, S. J., & Skaff, M. M. (1990). Caregiving and the stress process: An overview of concepts and their measures. *Gerontologist, 30*(5), 583–594.

Pinquart, M., & Sorensen, S. (2006) Helping caregivers of persons with dementia: Which interventions work and how large are their effects? Helping caregivers of persons with dementia: Which interventions work and how large are their effects? *International Psychogeriatrics, 18*, 577–595.

Reever, K. E., Mathieu, E., Dennis, M. P., & Gitlin, L. N. (2004). Adult day services plus: Augmenting adult day centers with systematic care management for family caregivers. *Alzheimer's Care Quarterly, 5*, 332–339.

Sörensen, S., Pinquart, M., & Duberstein, P. (2002). How effective are interventions with caregivers? An updated meta-analysis. *The Gerontologist, 42*(3), 356–372.

Teri, L., Gibbons, L. E., McCurry, S. M., Logsdon, R. G., Buchner, D. M., Barlow, W. E., et al. (2003). Exercise plus behavioral management in patients with Alzheimer's disease: A randomized controlled trial. *Journal of the American Medical Association, 290*(15), 2015–2022.

Teri, L., Logsdon, R. G., Uomoto, J., & McCurry, S. M. (1997). Behavioral treatment of depression in dementia patients: A controlled clinical trial. *Journals of Gerontology Series B: Psychological Sciences & Social Sciences*, 52B(4), 159–166.

Von Eye, A., & Brandstädter, J. (1988). Application of prediction analysis to cross classifications of ordinal data. *Biometric Journal*, 30, 651–665.

Whitlatch, C. J., Zarit, S. H., & von Eye, A. (1991). Efficacy of interventions with caregivers: A reanalysis. *Gerontologist*, 31, 9–14.

Wolff, J. L., & Kasper, J. D. (2006). Caregivers of frail elders: Updating a national profile. *Gerontologist*, 46, 344–356.

Zarit, S. H., & Femia, E. E. (2008). A future for family care and dementia intervention research? Challenges and strategies. *Aging and Mental Health*, 12, 5–13.

Zarit, S. H., Orr, N. K., & Zarit, J. M. (1985). *The hidden victims of Alzheimer's Disease: Families under stress*. New York: New York University Press.

Zarit, S. H., Stephens, M. A. P., Townsend, A., & Greene, R. (1998). Stress reduction for family caregivers: Effects of day care use. *Journal of Gerontology: Social Sciences*, 53B, S267–S277.

Zarit, S. H., Stephens, M. A. P., Townsend, A., Greene, R., & Leitsch, S. A. (1999). Patterns of adult day service use by family caregivers: A comparison of brief versus sustained use. *Family Relations*, 48, 355–361.

Zarit, S. H., & Zarit, J. M. (2007). *Mental disorders in older adults* (2nd ed.). New York: Guilford.

8

Caregiver Family Therapy for Conflicted Families

SARA HONN QUALLS AND TARA L. NOECKER

As the primary context for caregiving, families are an appropriate and often critical focus for therapy. Families care for each other across the lifespan (Rossi & Rossi, 1990), implementing obligations of solidarity (Bengtson, Giarrusso, Mabry, & Silverstein, 2002; Bengtson & Roberts, 1991; Katz, Lowenstein, Phillips, & Daatland, 2005) and reciprocity (Beel-Bates, Ingersoll-Dayton, & Nelson, 2007; Boszormenyi-Nagy & Spark, 1984; Cantor, 1975, 1989; Carruth, Tate, Moffett, & Hill, 1997; Lewinter, 2003). Although some relationships have stronger norms of obligation than others (Rossi & Rossi, 1990), families demonstrate remarkable flexibility in working together to meet members' needs (Carstensen, 1992; Minuchin, 1974; Qualls, 1996). The general pattern in elder care is for one or a few individuals to take charge—defined as *primary caregiver(s)*—with secondary caregivers offering important support roles (Cantor, 1979, 1991; Kahn & Antonucci, 1981; Sims-Gould & Martin-Matthews, 2007) such as providing emotional and family support or participating in family-based decision making (Fisher & Lieberman, 1994, 1996; Lieberman & Fisher, 1995). Many members of the family are involved in providing care, so a family-wide lens for intervention warrants consideration.

Family dynamics influence outcomes and well-being of caregivers and care recipients. Fisher and Lieberman (1999) found that families with greater emotional intensity (both closeness and negative family feelings) and with lower levels of efficiency in problem solving were more likely to institutionalize elders with dementia. Structural characteristics such as cross-generational boundaries, good conflict-avoidance skills, and family organization provided protection against caregiving intrusions on other roles (Lieberman & Fisher, 1999b). A focused decision-making style and positive conflict-resolution methods were correlated with more help provided to elders (Lieberman & Fisher, 1999a). One could extrapolate from these findings that clear, organized family structures that support interpersonal emotion regulation and proactive problem solving are useful to families in the latest stage of the life cycle.

The quality of supportive relationships has been a consistent predictor of well-being in primary caregivers. Quite simply, primary caregivers need to feel supported by other members of the family (Aneshensel, Pearlin, Mullan, Zarit, & Whitlatch, 1995). In fact, Roth, Mittelman, Clay, Madan, and Haley (2005) believe their findings indicate that improvement in the quality of relationships with key family members was more important than increasing the actual amount of assistance received. In addition, perceived social support alters a caregiver's appraisal of a threatening stressor and improves caregiver well-being despite sustained stressors (Roth et al., 2005). Remarkably, the literature to date offers us very little understanding of the process by which roles transition into caregiver–care receiver from the mutually autonomous position experienced during the middle adult years (Bedford, 1995), nor about the reverberations within the *life event web* of families (Pruchno, Blow, & Smyer, 1984) as those roles shift over time.

Family conflict is a particularly important mediator of the impact of care-recipient mental impairment on caregiver strain (Scharlach, Li, & Dalvi, 2006). Higher rates of family conflict are found in families that coreside with the care recipient, have lower caregiver household income levels but greater caregiver education levels, and when the care recipient is someone other than a spouse.

Few family-level interventions have been developed despite the fact that most caregivers for frail elderly persons are family members and family dynamics are strongly related to outcomes for care recipients and caregivers. The impact of the few existing family caregiver interventions has been impressive, demonstrating increases in caregiver well-being and perceived social support and reductions in caregiver perceived stress and depression (Drentea, Clay, Roth, & Mittelman, 2006; Mittelman, Roth, Coon, & Haley, 2004; Mittelman, Roth, Haley, & Zarit, 2004; Roth et al., 2005). The value of working with an entire family to benefit the care recipient, caregiver, and other family members has been demonstrated repeatedly (Czaja, Eisdorfer, & Schulz, 2000; Knight & McCallum, 1998; Mitriani & Czaja, 2000; Whitlatch, Judge, Zarit, & Femia, 2006; Zarit, Johansson, & Jarrott, 1998; Zarit & Zarit, 1982). Thus, clinicians have been encouraged to view the caregiver–care recipient dyad within a broader family framework. The logic of this seems obvious when we note that family members are involved in care all across the lifespan.

Three approaches to family therapy inform our own. Zarit, Orr, and Zarit (1985) pointed to caregivers as the hidden victims of Alzheimer's Disease, a point so compelling that it fed a stream of intervention research to support caregivers (Pinquart & Sörensen, 2003, 2007). Mittelman and colleagues (1993) have run the longest continual study of family caregiving intervention to date with spousal caregivers at New York University School of Medicine's Alzheimer's Disease Center. Their findings show the strongest benefits of any caregiver intervention: an approximately 1-year delay (329 days) in, and in some cases avoiding entirely, institutional placement in addition to improvement in caregivers' and family members' well-being, practical support, and social support (Hirsch & Mittelman, 1997; Mittelman et al., 1993; Mittelman, Epstein, & Pierzchala, 2003; Mittelman, Ferris, Shulman, Steinberg, & Levin, 1996). A more recent study demonstrated a more prolonged time for placement (557 days) for caregivers who received six sessions of individual and family counseling, had continuously available ad hoc telephone counseling, and participated in support groups (Mittelman, Haley, Clay, & Roth, 2006).

An adaptation of structural-strategic family therapy was tested with Cuban American caregivers of dementia patients at the REACH site at the University of Miami. Using computer-telephone technology, these families received in-home family therapy, accessed resources, and participated in family conferences and online support groups (Eisdorfer et al., 2003). A meta-analysis of all REACH sites found small but significant effects of reduced burden for caregivers in active treatment conditions compared to those in control conditions. However, active treatments in most REACH sites failed to produce significant reductions in depression. The Miami site was the exception; the therapy and technology intervention yielded a significant reduction in depressive symptoms for caregivers (Eisdorfer et al., 2003; Gitlin et al., 2003; Schulz et al., 2003).

We are indebted to colleagues for teaching us these key lessons we take from their work: (a) Caregivers and family members are invisible within the care services systems despite their critical roles, (b) family-level counseling is powerful if provided flexibly with regard to whom to include as well as when and how sessions are structured, and (c) adaptation of family therapies that target the family structures and processes explicitly have potential to benefit the caregivers' mental health, especially when they improve communication among family members.

Our approach, Caregiver Family Therapy, has developed within a particular clinical setting—a community mental health services and research center run by a university psychology program in a location near other senior services. Despite the original expectation that we primarily would provide psychotherapy for individuals with mental disorders, we found our caseload filled with family members whose psychological distress seemed directly related to their worry about a loved one and how to renegotiate their own roles vis-à-vis that person's decline. We then initiated the Aging Families and Caregiver Program and obtained funding through the local Area Agency on Aging, who administers caregiving funding available within the Older American's Act. The program offers psychoeducational classes for caregivers that are adapted from the work of Dolores Gallagher-Thompson and colleagues (Coon, Gallagher-Thompson, & Thompson, 2003), along with interventions for families, and a men's caregiver group. As we continued to work with caregivers to address their struggles to adapt to new relationship structures produced by declining health and cognition in an elderly member, we realized that we were adapting a family systems approach in a relatively consistent way. Over time, we are defining, exploring, and setting parameters for this work based on the data we collect from our clients and our own clinical observations and analyses. This chapter shares our current state of understanding that is shaped by previous statements of the model (Qualls, 1996, 1999a, b, c, 2006, 2008).

Clients and clinicians working together in the Aging Families and Caregiver Program have taught each other a lot about how to help families restructure themselves to meet the continually changing needs of older adults with declining health. This chapter is dedicated to them and is an effort to describe the model that has emerged from our work together.

CAREGIVER FAMILY THERAPY MODEL

The core tenets of the Caregiver Family Therapy (CFT) model are presented in Qualls (2006) and elaborated in Qualls (2008). The four goals of CFT are to (a) empower families to make decisions that manage safety risks and support the highest potential level of autonomy of the impaired person, (b) assist caregivers in relating with other family members in ways that yield a substantive as well as a subjective sense of support and healthy family functioning, (c) balance the needs and growth of all family members according to the values of the family, and (d) facilitate restructuring of family members' roles and processes for providing care in ways that maximize the quality of life for the elder, caregiver(s), and other family members.

To accomplish those goals, the therapy is organized around three tasks. The caregiving situation must be named accurately, which involves identifying the etiology of the care recipient's functional difficulties, along with a detailed analysis of the contexts in which care is provided. The family roles and relationships need to be adapted or restructured to facilitate caregiving. Finally, the caregiving family structures also are reviewed and revised to ensure that the needs of all family members are met.

The following CFT case description is provided by the second author, with significant details masked or changed to protect the identity of the family. This case description will be used to demonstrate and illustrate aspects of CFT, including assessment and intervention techniques with a loving and complex family facing a difficult transition.

Sally, a blind caregiver who used a guide dog companion to navigate, had recently moved from another state with her partner, Jim. They moved because Jim's son was no longer providing adequate support and Sally's daughter offered to help. Jim had already had two incidents of congestive heart failure, advanced Alzheimer's dementia, and diabetes, for which he gave himself insulin injections. Jim was still driving and Sally's tales of near accidents each week made my hair stand on end.

Sally and Jim partnered after childrearing and had lived together for approximately 20 years. Thus, Jim and Sally's children did not know each other well. Sally's daughter was attempting to assist the couple yet was not fully trusted by Jim's children. After the move, Jim continued to decline but his children had no direct experience of his growing deficits. Lacking a means to communicate with Jim's children, who were the legal next of kin, Sally and her daughter were frustrated and unable to appropriately assist with Jim's safety, health, and finances. Jim's health deteriorated to the point where he was unhappy, frustrated, incapable of managing his own medications and injections, and appeared to be at risk for medication mismanagement or injuring Sally. He had pushed and slapped Sally on several occasions when he was unable to vocalize his frustration. I decided that an in-home assessment was needed, along with a review of his treatment plan.

With some coaching, Sally allowed palliative care to visit her home and assess the living situation. Within hours, the physician from palliative care called me to express his concerns. He felt that

Jim and Sally were no longer safe in their home because Jim needed assistance remembering his medications and insulin injections. He was also concerned about Jim's growing physical aggression toward Sally. The palliative-care physician suggested medication to calm Jim, to reduce the possibility that Sally would be injured. The physician also recommended placing Jim in a 24-hour, skilled, care facility that could monitor his health and care needs as soon as possible. He also felt that hospice was an option, as Jim would probably pass away within 6 months.

Although Jim and Sally's case is complex, it is not atypical. Many caregivers manage their own health concerns as well as their partners and will move closer to family (often miles away from their social support network) to be closer to children. Often, adult children cannot provide the support that multiple longstanding friends did, and these adult children often find it difficult to communicate and trust other adult children. Finally, multiple sources of information are required to complete a full assessment. For Sally's family, the strength of the intervention was grounded in a complete and accurate assessment. Sally's case will be used to illustrate several points that will be discussed in more detail later in the chapter.

ASSESSMENT

Typically completed in the first three sessions, the assessment focuses on gathering information about the caregiving situation. The process begins with questionnaires in which the caregiver(s) describes concerns, IADL and ADL difficulties, behavioral problems, and cognitive problems. An interview is used to gather information about family history and structure along with detailed information about the care recipient: medical diagnoses and medications, cognitive and physical capacity, personality, and how the individual interacts with others. The clinician also gathers information on use of support services (both formal and informal) and the level of involvement of caregivers and family members. The clinician evaluates the caregiver's knowledge of and openness to using community resources. Throughout the assessment and therapy, the clinician remains vigilant for possible abuse, safety risks, or exploitation.

During the information-gathering phase, clinicians need to distinguish carefully between descriptions of the behavior problem and the client's label for the problem. We find that caregivers are able to describe the problem accurately but are less accurate in their label for it. Careful description of worrisome behavior patterns, safety risks, and any other behavior changes all help clarify the types of additional assessment needed to obtain an accurate understanding of the etiology of the problem.

The key focus of the first session is on the caregiver's initial statement of the problem(s) he or she has come to psychotherapy to resolve. By the time the caregiver seeks professional services he or she often feels hopeless after trying many options to help, cajole, motivate, entice, soothe, or manipulate the care recipient into cooperation. His or her problem-solving methods thus far have been minimally effective or ineffective. By focusing on the client's primary concern, the therapist will provide much-needed hope that change can indeed occur.

The clinician should not be surprised if the caregiver desires nothing short of a miracle in the first few sessions, when the clinician's goal is primarily to collect information. The therapist must understand and acknowledge to the client that reaching out for assistance is an excellent step. Acknowledging how much the client has already overcome as a caregiver is a supportive intervention that focuses the therapy back on the client's strengths and dedication. Besides searching for and acknowledging strengths, encouraging the client that there is hope and help is a first step in rapport building. Through this process, the client is apt to feel calmed and soothed, which will allow the clinician the time to become oriented to the family and caregiver's situation.

Alternatively, some family members are so uncertain as to whether there really is a problem that they approach therapy apologetically, as if embarrassed that they are wasting our precious time. Instead of hope, these families need a strong reality check about their concerns. If they are understating the problem, we have to help them face the reality of the problem before offering hope or other interventions. Even many of these hesitant families have begun to address growing problems in subtle ways that are not recognized until the interviewer explicitly asks questions about changes in functioning and patterns of assistance in recent years.

Close attention to previous failed solutions protects the therapist from diminishing hope by offering the same problematic solutions that the client has attempted and failed. The assessment strategy is simple: Ask the caregiver what has and has not worked. Some of the previous failed efforts will still be viable options once the clinician knows exactly what and how they were implemented. In other words, assessment extends beyond assessment of the problem to include previous strategies employed to resolve it and the interpersonal contexts in which those strategies were attempted.

The assessment phase culminates in a discussion between client and therapist about the recommended course of therapy, including number of predicted sessions, who will be involved, and the goals of therapy. Despite the fact that the range of potential presenting problems is vast, caregivers often only present with one or two major complaints that point directly to the goals of therapy. Once the goals are established, the therapist can make a reasonable determination of whether the caregiver is capable of effecting change within a brief format (i.e., a couple of sessions) or if he or she will need more time to create change. Broaching the topic of limited sessions often elicits the caregiver's beliefs about self-efficacy as well as the sense of urgency behind the complaints. The discussion of short- versus longer-term intervention is really a negotiation of the depth of change embedded in the goals.

An additional issue to address before launching into therapy is whether the care recipient can stay alone while the caregiver comes to sessions. If the caregiver is uncomfortable and concerned about the care recipient's safety during the period of absence, he or she will be ambivalent about therapy just because it costs so much effort to arrange coverage. We also have seen caregivers who are confused about what to tell the care recipient regarding their whereabouts during therapy sessions. This can become an opportunity for psychoeducation on role transitions.

Caregiver Family Therapists often begin an assessment with only one viewpoint in a complex, dynamic family negotiating a difficult transition.

Many times the first person in the family presenting for treatment is angry with other members for failing to give adequate support, assistance, or decision-making ability to him or her. The caregiver often expresses grief and even depression regarding his or her loss of independence, time, and the care recipient as he or she was previously known. Although it is appealing to take sides or draw conclusions, the therapist must be careful to remain neutral, especially when the family is the client or other family members are likely to become clients.

STRUCTURE OF FAMILY SESSIONS

The structure of CFT varies substantially across families and over time within a family, exhibiting tremendous flexibility in who gets involved, when and how the sessions are scheduled, and whether family members are in the therapy room or connected electronically. Clinical judgment about the best strategy to achieve the goal combines with client preference to negotiate the specific choices. Sometimes family members who would not otherwise be involved are included to ensure the safety of the care recipient or caregiver and avoid involvement of Adult Protective Services. Even nonfamily members participate in family therapy when their communication is part of the leveraging of change within the family structure. For instance, a primary health-care provider may be the intolerable voice that restricts driving or living in the community when the care recipient is in danger and the family cannot otherwise provide the voice. Most often, a multiperson family session is used to share accurate information that can be used to get the family "on the same page" about a recent diagnosis or change in the health or functional status of the caregiver or care recipient. Other clients request or require a third party to assist in family *negotiations*. Variation is the rule, with thoughtful justification of how and why various members are involved based on the treatment plan.

The timing of therapy sessions is also variable. Family sessions generally continue until the crisis has passed or the family is able to make decisions and communicate more independently. Often, only one or two family sessions are needed per episode, but several family sessions may occur over a period of years as new crises or transitions arise. Family sessions are often longer than the typical 45- to 50-minute therapy hour, running 1½ to 3 hours. Sessions may occur on weekends, over holidays, in the evening, or at other times when the entire family is present. Sessions may include family members who are conferenced into the meeting by phone or who are visiting. Often, nonfamily members are included such as physicians, neuropsychologists, care planners, friends who assist in caregiving, staff at nursing facilities, and even clergy. The family usually names the participants and is assisted by the therapist in structuring the family session and inviting outside members.

Family conferences focused on their declining health or behavior can be too stimulating for care recipients, but the decision about including the elderly member who is the focus of concern needs to be considered explicitly in every case. Care recipients with cognitive impairment can become quite distressed by other family members' efforts to force them to achieve insight into their deficit and/or reach consensus on a plan of action. When a crisis in the elder's care is the focus of hot debate by the family, a cognitive-impaired elder will become upset at being helpless to think through the issue or manage the conflict. The therapist can use the choice about including the elder as an opportunity to collaborate with the family and elder in making a decision based on cognitive functioning data. Neuropsychological report data can guide the discussion of what "he/she *can* do" and the elder's stated preferences can guide the family to honor his or her preferences about being involved. An elder who wants to be involved, but whose cognitive functioning disallows him or her to process others' language, needs the therapist to recognize his or her role and assist him or her in finding a way to participate meaningfully. The family may also need assistance honoring their need *not* to have the elder participate when the elder truly cannot process what is being discussed. The family can be guided to engage the elder in statements of values and preferences without allowing the elder to choose unsafe options that will bring distress later.

In Sally's case, two family sessions were needed and prior to these, information was gathered from multiple sources, professionals, and family members to complete a full assessment and understanding of the family and its transition. Jim was not involved in the family session because

Sally did not believe that he or the family would benefit from his presence. Sally, however, did invite many family and nonfamily caregivers in order to share Jim's health information and to make plans for his future with the family and a therapist on hand.

Therapist Reflections on Case 1

Assessment of Sally's caregiving situation required gathering all of the information from Sally, her doctors, and the AAA care planner. Sally and I discussed her options for dissemination of the palliative-care physician's recommendations amongst the family. In addition, in the face of Jim's rapid decline, Sally decided that she wanted to take Jim for one last trip to see his children and to go to Hawaii. I believed the safety risks on this trip were substantial so I suggested that the family should be included in planning and preparations for the trip. In addition, Sally wanted to share Jim's prognosis with her family. Sally also noted that Jim was losing his capacity to speak English and reverting more and more to his native language. So Sally invited Jim's sister from Europe, who did not speak or understand English. Sally believed Jim's sister would be helpful as a companion for Jim who could speak with him in their childhood language.

Sally wanted to meet with Jim's sister privately to ensure that she understood Jim's condition. The first *family* session included Sally, Jim's sister, a translator, and me. Jim's sister was stunned that Jim was so ill, as she had been unable to adequately communicate with her sister-in-law prior to this meeting. It became clear that much of the family was ill-informed about Jim's rapidly deteriorating health. The session allowed Sally and Jim's sister to express their concerns, comfort each other, and to form a plan for the trip without a language barrier.

At this point, Sally, who had originally asked for individual assistance with caregiving, found it necessary to include the rest of the family in Caregiver Family Therapy. A larger family session was scheduled including Sally's daughter and son-in-law, who also were heavily involved in caring for Jim and assisting Sally with aspects of IADLs that were difficult for her due to blindness, such as finances and cleaning. An immediate goal of this session was to reorganize family roles, responsibilities, and power over finances. Jim's son had power of attorney for medical and financial decisions but lived hundreds of miles away and was virtually unreachable much of the time. Sally's daughter, who accompanied them to doctor's visits and paid their bills, needed power of attorney to accomplish her tasks and to ensure that she could get federal assistance to place Jim. The trip and the palliative-care physician's report were used as a catalyst for engaging the family in role transitions that were long overdue.

Sally helped identify participants. Most of Sally and Jim's family members participated, including Jim's son (by phone) and sister and Sally's daughter, son-in-law, granddaughter, and niece. A care planner attended the meeting to bring knowledge and experience with local nursing homes that would assist the family in narrowing options for Jim's future placement. Other participants included Sally's pastor, the interpreter, and me.

I prepared for the family session by compiling the assessment information, structuring the session, and making a to-do list for the family. After introductions, Jim's condition was discussed. The physician's assessment of the home situation was provided. This included items such as Sally and Jim's questionable safety and the physician's concerns for managing Jim's pain. At this point the family realized they had been misinformed about the severity of his condition and his impending death. The culmination of the assessment phase in the clear, unequivocal naming of Jim's diagnoses represented the first major intervention for this family.

Although specific actions were laid out by the therapist in Sally's case, other families bring an action list with them. Sometimes, that list is a source of conflict within the family as members not only have opposing preferred action (e.g., nursing home placement versus home care), but they have also begun to make negative attributions for each others' motives.

Prior to discussion of preferred caregiving strategies, families are led in a discussion of values. The purpose of this intervention is twofold. First, the family needs to figure out whether there are shared values or not. Second, assuming they can rally around common values (which is typical), they need to state their commitment to valuing the diverse contributions of different individuals to the caregiving effort.

Clear value statements typically make it obvious that everyone desires support of autonomy that is balanced by a concern for safety. In many families, the core values that underlie our most basic ethical struggles as humans have been polarized so one person has become the voice for one value and another embodies another value. A sister may speak about her value of safety each time her brother speaks about the value of support for autonomy. Family members find it easy to forget that they all hold dear both of those values unless the therapist interrupts the urge to project and polarize them as if each value was held only by one person.

Therapist Reflections on Case 1

Next, I led a discussion of core values. The group shared the goal of providing the best care possible for Jim that would maximize his independence, comfort, and safety. Although Sally's family had negative feelings about Jim's children, when Sally and her family realized that everyone hoped for the same outcome for Jim, it united the family to focus on and work toward the greater shared goal.

The second half of the values discussion focused on the varied gifts of members of the group: the hands-on care provided by Sally's daughter's family, the love and loyalty of his son, and his sister's ability to communicate with him when no one else was able and their shared early history to which he would occasionally relate. Also, the family's religious values and the importance of having the pastor's involvement were acknowledged. With structure, direction, and new-found respect for each other, the family was forced to create new patterns of interaction and resolution.

The assessment process that began during individual sessions with Sally proceeded to include her primary support—her daughter—and her core support network. During these assessment sessions, the majority of which were conducted only with Sally until the larger family session occurred, information was gathered, disseminated, written, and repeated until the family had reached some degree of shared understanding through their shock. The larger family session was task focused, launched with strong statements about the fact that Jim was dying and needed 24-hour, skilled care. The conversation was difficult because family members struggled to accept the reality and severity of Jim's condition. Once everyone was able to accept this reality, practical issues arose—how should the care be provided.

The long conversation about the severity of Jim's illness opened his family to the limited level of trust needed to discuss the values underlying care options. The values discussion was used as a basis for planning specific care options. Even this assessment process functioned as intervention. Although generated primarily from Sally and the palliative-care physician, the list of major areas for change motivated and focused the participants on the tasks that would change their roles and relationships.

CAREGIVER FAMILY THERAPY TASKS

CFT centers around three therapeutic tasks that unfold only somewhat sequentially, so they are not considered stages. At some point in successful caregiving, families need to name the problem, restructure themselves to meet the care recipient's needs, and balance caring across all family members. Generally, caregiving families we see are unsuccessful in one of these tasks.

Naming the Problem

Caregivers may enter into CFT describing a problem that has not yet been identified by the medical community. Alternatively, the problem may have a name, but the treating physician has not given additional information on course, prognosis, resources, or even what the caregiver should or should not do. Families sometimes have useful information but have not assimilated it because it is too technical or simply because they are in shock about labels that were applied, such as *terminal* or *dementia*.

The assessment process gathers what information is available and determines whether an adequate name for the problem already exists. If not, the caregiver is assigned specific evaluations to obtain. Naming the problem includes identifying the source, nature, and implications of the problem. Safety risks, family roles, family decision-making processes, and caregiver burdens are spelled out and structural ambiguities are acknowledged. The therapist validates the meaning of family boundaries, especially hierarchical boundaries between generations; he or she also grants permission to revisit them in light of the current situation. Validating meaning also communicates to the client that the therapist recognizes and understands the role confusion that the client faces regarding the deteriorating elderly family member.

Once a diagnosis is given or neuropsychological assessment is completed, we routinely write a summary of the assessment data in language accessible to the family because technical reports are so difficult to understand. The summary includes the name of the problem (e.g., diagnosis or functional status) and a detailed description of cognitive and physical functioning with application to everyday tasks. Books may be recommended for more details on care or on family dynamics. Finally, the therapist clarifies any risks and makes an immediate plan for them.

When sharing information with a family, stating the information once is not enough; repetition is crucial for family work. Family members may only hear the one or two key pieces of information that answered their most compelling question. Almost every family session that we have *mediated* has left the family reeling. Members need time to adapt to their changing views of other family members and create a new response. Written information offers them a chance to review it on their own time, repeatedly, and to share it with other key members of the caring network. Each subsequent session will likely include at least one request for clarification or one question that shows which pieces of information are not yet understood. Repetition is also useful because the information literally means something new as the family begins to function in a new way.

Levels of Structural Change

Family therapists distinguish between first-order and second-order change, which represent two levels of reorganization intensity (Olsen, 2000). We find this distinction meaningful within CFT because the process of therapy varies substantially across the two levels of intervention. First-order change is often faster and less demanding on the therapist than second-order change.

In first-order change, the less intrusive option, the family fosters adaptation of existing structures to meet the care recipient's needs without excessively burdening any one person. The three stages of CFT can be accomplished within existing relationship structures by adding information, skills, or resources to improve the caregiving situation for everyone involved. The family is structured well to accomplish the tasks of assessment that lead to adequate naming of the problem and the needed caregiving tasks. In addition, no family member's development is sacrificed by the caregiving structures and processes. Psychoeducational and problem-solving counseling approaches are highly effective at helping most families meet the care recipient's needs, while ensuring that the burden and stress of caregiving does not put the primary caregiver at risk (Drentea et al., 2006; Mittelman et al., 2003; Mittelman, Roth, Coon, & Haley, 2004; Mittelman, Roth, Haley, & Zarit, 2004).

Sally's family required only first-order change because they had already engaged in role transitions that defined Sally and her daughter's family as caregivers for Jim, the care recipient. Sally also received care in domains affected by her blindness. The basic role structures were in place, but the intensity of caregiving behavior needed to be increased due to Jim's deteriorating health and cognition. The therapist focused on first-order change strategies to strengthen roles in order to more effectively support Jim and Sally, especially in light of growing risks.

Sally's family illustrates the nonlinear sequencing of the three core CFT tasks. Although the problem had been named for months, family members did not share an understanding of that name. Different family members had very different views about the problem primarily because they lacked shared access to assessment results or interpretations of those results. Although time-consuming, the process of getting everyone on the same page about the care recipient's problem pays off in the role-restructuring phase of therapy. Sally's family cycled back to the first task long enough to get everyone on the same page about the problem.

Following the discussion of values, the family was focused on how transitions would occur. It was clear from limited contact with the family prior to the meeting that they desired more structure and guidance in their transition. Thus, prior to the meeting, I developed an agenda that included the tasks that would be necessary to accomplish in order to ensure a safe trip and easy transition to 24-hour, skilled care upon their return. The family agreed that placing Jim directly after his return would be the option of least resistance for Jim. They planned to have a room in a facility in which family pictures and his favorite chair would be waiting. Jim's memory was so poor that he probably would not remember where he had been living prior to the trip.

The to-do list tasks were placed in a chart and everyone was given a copy to follow. The chart left spaces next to each task to record the names of family members who volunteered to accomplish that task. It also left spaces for tasks to be added by other family members.

Family members engaged actively in completing the chart. They recognized that Sally was still reeling from all of the diagnostic information and was struggling to think clearly. They discussed the tasks, added tasks to the chart, and divided these tasks. The care planner provided Jim's son with several reasons to include Sally's daughter as power of attorney for Jim and discussed options for his placement. As the tasks were split up among the family, it became clear to both Sally's and Jim's children and extended family how much of the burden Sally and her daughter had been handling. It was obvious that Sally's daughter was attempting to balance Jim's autonomy and safety. Jim's son realized that Sally's daughter was not asking for power of attorney to steal Jim's money. She had only begun to manage Jim and Sally's finances when Jim began to make poor financial decisions and failed to pay bills. When Jim's son understood the extent of his father's illness and how advanced his deficits were, he finally realized that Sally's daughter was attempting to ensure appropriate care and treatment for Jim. Jim's son thanked Sally and her daughter for their care of his father. Sally's daughter and Jim's son had their first productive conversation about *their* parents' future, and they were able to continue these conversations without the problems that had occurred in the past.

Putting the to-do list of urgent actions in writing for the family members not only kept the meeting on task, but it also guided the family to the kinds of caregiving roles and relationships that Jim and Sally required. Over the next few weeks, family members accomplished their tasks. Sally, Jim, and his sister flew for one last visit to see Jim's children. Following this, the trio went to Hawaii.

Within 2 days of landing in Hawaii, Jim was having bowel incontinence. Sally and Jim's sister were disgusted and angry with him for the mess and his increased fighting and agitation. After 2 days of increasingly severe symptoms, Sally finally called the ambulance, just in time. Jim was in renal failure. Unfortunately, Jim's sister's role as a translator and support person was not realized. In the hospital, it became apparent that Jim's sister was also in the beginning stages of dementia and causing trouble in paradise.

Sally called her daughter who immediately got on a plane and traveled to Hawaii with medical power of attorney in hand, travel insurance in place, funeral plans completed, and the room at the nursing home ready because the family had completed all of the tasks asked of them during the family session. Sally called me for moral support before her daughter arrived. We used the brief telephone therapy session to discuss strategies to quiet Jim's sister, manage her problem behavior, and to anticipate the possibility of Jim's death. Jim stabilized within a few days of Sally's daughter's arrival. Travel insurance provided a nurse that accompanied Jim, his sister, Sally, and her daughter on the plane. The nurse even traveled to the nursing home to hand over Jim's files and explain his hospitalization, condition, and situation.

Jim settled in comfortably to the nursing home for the final 6 months of his life, believing it was his home. Sally's daughter had even learned enough of his childhood language to speak and sing to Jim in his childhood tongue while he quietly passed away from his third congestive heart failure. When Jim died, Sally's daughter called me to express appreciation for the way family therapy had allowed Jim to die peacefully in a comfortable facility with hospice caring for his pain. Sally and her family loved Jim and grieved together. They returned to the ocean, where Jim and Sally met, to spread his ashes with both families. Sally continued in psychotherapy individually for grief counseling and to work through another role transition, life after caregiving.

Sally's family is a prototypical well-functioning family that simply had not recognized how much the care recipient deteriorated and, thus, had not adapted. As a consequence, families like Sally's do not manage the situation effectively, lack resources, or do not work as a team to solve the problem of maximizing independence *and* safety for the care recipient. Even these healthy families sometimes require assistance for caregiving transitions because they need support through grief, referrals for resources, validation, and for the situation to be normalized by a professional whose permission to change is meaningful.

CFT that is successful with only first-order change strategies usually leaves the therapist highly gratified because caregivers easily follow through on practical problem-solving strategies that enhance the care recipient's comfort and safety while maximizing independence. Additional interventions may not ever be needed, or at least not until the next major transition confuses the family in months or even years. Furthermore, the caregivers are grateful for the assistance that transformed their caregiving experience.

Some of our CFT work is not so easy, requiring more intensive, second-order change. In second-order change, the basic family structures (roles, responsibilities, and power) are reorganized so the family can better meet members' needs. Second-order change is the more intrusive intervention and requires family restructuring of decision-making structures, nurturance structures, and roles that no longer (or perhaps never did) meet family members' needs. Caregiving tasks are the medium in which restructuring work is done.

Second-order change becomes necessary when families simply cannot accomplish needed or desirable first-order changes. Occasionally, the assessment process reveals that there are no caregiving structures in place on which to build either, because there is no one capable of providing care or no one will accept that care needs to be provided. The latter families are resisting any shift from the illusion of mutual autonomous roles even though one person's functional abilities have deteriorated so significantly that he or she really needs a caregiver. Information and problem-solving suggestions are insufficient to help these families who will incorporate the information within their myth and maintain the status quo, leaving the ill person at risk. However, the assessment process does not always show the structural problems that become evident during implementation of first-order interventions. When the problem-solving strategies simply cannot be implemented by the family in its current configuration, second-order change strategies are needed.

Therapists implement second-order change by engaging family members in new communication patterns. Family members are often stuck in redundant, ineffective communication during conflict. Satir (1967) summarized the basic positions that family members can take as blaming, placating, avoiding, and intellectualizing. The therapist has to interrupt familiar patterns sufficiently to allow novel interaction patterns to emerge.

Second-order change usually includes family meetings to get everyone on the same page about problems and to discuss a long-term care plan for the care recipient. The family usually will have to renegotiate decision-making structures that define who will assist in making formal or informal decisions. The therapist can help the family assign members different tasks based on their family roles as well as the skills and abilities needed by the family or care recipient.

What background factors account for the inflexibility within families that would require second-order change processes? Some caregivers have great difficulty accepting the process of reconceptualizing their marriage or parent-child relationships in ways that allow them to act effectively. For example, a daughter who cannot imagine discussing body care with her father is adhering so strongly to culturally sanctioned boundaries that she is hindered from providing needed care. A husband who cannot look at his wife's checkbook (in her purse) to see if bills have been paid and instead allows their utilities to be turned off is an ineffective caregiver who endangers his wife and himself as they stumble in the dark. Thus, providing information about the care recipient's illness is a necessary but insufficient intervention for some families. These families are in much the same position as parents who do not change their child-rearing practices as their children move into adolescence. These families require clearer interventions to restructure their relationships so that effective caregiving can occur.

Systemic problems within families also set the stage for second-order change. Personality disorders in caregiver clients or care recipients are usually characterized by rigid interaction styles that limit openness and effectiveness in problem solving. Early experiences with family members who were critical and rejecting may have produced poor or complicated attachments that are too weak to support the ongoing work of caregiving. Families also may have a history of poor processes and outcomes in previous family transitions. Family transitions that occur when members enter and exit (e.g., a child going to college, death, divorce) require flexibility in family interactions. Yet, family systems are based on familiar patterns and are complex homeostatic mechanisms that resist change, making transitions particularly challenging. For instance, parenting styles that assist young children in development may hinder launching and later development if applied continuously in early adulthood (Aquilino, 2006). When the outcome of one family transition is an ossified structure that hurts members, that experience makes family members cautious or rigid about future transitions. In sum, elder care occurs within families with personality problems, attachment problems, and problems with previous transitions.

The second case presented is an example of second-order change occurring in the context of a family with a long history of abuse and mistrust. This case provides a more concrete example of the primary caregiver, Barbara, reconceptualizing her role, which produces a shift in power in the family and a role transition. Barbara's new status in the family allows other members to act more flexibly and effectively, and new patterns of interaction between members emerge.

Therapist Reflections on Case 2

Barbara, a caregiver to her mother (Sheila), was previously diagnosed with Borderline Personality Disorder that was consistent with her histrionic presentation. Sheila had dementia that had progressed to the point that she moved in with Barbara and Barbara's second husband. Sheila also showed some personality-disorder features such as consistently finding it humorous when she called Barbara's second husband by her first husband's name and using "her poor memory" as her excuse to continue this behavior. In all other situations she vehemently denied her deficits (driving, walking alone, etc.) and accurately recalled family members' names.

Barbara was raised with one brother, Tom, an attorney who lived hundreds of miles away and maintained little or no contact with Barbara or their mother. Barbara's mother had been widowed for approximately 30 years. Nonetheless, Sheila gave power of attorney for her health and finances to Tom. He refused to arrange appropriate decision-making authority for Barbara, the primary caregiver, and accused Barbara of exaggerating their mother's cognitive decline. Barbara had never held authority within the family structure, at least in part due to her launching. Intellectually gifted but troubled, Barbara finished high school early and moved across the country where she used drugs, alcohol, and was promiscuous. Prompted by her father's death and her subsequent depression, she returned home and attempted suicide. After 30 years, Barbara still lamented missing her father's final hours. Barbara had raised her children and built a relatively stable career in the 3 decades since leaving home. She was bright and very aware of her mother's deficits. In her histrionic way, she let Tom know that their mother was declining. He maintained his lifelong reaction to her: He minimized her concerns, which was neither realistic nor helpful.

The family roles ossified as they were when Barbara left home. Tom created unapproachable distance to protect himself from his narcissistic mother and borderline and histrionic sister. He continued to view Barbara as the irresponsible baby of the family, a teenage rebel, and an attention-seeking troublemaker. Sheila continued to favor Tom as the "successful" child while relying on Barbara to meet her narcissistic needs. Barbara tried but failed to make Sheila happy and worked in individual psychotherapy to make peace with her absence during her father's death. Caregiving was a natural extension of her indentured servitude to a mother who could never be satisfied, but the growing burden was exceeding her capabilities either practically or emotionally.

Tom agreed with obvious reluctance and hostility to attend a family meeting to review the results of a neuropsychological evaluation of Sheila and develop a long-term care plan in which the entire family could be involved. Tom was abusive and aggressive toward me in the meeting. I listened to his arguments and after explaining neuropsychological assessment to Tom, attempted to join him by asking him for his view about his mother's current condition. He responded to my concerns in the same manner in which he normally responded to Barbara. Tom denied the accuracy of the report and the suggestions for care, and he vehemently denied his mother's deficits. Instead, he decided that he would fly Sheila across the country to stay with him. After all, Sheila had regaled Tom with tales of the "terrible" treatment she received from Barbara and her husband. Tom believed his mother had symptoms of normal aging and just needed a break from the stress of Barbara's home and to feel as if someone cared about her. Further, Tom was angry that Barbara had initiated in-home care services for their mother when Barbara was at work. Tom believed that Barbara was wasting their mother's inheritance for services that she did not need. Tom lived with his girlfriend (Linda) who would take responsibility for Sheila while Tom was at work, and, reportedly, she was excited to meet and help his mother. I suggested that Tom should evaluate Sheila in her current state for a longer period of time than his normal visit and assist the family with suggestions for her care. The meeting ended with family agreement that Tom would indeed fly with Sheila back to his home for 2 weeks. Barbara was thankful for the respite.

Barbara reported that she did not hear from Tom for several days. When he called, Tom and Linda were both on the line to discuss "Sheila's serious problems." They reported problems very similar to what Barbara experienced. At this point, another family therapy session was scheduled, and Linda decided to accompany them when Sheila returned to Barbara's home. At the arrival airport, Sheila was unable to plan adequately to make it to the bathroom before losing bladder control. Linda described accompanying an argumentative and smelly Sheila into the airport restroom. Sheila stripped and paced around the restroom threatening to leave, with her bottom half-naked, while Linda dumped the urine out of her shoes and rinsed and dried Sheila's clothing. Whatever doubts Tom had about Sheila's deficits were washed away in the airport.

Tom, Barbara, Linda, and Barbara's husband attended a second session. Tom was cooperative in this meeting, and he was able to hear the feedback from the neuropsychological assessment, with which he was now in complete agreement. Linda also confirmed that the assessment was accurate according to her experience. Although Tom did not apologize, he acknowledged that their mother was declining and thanked Barbara for her assistance. This was clearly uncomfortable for Tom, as Barbara understood the message behind his words to mean "you were right and I was wrong." Tom and Barbara agreed to continue to openly discuss their mother's problems and health through weekly e-mails. Barbara was wary that Tom would fail to fulfill his obligations, as he had done many times in the past. She had often spoken in individual sessions about how her brother would criticize her care of their mother but would not pitch in even to cheer up their mother with regular calls. After several hours in the session, the group ultimately negotiated for Barbara to be in charge of Sheila's care, with power of attorney for medical decisions. Tom would continue to handle Sheila's finances and agreed to pay for supportive services that Barbara chose. In the lobby on the way out of the building, Tom and Barbara hugged each other and tearfully acknowledged how much they both had been through growing up in their chaotic family.

Second-order change can produce remarkably gratifying outcomes when they are successful. Barbara's story demonstrates that complex families with multiple difficult personalities also can restructure in ways that reduce conflict, build respect, and set the stage for at least some nurturance. Despite their history of low functioning, this family was able to grow stronger bonds and broaden conflict-resolution strategies during a challenging family transition. Without the therapy, the siblings were almost inevitably headed for a fight in guardianship court.

The first step in therapy required restructuring work to get family members to accept the same name for the problem. In other words, the therapist had to do more than just share information to get Tom on the same page with Barbara about the name and nature of the problem. Tom started with strong resistance to information conflicting with his conceptualization of the problem. Two factors maintained his resistance. Tom actually had information that contradicted what Barbara told him. Even Barbara acknowledged with great frustration that Sheila seemed to rally and be more cognitively intact when Tom was visiting, ensuring that he would view her unrealistically. Additionally, Tom's past interactions and knowledge of his sister hindered him from trusting her judgment about whose evaluation to accept. Tom simply had to have a different role with his mother (i.e., caregiver) that would open him up to a new perspective on the medical and neuropsychological evaluation data. Tom and Barbara got on the same page about their mother's decline when Sheila was placed in Tom's care temporarily, with his girlfriend as the hands-on caregiver. Tom's home was a new setting where Sheila was unable to use her old strategies to compensate for memory losses as effectively. After observing Linda struggle without paid assistance for only 2 weeks, Tom realized that Barbara, who had been caring for her mother for years, indeed needed a new caregiving structure that included outside resources.

The second step of CFT produced two specific structural changes within the family: Barbara and Tom became allied as cocaregivers of their mother, and Barbara's excessive burden for care was distributed to Tom and paid care providers. Once the siblings were on the same page, Tom accepted a collaborative role with Barbara to share responsibility for decisions and resources needed by their mother. The siblings altered the frequency, style, and content of their communication in ways that fundamentally altered their relationship. Sheila's care became a medium through which they began to know each other as adults and to respect their mutual strengths. Their renewed skills at communicating allowed them to address problems together, leading to new solutions for care that relieved Barbara of the excessive burden she carried.

Balancing Needs

The final step of CFT, balancing needs of all members in the family, was accomplished as Barbara was able to attend to her own needs once again. Psychotherapy truly began when Barbara expressed a growing interest in discovering her wants and needs and in investing in self-care. Formerly, she let her desires be dictated by others, ignored her pain, and failed to acknowledge or examine herself by continuously engaging in self-perpetuated crises and overinvesting in caregiving. For many years, Barbara was paralyzed with rage by her brother's power over their mother and her mother's discounting of herself. Once Barbara's needs, limits, and burden of caregiving were understood and acknowledged by her brother, the power in the family shifted. Barbara claimed power with her brother, the only elder family member that was psychologically available. This shift in power allowed Barbara and her brother to partner in the care of their mother, and it allowed her brother to view her as an adult. Their relationship is not likely to grow into intimacy or even power equality, but the changes they accomplished were sufficient to get Barbara back on track with her own self-care, reduced the caregiving burden, and unhooked Tom and Barbara from the destructive patterns they had used to cope with a painful childhood.

Complex families sometimes require the CFT therapist to work on individual and family development concurrently. For instance, Barbara completed CFT with little or no progress toward her personal growth goals because the structural changes required all of the allocated time. Barbara could not accomplish these in the absence of family cooperation. However, as a result of the second-order changes noted, in subsequent individual psychotherapy with the same therapist, Barbara was able to work on her individual development. Building on the positive effects of CFT, she focused on growing into her position of increased authority within the family structure. She also gained self-regulation skills as she oversaw her mother's care, ultimately even improving the quality and intimacy of her interactions with her mother.

Barbara benefited from the flexibility to have individual therapy interspersed with couple and family sessions. She was able to negotiate with individual members on specific problems in these relationships then retreat to individual sessions to examine the meaning of the negotiations and clarify how to continue to improve her own well-being. By the end of therapy, Barbara renegotiated roles with almost everyone in the family system.

PRAGMATIC ASPECTS OF INTERVENTION

CFT is structured according to general guidelines and principles rather than a specific format because of the diversity of families and caregiving situations. Some general rules we try to follow include the following.

Intervention strategies must include all key players. Operationally, this means that individuals listed by the primary caregiver as involved in decisions that affect the day-to-day well-being of either the caregiver or care recipient must be represented in family sessions. Family sessions may be scheduled on weekends or holidays when the family is gathered. Otherwise we rely on e-mail, phone, fax, and conference calls to engage family members sequentially or simultaneously as needed to accomplish the task at hand.

The therapist must acknowledge the diverse roles, perspectives, and challenges faced by the various players (Boszormenyi-Nagy & Spark, 1984). Each family member has a niche in the family with gifts, interaction styles, and values that will be needed during the caregiving phase. These values must be recognized and acknowledged by the therapist.

The therapist must be flexible with the frequency, format, and length of sessions. Similar to what Mittelman, Epstein, and Pierzchala (2003) describe, we break the tradition of weekly sessions to respond to the practical demands of the caregiving challenges. Instead, sessions may occur several times in a short period and resume when the system encounters new transitions, often after several months or sometimes years.

We focus on goals directly tied to the caregiving challenges that are realistic in a relatively short-term format. The therapist must consider what can be accomplished in a short-term therapy. Simpler goals that are more easily accomplished provide the caregiver or family with confidence and mastery to tackle more complex or frightening problems.

Within the session, the therapist is responsible for maintaining the task focus because most families cannot. Although flexible, the therapist starts the session by stating or negotiating the immediate goals that center on core questions. Why is the family gathering? What are the problems with care?

The care recipient should be empowered and encouraged to participate as much as possible. Cognitively impaired individuals may find participation to be difficult. In addition to latent fears about how family decisions might affect his or her life, a cognitively impaired care recipient can become overwhelmed in a family session with a large number of people who change conversations rapidly, toss about large amounts of information, and discuss unfamiliar service systems. Hearing impairment in addition to cognitive impairment tends to increase the struggle of the care recipient. In many cases, participation in such an environment creates the exact opposite of the caring, engaged, respectful outcomes the family desires. Participation by the cognitively impaired family member should be considered on a case-by-case basis.

ENDING THE SESSION OR TERMINATING CAREGIVER FAMILY THERAPY

The therapist's final role is to anticipate future transitions along with the caregiving family. At the conclusion of caregiver family therapy the therapist is acutely aware of the health of the care recipient, the caregiver situation, and the pace of family members' development. The therapist can help family members identify signs of stress and family tension that can be used to signal review of the caregiving situation either on their own or in a CFT booster session. Also, the therapist can help the family identify future transitions, such as the death of the care recipient and the transition to life after caregiving, that may prompt additional sessions. At the conclusion of CFT, most families have new community resources and, perhaps most importantly, have identified resources in other members that can be useful in future transitions.

REFERENCES

Aneshensel, C. S., Pearlin, L. I., Mullan, J. T., Zarit, S. H., & Whitlatch, C. J. (1995). *Profiles in caregiving: The unexpected career*. San Diego, CA: Academic Press.

Aquilino, W. S. (2006). Family relationships and support systems in early adulthood. In J. J. Arnett & J. L. Tanner (Eds.), *Emerging adults in America: Coming of age in the 21st century* (pp. 193–217). Washington, DC: American Psychological Association.

Bedford, V. H. (1995). Sibling relationships in middle and old age. In R.Blieszer & V. H. Bedford (Eds.), *Handbook of aging and the family* (pp. 201–222). Westport, CT: Greenwood.

Beel-Bates, C. A., Ingersoll-Dayton, B., & Nelson, E. (2007). Deference as a form of reciprocity among residents in assisted living. *Research on Aging*, 29(6), 626–643.

Bengtson, V. L., Giarrusso, R., Mabry, J. B., & Silverstein, M. (2002). Solidarity, conflict, and ambivalence: Complementary or competing perspectives on intergenerational relationships? *Journal of Marriage and Family*, 63, 1–16.

Bengtson, V. L., & Roberts, R. E. L. (1991). Intergenerational solidarity in aging families: An example of formal theory construction. *Journal of Marriage and Family*, 53, 856–870.

Boszormenyi-Nagy, I., & Spark, G. M. (1984). *Invisible loyalties: Reciprocity in intergenerational family therapy*. New York: Brunner/Mazel, Inc.

Cantor, M. H. (1975). Lifespace and the support of the inner city elderly. *The Gerontologist, 15*(1), 23–27.

Cantor, M. H. (1979). Neighbors and friends: An overlooked resource in the informal support system. *Research on Aging, 1*(4), 434–463.

Cantor, M. H. (1989). Social care: Family and community support systems. *Annals of the American Academy of Political and Social Science, 503,* 99–112.

Cantor, M. H. (1991). Family and community: Changing roles in an aging society. *The Gerontologist, 31*(3), 337–346.

Carruth, A. K., Tate, U. S., Moffett, B. S., & Hill, K. (1997). Reciprocity, emotional well-being, and family functioning as determinants of family satisfaction in caregivers of elderly patients. *Nursing Research, 46*(2), 93–100.

Carstensen, L. L. (1992). Social and emotional patterns in adulthood: Support for socioemotional selectivity theory. *Psychology and Aging, 7*(3), 331–338.

Coon, D. W., Gallagher-Thompson, D., & Thompson, L. W. (2003). *Innovative interventions to reduce dementia caregiver distress: A clinical guide.* New York: Springer Publishing Company.

Czaja, S. J., Eisdorfer, C., & Schulz, R. (2000). Future directions in caregiving: Implications for intervention research. In R. Schulz (Ed.), *Handbook on dementia caregiving: Evidence based interactions for family caregivers* (pp. 283–319). New York: Springer.

Drentea, P., Clay, O. J., Roth, D. L., & Mittelman, M. S. (2006). Predictors of improvement in social support: Five-year effects of a structured intervention for caregivers of spouses with Alzheimer's disease. *Social Science and Medicine, 63,* 957–967.

Eisdorfer, C., Czaja, S. J., Loewenstein, D. A., Rubert, M. P., Argüelles, S., Mitrani, V. B., et al. (2003). The effect of a family therapy and technology based intervention on caregiver depression. *The Gerontologist, 43*(4), 521–531.

Fisher, L., & Lieberman, M. A. (1994). Alzheimer's disease: The impact of the family on spouses, offspring, and inlaws. *Family Process, 33*(3), 305–325.

Fisher, L., & Lieberman, M. A. (1996). The effects of family context on adult offspring of patients with Alzheimer's disease: A longitudinal study. *Journal of Family Psychology, 10*(2), 180–191.

Fisher, L., & Lieberman, M. A. (1999). A longitudinal study of nursing home placement for patients with dementia: The contribution of family characteristics. *The Gerontologist, 39*(6), 677–686.

Gitlin, L. N., Belle, S. H., Burgio, L. D., Czaja, S. J., Mahoney, D., Gallagher-Thompson, D., et al. (2003). Effect of multicomponent interventions on caregiver burden and depression: The REACH multisite initiative at 6-month follow-up. *Psychology and Aging, 18*(3), 361–374.

Hirsch, C. H., & Mittelman, M. S. (1997). Support for caregivers delayed time to nursing home placement in Alzheimer's disease. *Evidence-Based Medicine*, *2*(3), 85.

Kahn, R. L., & Antonucci, T. C. (1981). Convoys of social support: A life-course approach. In J. G. March, S. B. Keisler, J. N. Morgan, & V. K. Oppenheimer (Eds.), *Aging: Social change* (pp. 383–405). New York: Academic Press.

Katz, R., Lowenstein, A., Phillips, J., & Daatland, S. O. (2005). Theorizing intergenerational family relations: Solidarity, conflict and ambivalence in cross-national contexts. In V. L. Bengtson, A. C. Acock, K. R. Allen, P. Dilworth-Anderson, & D. M. Klein (Eds.), *Sourcebook of family theory and research* (pp. 393–420). Thousand Oaks, CA: Sage.

Knight, B. G., & McCallum, T. J. (1998). Family therapy with older clients: The contextual, cohort-based, maturity/specific challenge model. In I. H. Nordhus, G. VandenBos, S. Berg, & P. Fromholt (Eds.), *Clinical geropsychology* (pp. 313–328). Washington, DC: American Psychological Association.

Lewinter, M. (2003). Reciprocities in caregiving relationships in Danish elder care. *Journal of Aging Studies*, *17*, 357–377.

Lieberman, M. A., & Fisher, L. (1995). The impact of chronic illness on the health and well-being of family members. *The Gerontologist*, *35*, 94–102.

Lieberman, M. A., & Fisher, L. (1999a). The effects of family conflict resolution and decision making on the provision of help for an elder with Alzheimer's disease. *The Gerontologist*, *39*, 159–166.

Lieberman, M. A., & Fisher, L. (1999b). The impact of a parent's dementia on adult offspring and their spouses: The contribution of family characteristics. *Journal of Mental Health and Aging*, *5*(3), 207–222.

Minuchin, S. (1974). *Families and family therapy*. Cambridge, MA: Harvard University Press.

Mitriani, V. B., & Czaja, S. J. (2000). Family-based therapy for dementia caregivers: Clinical observations. *Aging and Mental Health*, *4*(3), 200–209.

Mittelman, M. S., Epstein, C., & Pierzchala, A. (2003). *Counseling the Alzheimer's caregiver: A resource guide for health care professionals*. Chicago: American Medical Association.

Mittelman, M. S., Ferris, S. H., Shulman, E., Steinberg, G., & Levin, B. (1996). A family intervention to delay nursing home placement of patients with Alzheimer's disease: A randomized controlled trial. *Journal of the American Medical Association*, *276*(21), 1725–1731.

Mittelman, M. S., Ferris, S. H., Steinberg, G., Shulman, E., Mackell, J. A., Ambinder, A., et al. (1993). An intervention that delays institutionalization of

Alzheimer's disease patients: Treatment of spouse caregivers. *The Gerontologist,* 33(6), 730–740.

Mittelman, M. S., Haley, W. E., Clay, O. J., & Roth, D. L. (2006). Improving caregiver well-being delays nursing home placement of patients with Alzheimer's disease. *Neurology, 67,* 1592–1599.

Mittelman, M. S., Roth, D. L., Coon, D. W., & Haley, W. E. (2004). Sustained benefit of supportive intervention for depressive symptoms in caregivers of patients with Alzheimer's disease. *American Journal of Psychiatry, 161,* 850–856.

Mittelman, M. S., Roth, D. L., Haley, W. E., & Zarit, S. H. (2004). Effects of a caregiver intervention on negative caregiver appraisals of behavior problems in patients with Alzheimer's disease: Results of a randomized trial. *Journal of Gerontology: Psychological Sciences, 59B*(1), 27–34.

Olsen, D. H. (2000). Circumplex model of marital and family systems. *Journal of Family Therapy, 22,* 144–167.

Pinquart, M., & Sörensen, S. (2003). Differences between caregivers and non-caregivers in psychological health and physical health: A meta-analysis. *Psychology and Aging, 18,* 250–267.

Pinquart, M., & Sörensen, S. (2007). Correlates of physical health of informal caregivers: A meta-analysis. *Journal of Gerontology: Psychological Sciences, 62B,* 126–137.

Pruchno, R. A., Blow, F. C., & Smyer, M. A. (1984). Life events and interdependent lives: Implications for research and intervention. *Human Development, 27,* 31–41.

Qualls, S. H. (1996). Family therapy with aging families. In S. H. Zarit and B. G. Knight (Eds.), *Effective clinical interventions in a life stage context: A guide to psychotherapy and aging* (pp. 121–137.) Washington, DC: American Psychological Association.

Qualls, S. H. (1999a). Family therapy with older adult clients. *In Session: Psychotherapy in Practice, 55*(8), 1–14.

Qualls, S. H. (1999b). Family therapy with older adult clients. *Journal of Clinical Psychology, 55,* 977–990.

Qualls, S. H. (1999c). Realizing power in intergenerational family hierarchies: Family reorganization when older adults decline. In M. Duffy (Ed.), *Handbook of counseling and psychotherapy with older adults* (pp. 228–241). New York: Wiley.

Qualls, S. H. (2006). *Alzheimer's Caregiver Family Therapy [video].* American Psychological Association.

Qualls, S. H. (2008). Caregiver family therapy. In B. Knight & K. Laidlaw (Eds.), *Handbook of emotional disorders in older adults* (pp. 183–209) Oxford, England: Oxford University Press.

Rossi, A. S., & Rossi, P. H. (1990). Help exchange between the generations. In A. S. Rossi & P. H. Rossi (Eds.), *Of human bonding: Parent-child relations across the life course* (pp. 391–460). New York: Aldine de Gruyter.

Roth, D. L., Mittelman, M. S., Clay, O. J., Madan, A., & Haley, W. E. (2005). Changes in social support as mediators of the impact of a psychosocial intervention for spouse caregivers of persons with Alzheimer's disease. *Psychology and Aging, 20*(4), 634–644.

Satir, V. (1967). *Conjoint family therapy.* Palo Alto, CA: Science and Behavior Books.

Scharlach, A. E., Li, W., & Dalvi, T. B. (2006). Family conflict as a mediator of caregiver strain. *Family Relations, 55,* 625–635.

Schulz, R., Burgio, L., Burns, R., Eisdorfer, C., Gallagher-Thompson, D., Gitlin, L. N., et al. (2003). Resources for enhancing Alzheimer's caregiver health (REACH): Overview, site-specific outcomes, and future directions. *The Gerontologist, 43*(4), 514–520.

Sims-Gould, J., & Martin-Matthews, A. (2007). Family caregiving or caregiving alone: Who helps the helper? *Canadian Journal on Aging, 26*(1), 27–45.

Whitlatch, C. J., Judge, K., Zarit, S. H., & Femia, E. (2006). Dyadic intervention for family caregivers and care receivers in early-stage dementia. *The Gerontologist, 46*(5), 688–694.

Zarit, S. H., Johansson, L., & Jarrott, S. E. (1998). Family caregiving: Stresses, social programs, and clinical interventions. In I. H. Nordhus, G. R. VandenBos, S. Berg, & P. Fromholt (Eds.) *Clinical geropsychology* (pp. 345–360). Washington, DC: American Psychological Association.

Zarit, S. H., Orr, N. K., & Zarit, J. M. (1985). *The hidden victims of Alzheimer's disease: Families under stress.* New York: New York University Press.

Zarit, S. H., & Zarit, J. M. (1982). Families under stress: Interventions for caregivers of senile dementia patients. *Psychotherapy, 19*(4), 461–471.

CHAPTER

9

Integrating Families into Long-Term-Care Psychology Services: Orchestrating Cacophonies and Symphonies

MARGARET P. NORRIS

Mental health care for older adults has precipitously increased since Medicare eliminated the restrictions on mental health benefits in 1987 and again in 1989. The impact has been felt especially in long-term care (LTC) settings where the rates of mental illness are as high as 65% (Strahan & Burns, 1991), compared to only 12% in community-dwelling older adults (Rabins, 1992)—more than a fivefold increase. Given the need for mental health services among LTC residents and greater access to care with improved Medicare coverage, there is ample opportunity for psychologists to expand their work to these settings (Spira, Koven, & Norris, 2005). This opportunity is especially appealing to psychologists who offer family therapy services. A premise of this chapter is that the emotional state of LTC residents is greatly affected by family relationships. LTC residents' mental health may be harmed by family cacophony or may be improved by family cohesion. Because family involvement

189

with LTC residents is substantial, mental health services often necessitate family therapy.

Many psychologists, even seasoned geropsychologists, may come into LTC work with little understanding of the environment, the residents in LTC, and their unique needs. This chapter begins with edification of many common myths and stereotypes about LTC residents and their families. Following this foundation, assessment and treatment issues pertinent to psychological services with LTC residents and their families are addressed. Finally, the complex legal and ethical issues that are unique to this mental health service are reviewed. Case examples will also be included throughout the chapter to highlight intricacies.

MYTHS AND STEREOTYPES ABOUT LTC RESIDENTS AND FAMILIES

Myth 1: LTC residents are alone, often abandoned by their families.

In fact, the vast majority of LTC residents have regular contact with their families (Cohn & Jay, 1988). While most residents' family members are actively involved in their care, the characteristics of uninvolved families mirror disconnected families in the general population. Residents who have no family involvement typically severed ties with their families long before placement, and similarly, residents with minimal family contact often have a history of family disharmony. These residents are among the more likely to be referred for psychological services for two reasons. First, these residents need emotional support from other sources in the absence of family. Second, a history of conflict so serious as to dissolve family relations often reflects deficits in relationship skills, which impair a person's ability to adapt in the social environment of LTC settings. Residential care requires a person to interact and cooperate with many individuals. Those who have difficulty assimilating in this social arena are often in need of psychological services.

Another unique demographic factor may also contribute to the absence of family members for some LTC residents. Many of the old-old LTC residents (especially those approaching centenarians) may have survived most of their close offspring. Ruth is an example of this outcome of longevity. She is 100-years-old and her only child died at the age of 62, many years before she went into the nursing home. Years later, as a nursing-home resident, she was referred for psychological services for depression and prolonged grief. Her other relatives included a step-granddaughter whom she raised and two grandchildren who lived out of state and had infrequent phone contact. Her step-granddaughter was closely involved in Ruth's life at the nursing home. They were deeply attached and enjoyed regular visits. Ruth then faced the worst tragedy that could have happened when her step-granddaughter was diagnosed with cancer and died in her early 50s. Ruth fell into a deep depression and her health took a precipitous dive. At 100-years-old, she has no living family in her community to watch over and care for her.

Myth 2: Traditional individual psychotherapy is a viable option in LTC.

Family therapy is far more common in LTC than in outpatient settings. In my predominantly geriatric practice, a review of cases over a 1-year period revealed at least some family involvement in therapy in 40% of my outpatient geriatric patients, compared to 70% of my nursing-home patients. These rates reflect the frequency and necessity of family participation in geriatric mental health care, which is the norm, not the exception, in LTC settings.

The outpatient model of psychotherapy services as an entirely private interaction between a patient and a therapist does not apply in an LTC setting (Lichtenberg et al., 1997). Models of consultation services and interdisciplinary services (Ogland-Hand & Florsheim, 2002; Smyer & Qualls, 1999b) are far more applicable to the inpatient context of LTC settings. In fact, a consultant role should be considered obligatory for successful services in LTC. Services are more highly valued when the psychologist understands he or she is serving multiple roles and providing a service to the residents, staff, and the families. In addition to direct clinical services for individual residents, the psychologist must also sometimes include family in treatment, as family problems may be the focus of treatment, and he or she must consult with staff, which have a great impact on the resident's day-to-day well-being. Needless to say, these multiple roles also create a complicated balancing act for the psychologist. Adopting a systems-theory model rather than traditional individual therapy will help the psychologist meet the needs of the multiple parties impacting one another.

Recognizing the social unit of the LTC facility is imperative. The key players are the residents, the facility staff, residents' family members (often referred to as *sponsor* or *responsible party*), and of course, numerous regulatory agencies. Key staff members include the certified nursing aides, who provide most of the direct personal care; administrators, who set policy and an institutional tone in the facility; social workers, who are often the contact person for the psychologist and the source of referrals; and nurses, who provide medical care and are the direct link to residents' physicians. Physically outside of the facility, but no less influential, are numerous state and federal agencies that establish laws and regulations. The Nursing Home Reform Act of 1987 established the first major revision of the federal standards for nursing-home care. This landmark legislation entitles all residents to receive care that improves or maintains their highest level of physical, mental, and psychosocial well-being. These standards are enforced by Medicare, Medicaid, and authorized state departments of aging and disability services. Importantly, psychologists working in LTC settings must become familiar with the federal and state regulations that govern mental health care provided in LTC settings.

The following example illustrates the benefit of replacing individual psychotherapy with systems therapy. Faye, a 77-year-old widow, was referred for therapy when her infatuation with a middle-aged male volunteer became quite public. She also spoke openly in therapy of her desire for a relationship with the volunteer, as well as her deep distress that her daughter and grandchildren were rarely visiting and often would not answer the phone when she called. With the patient's consent, the psychologist contacted the patient's family to encourage more frequent visits. While the frequency of visits did not improve, the tone of the visits became more positive and supportive, which significantly reduced the patient's depression. The plot thickened when it was learned that a female resident at another nursing home had also developed a romantic fantasy for the same volunteer. A focus on only individual therapy would not have served this patient well. In addition to individual therapy sessions, the psychologist worked with the nursing-home administrators and social workers to counsel the volunteer that his overly solicitous attention could be easily misinterpreted by female residents. He was a naïve *do-gooder* without ill intent but in need of guidance about his relationship with residents. Additional corrective measures to prevent harm were put into place, including the volunteer not being permitted to be with residents other than in public areas of the nursing home. This case illustrates that individual therapy would not have been sufficient to address the family problems and the broad social setting of the nursing home.

Who pays for the consultation services the psychologist provides in LTC? Typically, psychologists offer this time gratis; however, many LTC facilities will compensate the psychologist for this service. They are often willing to pay when they see the psychologist's presence and contribution benefits not only the referred residents but also the staff, families, and the LTC milieu. A major development in the acknowledgment of consultation services was the CMS approval in January 2008 of two new codes, 99366 and 99368, team conference services in meetings of at least 30 minutes with at least three disciplines to assess a patient's care plan and progress. The team conference codes are specifically intended for use by nonphysician practitioners; whereas, in the past, similar CPT codes were available exclusively to physicians (www.apapractice.org October 25, 2007, Vol 4, Number 12). Unfortunately, reimbursement values have not been assigned (as of this writing), but it is a step in the right direction.

Myth 3: LTC residents are too demented to benefit from psychotherapy.

In fact, psychotherapy is highly effective for LTC residents including those with mild and moderate dementia (Cipher, Clifford, & Roper, 2007; Kasl-Godley & Gatz, 2000). In addition, effective behavioral treatments for patients with more advanced dementia are well-established (Allen-Burge, Stevens, & Burgio, 1999).

The high rate of mental illness in LTC (Strahan & Burns, 1991) certainly reflects the comorbidity of physical and mental illnesses. LTC residents often suffer from disabilities due to health problems such as diabetes, strokes, hip fractures, and so forth. In turn, these increase the risk for depression, anxiety, and behavioral disturbances. Along with the array of medical illnesses, many residents have declining cognitive function. While cognitive functioning is not the target of psychotherapy services, its presence does not preclude patients from receiving psychotherapy to reduce other targeted problems such as depression, anxiety, and behavioral disturbances. In an acknowledgment that patients with dementia can benefit from psychotherapy, CMS ruled in 2001 that carriers were not allowed to arbitrarily deny payment for services such as rehabilitation and mental health services based solely on the presence of a dementia diagnosis in patients' medical records.

The vast literature on providing psychological services to culturally diverse populations is highly relevant to services in LTC facilities (Hays, 2007). The treatment and assessment adjustments that are needed for working with outpatient versus LTC populations are analogous to the clinical adjustments needed in working with ethnically and culturally diverse populations. As argued throughout this chapter, including family members in treatment is a common adjustment needed in LTC work. Family and staff involvement is particularly important when treating patients with more advanced cognitive impairment.

The multiple levels at which treatment may be focused are illustrated in the case of Janet, an 84-year-old resident, who was referred for psychological services shortly after her placement in a nursing home. She had suffered a stroke and was acutely depressed about no longer being able to live independently in her home. Individual therapy targeted her grief. Her family (her son and daughter-in-law) were also seen twice to help them understand her depression and be more tolerant of her negative mood. Over time, Janet's cognitive functioning significantly deteriorated due to vascular dementia. Her behavior became repetitive and demanding, for example, asking aides to repeatedly adjust her pillow and screaming out when she was in her wheelchair for more than just short periods. The family insisted that she be up for all meals and kept in her wheelchair for 1 to 2 hours several times a day. Their efforts were well-intended as they believed too much bed rest would hasten her physical decline, which would be the case for some LTC residents. However, this goal was not realistic for Janet because her physical and cognitive abilities were precipitously and irreversibly declining. Psychotherapy had gradually moved from insight-oriented grief work, to behavioral- and solution-focused individual therapy, to family and staff training that helped them adjust to and accommodate her very different needs.

Myth 4: Family caregiving stops after placement in an LTC facility.

In fact, placing a family member in an LTC facility is a life-cycle transition much like other transitions that impact the whole family such as births, marriage, retirement, and so forth. The transition of placement necessitates an adjustment, a wandering through uncharted territories, that marks the beginning of a chapter in the family's life. Many families have a great sense of loss when their loved one is placed in LTC. The psychologist can help families understand this transition as a change, but not an end to their caregiver role.

After placement, family members shift *back* from instrumental care to emotional support. Prior to placement, physical illness and disability typically demanded greater family involvement and care. Many caregivers had to transition from being wife, daughter, or sibling to being a nursing aide, business manager, housekeeper, and so on. After placement, caregivers can and should be able to return to being a family member. Family members transfer instrumental care to the LTC staff and they may then focus on their emotional and supportive role. How well this shifting is done depends on past family history of nurturance, enmeshment versus independence, roles, and so forth.

The roles of various family members are often restructured after placement. Different family members often assume various tasks and responsibilities. One family member may oversee the vast financial and legal tasks that must be executed, other family members may be more adept at providing emotional support and regular visits, and others may be particularly suited to communicate with the nursing staff and physician about health-care issues. As the family, not just the resident, plod through these new roles and their responsibilities, psychologists can often help them support each other by valuing all individual contributions rather than trying to equalize each person's time or effort.

A not-so-uncommon discord develops when the LTC resident views and treats some children as favored and others as scapegoats. Sometimes the favored child is, in fact, a distant fantasy of a perfect child, while the scapegoat child may be the one who accepts the responsibility to do the unpleasant tasks, such as recognizing the need for the LTC placement. Often these roles go far back in the family's history.

Barbara, who resided with her husband in the nursing home, fell into this demarcation of her children. She and her husband had two adopted children, a daughter who lived in the community where they moved to for LTC placement and a son who lived 2 hours away. In the first therapy session with Barbara, she divulged an agonizing memory of her 6-year-old daughter emphatically telling her mother, "I will not be told what to do." She remained a willful child, resulting in disharmony and emotional distance between her and her mother. As an adult, she was the child who took on the filial responsibilities of caring for her ailing parents. Despite this care, Barbara regularly complained that her daughter did not visit often enough, talked to the nursing staff about her and her husband's care without including them, and lacked sympathy for her complaints about the nursing home. In contrast, Barbara boasted in therapy of her son's independence, his work accomplishments and long work hours, and his popularity among many friends. Only after the death of her husband did she open up in therapy that she was deeply hurt that her son came only on *required* and rare occasions, and that since his brief marriage ended many years ago, he had lived in impoverished and solitary conditions. In therapy, she continued to acknowledge her son's limitations and recognized that her daughter had many responsibilities, including overseeing her care, despite the poor emotional connection between them.

In summary, when persons are placed in LTC, they face many challenging transitions including loss of individual freedoms; loss of health, function, and independence; as well as the necessity to establish new relationships with staff, other residents, and roommates. The family also faces many emotional onslaughts: guilt, depression, anger, remorse, and so on. As with the many other life transitions, families can aid or hinder by how they respond. When family members are supportive, respectful, and charitable, harmony unfolds. When family members become disengaged, intolerant, or paternalistic, the result is often much cacophony.

ASSESSMENT OF LTC RESIDENTS AND THEIR FAMILIES

Psychological assessment must be adapted to meet the special needs of LTC patients. First, the legal status of the resident must be determined at the outset of services—that is, whether the patient is competent to make medical decisions. The physician's determination of competency is typically documented in the chart, but in some cases it is not accurate. If the resident is deemed not competent, his or her power-of-attorney must be notified prior to services, as he or she has the authority to consent to services.

Formal assessments with psychological measures are handicapped by lack of norms for institutionalized older adults. For LTC patients, the history of physical, mental, and cognitive functioning is usually far more illuminating than a battery of tests. Frequently, family members are the primary source for history of a patient's health. LTC residents who can give detailed medical histories are the exception, not the norm. Staff members are also often uninformed about important historical information. Initial assessments of LTC patients should often include contacting a close family member to determine critical information such as onset of cognitive impairments, prior incidents of depression, history of interpersonal relationships, and so on. A common and critical case in point is determining whether a new resident has dementia or delirium. A family member might be more knowledgeable than even the physician as to whether a patient's decline was recent and abrupt, as is often the case with delirium, or if he or she has been slowly declining for years—obviously, a critical factor in making numerous treatment decisions.

While family members often can provide crucial history, psychologists must always assess for bias in their reports. This is no different than outpatient families. A family member's attitude toward the patient inevitably influences his or her portrayal. A relative who has long-standing anger at the patient may be overly critical and personalize his or her deficits (e.g., "She just isn't trying hard enough."). Another family member who is anxious and guilt-ridden may be overly solicitous and foster his or her loved one's dependence on family and staff (e.g., "I must go everyday to feed her; otherwise she won't eat.").

An example illustrates the importance of obtaining accurate history and the potential for family to distort the facts. Jane was a recent admission, not yet well-known to the staff, and with a new primary care doctor who would follow her in the nursing home. At first, she appeared to have mild memory and cognitive deficits, but she soon started making reports of bizarre and violent events happening in the room next to hers, events that had certainly not taken place. She was referred for evaluation of dementia versus delirium. At the first interview she was unable to provide any accurate information about herself. Her daughter, Emily, was contacted and she reported a 1- to 2-year history of gradual decline. Jane had Parkinson's disease and her family had placed her in the nursing home because her husband was not able to meet her physical needs or manage her behavioral outbursts at home. The history seemed to point clearly in the direction of dementia secondary to Parkinson's and not to a drug-induced delirium, which is common in Parkinson's patients taking dopamine-enhancing medications. A report was given to the patient's physician and the nursing-home staff and psychological services were discontinued as she clearly could not benefit from psychotherapy.

One year later, the patient referred herself for psychological services to address problems with her roommate. (Self-referrals in LTC are a strong indication in and of themselves that the resident is cognitively intact.) She was not only cognitively intact, but she was among the highest-functioning residents in the nursing home. She provided an accurate history of several psychotic episodes that cleared after her medications were adjusted. In therapy, she also spoke of her deep sadness and frustration that her family would not allow her to go home for visits. While they took her out regularly, often to the home of Sarah (another daughter), they disregarded her requests to go to her home for visits. At her request, Emily was contacted about the home visits. Emily voiced significant anger at her mother and a considerable distortion in her mother's abilities. She placed her mother's overall ability at whatever had been her lowest level of functioning. The reason for the anger was never determined and her position on home visits was never altered. After addressing the roommate problem, therapy targeted grief issues the patient felt over her relationship with her family, which had become intensely and unnecessarily paternalistic.

In summary, the family relationship characteristics must be assessed and may become the focus of therapy. When there is cacophony, a first step is to learn if the family discord is chronic or acute. Is discord a result of a dysfunctional structure and impaired relationships that are tweaked by a major life transition such as LTC placement? Or is it a result of a functional family struggling with how to accommodate to this life transition?

It is also helpful to assess the patient's and family's history with LTC. Many will have had no experience with LTC facilities and may hold an antiquated stereotype of nursing homes as unregulated warehouses for very old persons who are hanging onto life by a thread. Some may have had a relative, likely a parent, in an LTC facility with either a positive or negative experience. The families' attitude toward the facility can have a beneficial or detrimental effect on the resident. A family's positive attitude can help the resident accept the staff and the LTC setting in general. In contrast, a family member who is frequently criticizing the staff is inadvertently not helping his or her loved one adjust to his or her new caregivers. A psychologist may be able to help the family set realistic expectations, deal with their guilt so they no longer project it onto staff, and make use of the staff as sources for support, information, and a communication link to the resident's physicians. The psychologist can encourage family to view the LTC staff members as partners, rather than obstacles, and thus, set an example for the resident's relationships with staff.

TREATMENT OF LTC RESIDENTS AND THEIR FAMILIES

As learned from the assessment, a patient's level of cognitive functioning determines what treatment approaches will be beneficial and whether treatment should be directed toward the resident, the staff, and/or the family. When direct psychological services are called for, both the individual patient and the family may be involved. When psychotherapy is contraindicated due to advanced dementia, behavior management targeted for staff and family intervention is often warranted.

As stated earlier, a systems approach is crucial to the therapy effort because it takes place in the social context of an LTC setting. Therapy goals may include both first-order and second-order interventions (Smyer & Qualls, 1999a). First-order interventions address issues such as grief and adjustment to the LTC placement. Second-order interventions address the family and social system (i.e., reorganizing relationships to accommodate the new transitions the family faces and the new relationships that develop between the resident and the staff).

A premise to all interventions is that the psychologist must be cautious about assigning blame to the family, or the resident, or the staff. While those individuals may present a picture of a family member who is uncaring, or a resident who is imposing guilt on the family, or an aide who is ignoring the resident, the truth may lie in all these perspectives, not just in one. Looking for the roles that all parties are playing in a dysfunctional situation will aid therapy.

Several taxonomies depict how families may or may not be involved in psychological services.

1. The resident needs services and the family is supportive. This scenario is most comparable to traditional outpatient individual therapy. Common issues targeted in individual therapy are loss, mood stabilization, pain management, and adjustment to disability. For some LTC residents, these goals may be adequately treated with traditional individual psychotherapy.

2. The resident is functioning well and the family needs services (Lebow & Kane, 1999). The staff may report to the psychologist that family members are making unreasonable demands, some of which are contradictory to the resident's well-being. Intervention may then target family members, with the goal of improving the resident's care.

3. Family relationships are chronically pathological. Placement then creates increased pressure on the ongoing family conflict. In addition, the resident may also develop difficult relationships with staff and other residents.

4. The resident and family relationship qualitatively changes after placement. Often, this takes the form of family members exerting more control over the resident. Objectively, there may be a need for family to take on more responsibility. But this goes awry when the family adopts a paternalistic attitude.

It is essential to recognize that a struggle between autonomy and dependency is a fundamental issue for LTC residents and their families. LTC facilities hold a great deal of the control over big and little daily decisions. By and large, state and federal agencies establish a myriad of rules and LTC facilities must enforce the rules. While residents have protected rights, there are countless decisions and actions that are not determined by residents' preferences (e.g., one's living space being confined to one room, sharing that small space with a stranger who probably has some disagreeable habits, taking showers in a chair that feels like a mobile commode along with numerous others also being showered, waiting for unreasonably long times for assistance from aides who do not always show patience or sympathy, eating institutional food that is stripped of flavor and texture). This is not *home*, either in terms of physical environment or who is king of the palace. Some families do not understand this. Family members can help the resident adjust to his or her new environment better when they recognize how vast this adjustment is for residents. The psychologist may be the key person to help the family members understand this adjustment.

A policy/reimbursement issue regarding family therapy is noteworthy. Two family therapy codes may be billed for family therapy, 90846 and 90847 (without the patient present and with the patient present, respectively). As with many Medicare reimbursement policies, the provider must become familiar with his or her Medicare carrier's Local Coverage Determination (LCD). All of the carriers adopt the national coverage policy that family therapy is covered only when treatment is directed at the patient's mental illness. For example, the Trailblazer carrier's LCD states:

> Codes 90846 and 90847 will be considered for payment under Medicare only for treatment of the Medicare beneficiary's mental illness. Family therapy is appropriate when intervention in the family interactions would be expected to improve or stabilize the patient's emotional/behavioral disturbance. Family therapy sessions with a patient whose emotional disturbance would be unaffected by changes in the patterns of family interaction (i.e., a comatose patient) would not be covered by Medicare. Similarly, an emotional disturbance in a family member, which does not impact on the Medicare patient's status, would not be covered by that patient's Medicare benefits. Family therapy is commonly the major treatment, especially for children and also for the elderly. Where both husband and wife are covered by Medicare, such therapy may be the most parsimonious treatment for both. (http://www.trailblazerhealth.com)

While all carriers adhere to this general guideline for family therapy, they differ regarding the coverage for 90846. Some carriers do not reimburse for this procedure because the patient is not present. Other carriers do pay for it; for example, Trailblazers and Noridian allow for coverage of 90846, but both LCDs stipulate that this code is used "rarely" (Noridian) or is "not routine" (Trailblazer). Again, 90846, like 90847, is covered only when treatment is directed toward the patient's condition, not the family's problems with the patient. It is imperative for geropsychologists to be knowledgeable of health-care policies that impact services for caregivers (Norris, 2006) as well as Medicare policies pertaining to mental health services in LTC (Norris, 2000).

LEGAL AND ETHICAL ISSUES

Psychologists consulting in LTC may have to wrestle with legal predicaments that often involve the patient's family. The capacity of a resident is the most common legal question to concern psychotherapy services.

Generally, physicians will document the patient's capacity to make medical decisions in the medical chart. The psychologist must be aware of the legal status because there are obvious implications for who has the right to consent to services. In a minority of cases, the psychologist, and perhaps the staff, will disagree with the physician's decision regarding capacity. This may result when the patient is not well-known to the physician or the physician has been unduly influenced by family members who may be trying to control the patient for illegitimate reasons.

An example involved Blanche, a new nursing resident who quickly got to know most staff and residents by name. According to her physician, she was not capable of making medical decisions, which was based on information he received from the patient's daughter. Blanche and her daughter had an extremely antagonistic relationship that preceded the LTC. Blanche had a serious somatization disorder and a long history of poor decisions (typically excessive use of medical procedures and medications). The daughter firmly believed that this behavior was grounds for incapacity and she wanted to handle the problem by taking charge of her mother's medical affairs. The psychologist and physician recommended a neuropsychological evaluation to resolve the competency question. Blanche scored above 90% on almost all measures. The right to make medical decisions was reinstated to the patient. Tragically, Blanche and her daughter remained on uncivil terms, mostly over who owned Blanche's few household belongings and jewelry, until her death.

On rare occasions, family legal predicaments become so serious that Adult Protective Services becomes involved or the family conflict is disputed in court. Adult Protective Services may be instrumental in placing an older adult in an LTC facility, or they may be asked to follow a case after a discharge that is against medical advice. A psychologist may become involved in numerous ways: conducting competency assessments (Moye & Marson, 2007), following a patient after discharge from LTC, or testifying in court regarding issues of capacity, neglect, or abuse.

The consultation component of psychological services in LTC settings introduces many challenges regarding patient confidentiality. As stated previously, psychotherapy in LTC facilities is different in many ways from traditional outpatient individual psychotherapy. Mental health services in LTC facilities should assume that consultation with multiple parties will facilitate the impact of the direct clinical services. In contrast, traditional outpatient treatment often involves no one other than the patient. Maintaining patient privacy, while at the same time including family and staff in treatment strategies, creates a rather complicated challenge (Norris, 2002).

Three central confidentiality issues are common. First, when documenting services and including family and staff in various ways in the treatment, it is important to adopt a *need-to-know* principle. That is, only general information that is needed to accomplish a specific purpose is communicated. Specific information, particularly information that would be detrimental for others to know, is never communicated. For example, family members should not be informed that the patient is talking about his or her daughter's oppositional and strong-willed behavior as a child. However, it may be quite helpful to speak with family members about the need to foster their mother's fragile sense of independence and control.

A second confidentiality issue concerns obtaining consent. When a resident is deemed incompetent, some of the formal procedures of receiving services must be modified. When a power of attorney is in effect, that person holds the legal rights that the patient would normally have, such as the right to consent to services. Prior to initiating services, the psychologist must determine who gives consent. It is also important to distinguish if power of attorney is presently in effect, or if it is a durable or springing power of attorney, which will go into effect if and when the person becomes incapacitated.

The third confidentiality issue is especially thorny and rarely recognized in the literature on ethics. We think of *confidentiality* in terms of not revealing patient information to others. However, sharing information is a two-directional exchange. In outpatient services, the psychologist does not obtain information from persons other than the patient. In contrast, in LTC or other inpatient settings, the psychologist regularly obtains significant information about the patient perhaps without the patient's awareness this is occurring. For example, the social worker referring the patient gives a great deal of information about the resident and why he or she is being referred for services. Throughout therapy, nurses, aides, and other staff may report on many updates regarding the patient such as roommate conflicts, progress in physical therapy, and changes in medical conditions. And the patient's family members may offer information and background that the patient has not yet chosen to reveal. At the outset of services, when LTC patients are given information about confidentiality and its limits, the patient should be informed about who (family or staff) might be wanting to provide updates and that the psychologist's role is to use this information only in ways that are beneficial for the patient.

CONCLUSION

Psychologists who seek to combine their expertise in geropsychology and family therapy will find no better setting to do so than in LTC facilities. Professional opportunities for geropsychology and family therapy abound in LTC settings. However, it is imperative to know that competency in working with this population requires education and training that is most always acquired after graduate training. Continuing-education resources are available through workshops, professional organizations such as Psychologists in Long Term Care and the American Psychological Association's Society of Clinical Geropsychology, and such readings as Ogland-Hand and Florsheim (2002) and Qualls (2002). As detailed in this chapter, the mental health needs of LTC residents are unique; thus mental health providers in LTC settings must develop a new knowledge base. The myths and stereotypes of LTC settings and their residents must be dispelled and replaced with expert knowledge of this patient population, the associated familial cacophonies and symphonies, the modifications needed for assessment and treatment in LTC, and the external systems and organizations that govern these services.

REFERENCES

Allen-Burge, R., Stevens, A. B., & Burgio, L. D. (1999). Effective behavioral interventions for decreasing dementia-related challenging behaviors in nursing homes. *International Journal of Geriatric Psychiatry, 14*, 213–232.

Cipher, D. J., Clifford, P. A., & Roper, K. D. (2007). The effectiveness of gero-psychological treatment in improving pain, depression, functionality disability, and health care utilization in long-term care. *Clinical Gerontologist, 30*, 23–40.

Cohn, M. D., & Jay, G. M. (1988). Families in long-term care settings. In M. A. Smyer, M. D. Cohn, & D. Brannon (Eds.), *Mental health consultation in nursing homes* (pp. 142–168). New York: New York University Press.

Hays, P. A. (2007). *Addressing cultural complexities in practice, Second Edition: Assessment, Diagnosis and Therapy.* Washington, DC: American Psychological Association.

Kasl-Godley, J., & Gatz, M. (2000). Psychosocial interventions for individuals with dementia: An integration of theory, therapy, and a clinical understanding of dementia. *Clinical Psychology Review, 20*, 755–782.

Lebow, G., & Kane, B. (1999). *Coping with your difficult older parent: A guide for stressed-out children.* New York: HarperCollins.

Lichtenberg, P. A., Smith, M., Frazer, D., Molinari, V., Rosowosky, E., Crose, R., et al. (1997). Standards for psychological services in long-tem care facilities. *The Gerontologist, 38*, 122–127.

Moye, J., & Marson, D. C. (2007). Assessment of decision-making capacity in older adults: An emerging area of practice and research. *Journal of Gerontology, 62B*, P3–P11.

Norris, M. P. (2000). Public policy and the delivery of mental health care to older adults. In V. Molinari (Ed.), *Professional psychology in long-term care: A comprehensive guide* (pp. 425–443). New York: Hatherleigh.

Norris, M. P. (2002). Psychologists' multiple roles in long-term care: Untangling confidentiality quandaries. *The Clinical Gerontologist, 25* (3–4), 261–275.

Norris, M. P. (2006). Health care policies and caregivers. In S. M. LoboPrabhu, V. A. Molinari, & J. W. Lomax (Eds.), *Supporting the caregiver in dementia: A guide for health care professionals* (pp. 223–236). Baltimore: Johns Hopkins Press.

Ogland-Hand, S. M., & Florsheim, M. (2002). Family work in a long term care setting. In M. P. Norris, V. Molinari, & S. Ogland-Hand (Eds.), *Emerging trends in psychological practice in long-term care* (pp. 105–123). New York: Haworth Press.

Rabins, P. V. (1992). Prevention of mental disorder in the elderly: Current perspectives and future prospects. *Journal of the American Geriatrics Society, 40*, 727–733.

Qualls, S. H. (2002). Working with families in nursing homes. In V. Molinari (Ed.), *Professional psychology in long-term care: A comprehensive guide* (pp. 91–112). New York: Hatherleigh.

Smyer, M. A., & Qualls, S. H. (1999a). Family systems model. In M. A. Smyer & S. H. Qualls (Eds.), *Aging and mental health* (pp. 103–120). Malden, MA: Blackwell.

Smyer, M. A., & Qualls, S. H. (1999b). Institutional contexts for mental health services. In M. A. Smyer & S. H. Qualls (Eds.), *Aging and mental health* (pp. 231–256). Malden MA: Blackwell.

Spira, A. P., Koven, L. P., & Norris, M. P. (2005). Long-term care: New challenges and opportunities for psychologists. *The Clinical Psychologist, 58* (1–2), 26–29.

Strahan, G. W., & Burns, B. J. (1991). Mental illness in nursing homes: United States, 1985. *Vital Health Statistics Series 13*, no. 105. Data from the National Health Survey; no. 97 DHHS publication; no. (PHS) 89–1758.

WEBSITES

APA Society for Clinical Geropsychology, http://geropsych.org.

CMS http://www.cms.hhs.gov/.

Local carrier LCDs http://www.cms.hhs.gov/mcd/overview.asp. Click on "Index", then scroll down and click on LMRPs / LCDs By State.

Psychologists In Long Term Care http://www.wvu.edu/~pltc/.

CHAPTER

10

Family Caregiving and
U.S. Federal Policy

DIANE L. ELMORE AND RONDA C. TALLEY

In recent years, federal policy makers in the United States have focused increasing attention on family caregiving issues. This attention has resulted in the enactment of important new policy initiatives aimed at reducing the physical, psychological, and financial burdens that family caregivers often face. This chapter will provide an overview of some of the existing federal policy initiatives that have been enacted in recent years as well as some new federal caregiving policy proposals that are under consideration. In addition, federal agency leadership efforts related to family caregiving will also be highlighted. Finally, some examples of the family caregiving policy efforts that are being undertaken and proposed to address the needs of military service members, veterans, and their families will be discussed.

EXISTING FEDERAL POLICY INITIATIVES
OF IMPORTANCE TO FAMILY CAREGIVERS

Over the last decade some important federal policy initiatives have been enacted and implemented to assist family caregivers and those for whom they provide care. Some of these policies were initiated through the legislative action of the U.S. Congress, while others were spearheaded by federal agency leaders. These initiatives can be primarily categorized into four areas, including direct services, consumer-directed approaches (e.g., cash & counseling model), employment-based mechanisms, and financial incentives and compensation (Feinberg, 1997). The following section will identify and discuss some of the most significant new federal policy initiatives for family caregivers in the last decade.

Direct Services for Family Caregivers

One of the ways to assist family caregivers is through direct services, such as in-home support services and respite care. Several important direct service initiatives have been established through the federal policy-making process. Among the most significant of these initiatives in recent years is the establishment of the National Family Caregiver Support Program, the creation of the Aging and Disability Resource Centers (ADRCs), and the enactment of the Lifespan Respite Care Act.

Older Americans Act Caregiving Programs

Because the aging of the population plays such a critical role in the family caregiving policy debate it is essential to begin with a discussion of one of the most significant federal laws related to the aging population, the Older Americans Act. This groundbreaking legislation was signed into law in 1965 (P.L. 89-73) and remains the primary vehicle for the delivery of nutrition and social services for older adults in the United States (O'Shaughnessy & Napili, 2006). The Older Americans Act established the Administration on Aging (AoA), which is part of the U.S. Department of Health and Human Services and responsible for providing home- and community-based care for older adults and their caregivers (AoA, 2005b). The Older Americans Act also established the aging services network, which is the network of federal, state, and local agencies/organizations dedicated to the needs of older adults, including the State Units on Aging and Area Agencies on Aging, which coordinate Older Americans Act services at the state and local levels.

The Older Americans Act Amendments of 2000 (P.L. 106-501) created a new federal program to provide assistance to family caregivers called the

National Family Caregiver Support Program. This program is administered by the AoA and has three components, the National Family Caregiver Support Program, the Native American Caregiver Support Program, and the National Innovation Programs. First, the National Family Caregiver Support Program provides a variety of services and supports for caregivers, including information about available services; assistance in gaining access to supportive services; individual counseling, organization of support groups, and caregiver training; respite care for temporary relief from caregiving responsibilities; and assistance with supplemental services to complement the care provided by caregivers (AoA, 2004a).

The second part of the National Family Caregiver Support Program is the Native American Caregiver Support Program, which was established to address the needs of the American Indian, Alaska Native, and Native Hawaiian family caregiving communities. Although this program is significantly smaller than the National Family Caregiver Support Program, it provides similar direct services and supports for family caregivers. Both the National Family Caregiver Support Program and the Native American Caregiver Support Program provide services to family caregivers of older adults as well as grandparents and kinship caregivers of children (AoA, 2004b). The Older Americans Act Amendments of 2000 established that priority for these services under the National Family Caregiver Support Program be given to caregivers who are older individuals (i.e., 60 years of age and older) with greatest economic or social need (Colello, 2007b).

The third component of the National Family Caregiver Support Program is the National Innovation Programs. This research and demonstration program authorizes competitive grants to develop and test new approaches to addressing the needs of caregivers and supports program evaluation, training, technical assistance, and research (AoA, 2004b).

In 2006, the U.S. Congress completed the first reauthorization of the Older Americans Act since the establishment of the National Family Caregiver Support Program. The Older Americans Act Amendments of 2006 (P.L. 109-365) made some important modifications related to priority of the National Family Caregiver Support Program services. Specifically, these amendments established that: (a) family caregivers of persons with Alzheimer's disease or a related dementia may be served regardless of the age of the care recipient with dementia; (b) grandparents and other relative caregivers providing care to children (under age 18 years) may receive services at 55 years of age and older; and (c) grandparent or relative caregivers providing care for adult children with a disability (between 19 and 59 years of age) can now be served under the program under certain circumstances (AoA, 2008).

To date, the programs within the National Family Caregiver Support Program have provided a variety of services and supports to family caregivers around the country. Many in the caregiving policy and advocacy communities continue to work in support of increasing and expanding this federal initiative. Some of the legislative proposals related to the National Family Caregiver Support Program are discussed in later sections of this chapter.

Lifespan Respite Care Act

Respite is a service for family caregivers that provides a break from their caregiving duties. Research indicates that respite care is among the most frequently requested direct services by family caregivers nationwide (National Alliance for Caregiving & American Association for Retired Persons, 1997). However, respite is not currently available, accessible, and affordable for all family caregivers in the United States.

Several years ago, a bipartisan group of federal legislators joined together with the local, state, and national family caregiving advocacy communities to draft a piece of legislation focused on respite services for family caregivers. This legislation, entitled the Lifespan Respite Care Act, was first introduced in the U.S. Congress in 2002 (S. 2489/H.R. 5241), and then it was reintroduced again in 2003 (S. 538/H.R. 1083), 2005 (S. 1283/H.R. 3248), and 2006 (H.R. 3248). This federal initiative was based on a group of successful state Lifespan Respite programs (i.e., Oregon, Wisconsin, Nebraska, Oklahoma) that each had unique components, yet all shared the common goal of improving the quality and accessibility of respite for families regardless of age or disability (Baker & Edgar, 2004). After several years of diligent advocacy and negotiation, the Lifespan Respite Care Act (P.L. 109-442) was passed by the U.S. Congress and signed into law in December 2006.

This new federal law authorizes planned and emergency respite for family caregivers, training/recruitment of respite workers and volunteers, provision of information to caregivers about respite/support services, assistance for caregivers in gaining access to such services, and the establishment of a National Resource Center on Lifespan Respite Care. Now that this initiative has become law, federal policy makers, caregiving experts, and advocates are working together to secure federal funding for the Lifespan Respite Care Act and ensure appropriate implementation of this new law.

Aging and Disability Resource Centers

The aging and disability resource center (ADRC) initiative was established by the AoA and the Centers for Medicare and Medicaid Services (CMS). ADRCs were "developed to assist states in their efforts to create a single, coordinated system of information and access for all persons seeking long term support to minimize confusion, enhance individual choice, and support informed decision-making" (AoA, 2007). In 2003, 12 initial grants were provided to states for the development of pilot programs (AoA, 2005a). Currently, 43 states and territories in total have received grants, with 12 grants allocated in 2004 and 19 grants in 2005 (Colello, 2007a). During the most recent reauthorization of the Older Americans Act in 2006, amendments were included to authorize ADRCs in all 50 states (O'Shaughnessy & Napili, 2006). Questions regarding the details of implementing ADRCs nationwide continue to arise; however, many in the aging and disability advocacy communities remain interested in the potential promise of this new initiative to streamline services to individuals who are aging and those living with disabilities.

Consumer-Directed Long-Term Care: Cash & Counseling and Beyond

In recent years, both the disability and the aging communities have focused growing attention on community-based options for long-term care. At the center of these efforts is often a focus on individual consumer choice. This interest has fostered an investment in innovative demonstration projects and new policy initiatives to address the long-term care needs of the population with a focus on individual differences and preferences.

Cash & Counseling

Cash & Counseling is a demonstration initiative that began in 1998 in three states—Arkansas, New Jersey, and Florida. This demonstration is a consumer-directed approach to community-based long-term care that "provides a flexible monthly allowance to recipients of Medicaid personal care services or home and community based services" (Cash & Counseling, 2007). The program is supported by the Robert Wood Johnson Foundation and the U.S. Department of Health and Human Services. In recent years, the demonstration was expanded to include Alabama, Illinois, Iowa, Kentucky, Michigan, Minnesota, New Mexico, Pennsylvania, Rhode Island, Vermont, Washington, and West Virginia. Support for the expansion of the Cash & Counseling initiative to Illinois comes from the Retirement Research Foundation (Cash & Counseling, 2007).

Evaluations of the demonstration programs in the first three states suggest benefits for family caregivers who participated in the program, including lowered levels of physical, emotional, and financial strain; improved feelings of satisfaction with life; fewer burdens on privacy, social life, and job performance; and increased feelings of satisfaction with care recipients' care arrangements (Foster, Brown, Phillips, & Carlson, 2005; Foster, Dale, & Brown, 2007). Evaluations of the programs in the expanded states are also being conducted.

The Cash & Counseling model is important in the caregiving policy debate because it allows consumers (or care recipients) to make choices about their care, including the ability to hire relatives and loved ones to provide their caregiving needs, which could help to ease caregiver burden (Foster et al., 2005). Such approaches provide a promising flexible alternative to traditional community-based long-term care that assists not only the care recipient, but also the loved ones who provide their care (Elmore, in press).

Deficit Reduction Act of 2005

In 2006, the Deficit Reduction Act of 2005 (P. L. 109-171) was signed into law, increasing opportunities for states to support home- and community-based and consumer-directed long-term care options. Several sections of this important new policy are of significance to family caregivers and those for whom they care. First, Section 1915(i) of the Deficit Reduction Act allows states to provide home- and community-based services as a State plan option. Next, Section 1915(j) of the Deficit Reduction Act allows states to offer consumer-directed models of service delivery, such as Cash & Counseling, as a State plan option. This initiative allows care recipients to pay family caregivers to provide personal assistance services (CMS, 2007). The new provisions enacted as part of the Deficit Reduction Act of 2005 allow states to expand their home- and community-based options and consumer-directed approaches to long-term care, thus further increasing flexibility for care recipients and caregivers.

Choices for Independence

During the reauthorization of the Older Americans Act in 2006, a new initiative was established, called Choices for Independence. This initiative, which is administered by the AoA, builds on consumer-directed models, such as Cash & Counseling, by focusing on "empowering individuals to make informed decisions about their long-term support options; providing more choices for individuals at high-risk of nursing home placement; and enabling older people to make behavioral changes that will reduce their risk of disease, disability, and injury" (U.S. Department of Health and Human Services, 2006, p. 2). While the specific details of this new initiative are still emerging, it appears to add to the growing consumer-directed movement in aging and disability services.

Employment-Based Supports for Family Caregivers

Evidence suggests that the majority of family caregivers maintain employment (MetLife Mature Market Institute & National Alliance for Caregiving, 2006). Balancing the roles of caregiver and employee can often be difficult for family caregivers. For this reason, employment-based policies to address the needs of family caregivers are critically important.

Family and Medical Leave Act

Among the most important federal employment-related laws of significance to family caregivers to date is the Family and Medical Leave Act (P.L. 103-3), which was signed into law in 1993. This federal policy allows 12 weeks of unpaid leave annually for full-time employees to care for a family member with an illness or new child (Feinberg, 1997). This initiative provides many family caregivers with the opportunity to care for their loved one, while also maintaining their employment. However, the Family and Medical Leave Act does not provide coverage for all workers/employment sites (e.g., employers with fewer than 50 employees) and does not assist those who cannot afford to take unpaid leave. In recent years, several attempts have been made to expand the Family and Medical Leave Act. Some of these efforts will be discussed in subsequent sections of this chapter.

Financial Incentives and Compensation for Family Caregivers

Family caregivers often struggle with significant financial burdens related to their role as caregivers. Federal policy makers have made efforts to respond to these financial challenges by enacting policy initiatives aimed at easing the economic burdens of caregiving. These policy initiatives include both direct payments and tax incentives for family caregivers in need (Feinberg, 1997).

One of the existing public policies that allows for a financial break for some family caregivers is the Child and Dependent Care Tax Credit. This policy option allows caregivers to claim a nonrefundable tax credit to assist in offsetting the cost of care for a child (under 13 years of age) or spouse/dependent with a physical or mental disability (Colello, 2007a). Another such tax incentive for family caregivers is the Dependent Care Assistance Program. This policy option currently allows caregivers to exclude up to $5,000 of their earnings used for qualified dependent-care expenses (Colello, 2007a). While these policies provide financial relief for some family caregivers, a variety of additional policy alternatives have been proposed to further address the economic burden of caregiving. Some of these proposals are identified in subsequent sections.

National Leadership Regarding Family Caregiving Policy

In addition to the actions taken in recent years by federal policy makers to enact policies aimed at assisting family caregivers (e.g., Family and Medical Leave Act, National Family Caregiver Support Program, Cash &

Counseling demonstrations, Lifespan Respite Care Act), other notable efforts have been made to ensure that family caregiving issues remain a national policy priority. There are several important examples of national leadership on issues of family caregiving by federal agencies, experts and advocates, and national coalitions.

White House Conference on Aging

In 1961, the first White House Conference on Aging was held to bring together a nationwide forum of citizens to focus on issues related to older Americans and make recommendations for policy makers (White House Conference on Aging, 2004). Since this time, such a conference has been held every 10 years. Issues of caregiving have often made their way onto the White House Conference on Aging agenda.

During the most recent White House Conference on Aging in 2005, efforts were made to focus attention on family caregiving. Specifically, two of the delegations' final resolutions directly addressed caregiving issues. These caregiving-related resolutions urged leaders to "Develop a National Strategy for Supporting Informal Caregivers of Seniors to Enable Adequate Quality and Supply of Services" and "Support Older Adult Caregivers Raising Their Relatives Children" (White House Conference on Aging, 2006a). While these two resolutions directly related to family caregiving, several additional 2005 White House Conference on Aging resolutions urged action on issues of importance to caregivers and their older adult care recipients.

In addition to the attention paid to family caregiving issues in the White House Conference on Aging resolutions, focus on these issues was also present during a series of preconference events that were hosted nationwide prior to the official conference. One of the largest of these events was a White House Conference on Aging miniconference on the "Future of Caregiving," which was hosted in June 2005 in Washington, DC by the National Alliance for Caregiving and MetLife Mature Market Institute. This event brought together 129 participants representing a variety of areas of expertise, including: policy, practice, business, research, education, aging, population diversity, disability, technology, and philanthropy (White House Conference on Aging, 2006b).

The miniconference included expert presentations and a keynote address by Senator Hillary Rodham Clinton (D-NY), lead sponsor of several pieces of caregiving legislation (i.e., Lifespan Respite Care Act, Kinship Caregiver Support Act).

Next, four small working groups were formed in which participants discussed key caregiving issues and developed policy recommendations. These recommendations included: (a) expand government programs to better support the diverse population of caregivers (e.g., increase funding for National Family Caregiver Support Program, enact Lifespan Respite Care Act); (b) encourage all employers, large and small, to develop voluntary, flexible workplace policies and programs that support employed caregivers; and (c) establish a bipartisan commission on caregiving to bring visibility to the issues of caregiving and the importance of supporting caregivers for our families and our society (White House Conference on Aging, 2006b). This event helped to create momentum related to national family caregiving policy issues and set the stage for caregiving as a key policy issue at the 2005 White House Conference on Aging.

Consumers, experts, advocates, and policy makers continue to look to the White House Conference on Aging for national aging policy guidance. The fact that caregiving issues were included as part of the most recent White House Conference on Aging priorities helps to promote the needs of family caregivers as an important part of the aging policy agenda.

Centers for Disease Control and Prevention Caregiving Leadership

It is important to recognize significant leadership on family caregiving issues at the federal agency level. In addition to the leadership shown by the AoA in this area (e.g., the National Family Caregiver Support Program), efforts are also being made by one of its partner agencies in the U.S. Department of Health and Human Services, the Centers for Disease Control and Prevention (CDC). The mission of the CDC is "to promote health and quality of life by preventing and controlling disease, injury, and disability" (CDC, 2006).

In particular, the CDC's efforts on caregiving have been led by the Disability and Health Team of their National Center on Birth Defects and Developmental Disabilities and the Healthy Aging Program of their National Center for Chronic Disease Prevention and Health Promotion. Since 2004, the Disability and Health Team has been funding family caregiving research across the life span. These efforts have included: (a) support to Harvard University to conduct extramural research on the health effects of caregiving for children with disabilities on their parents by analyzing data from the State and Local Area Integrated Telephone Survey (SLAITS); (b) funds to the University of Florida to examine data from the Behavioral Risk Factors Surveillance System (BRFSS) related to caregiving and to develop an optional BRFSS caregiver module; and (c) the creation of a web-based searchable database on caregiving research, unveiled in February 2008, which is designed to support scientists in conducting caregiving research (Talley, Crews, Lollar, Elmore, Crowther, & Valluzzi, in press).

In October 2007, CDC's caregiving leadership convened a small group of national caregiving experts, consumers, government officials, foundations, and businesses to assist in the development of strategic public health recommendations related to their ongoing and future work. This day-long strategic planning session included multiple break-out groups focused on issues of research, interventions, and partnerships to address family caregiving. Specifically, the expert panel recommended attention toward a number of caregiving efforts. These included: (a) encouraging states to adopt the optional BRFSS caregiver module as soon as possible; (b) collaborating with the Institute of Medicine of the National Academies to develop a report on caregiving; (c) sponsoring the development of evidence-based health-promotion interventions in caregiver health and disseminating intervention knowledge to states and communities; (d) promoting consistent, harmonic public-health messages and policies regarding the need for more caregiver supports that are flexible and tailored to family needs; (e) assuring a robust national research capacity in caregiving and health; and (f) establishing and linking public-health partnerships that advance research, policy, practice, and training in caregiving (CDC, in press).

Family Caregiving Coalitions

Several national coalitions dedicated to family caregiving issues have played an important role in the caregiving policy debate. Among the most active coalitions are the National Respite Coalition, the National Alliance for Caregiving, and the Rosalynn Carter Institute's National Quality Caregiving Coalition. These groups have been a driving force behind many of the caregiving policy successes in recent years (e.g., Lifespan Respite Care Act). These coalitions bring together and mobilize experts, consumers, and advocates to play critical leadership roles in the family caregiving policy arena.

FAMILY CAREGIVING POLICY: NEW FEDERAL PROPOSALS AND INITIATIVES

While strides have been made in recent years in the federal caregiving policy arena, a great deal of work remains ahead. There are several important federal legislative initiatives that have been proposed by policy makers to further address the needs of family caregivers. This section will provide an overview of some of the federal legislative initiatives related to caregiving that have been proposed in recent years.

Grandparent/Kinship Caregivers

Today, millions of children in the United States are being raised by grandparents or other kinship caregivers. These kinship caregivers often face unique caregiving challenges. In addition to the health problems frequently encountered by aging kinship caregivers, many face barriers in navigating the educational and health-care systems, have difficulty finding accessible and affordable housing and legal services, and may struggle to access and understand federal services and supports. As the number of grandparents and nonparent relatives raising children continues to rise in the United States, federal legislation to address the unique needs of kinship caregivers has emerged.

Kinship Caregiver Support Act

One piece of legislation to address these issues is entitled the Kinship Caregiver Support Act. This legislation, which was first introduced in 2004 (S. 2706), would authorize grants for kinship navigator programs to state agencies with experience in addressing needs of kinship caregivers or children and connecting them with services and assistance. This bill would allow states to provide kinship-guardianship assistance payments on behalf of children to grandparents and other relatives; authorize kinship-guardianship demonstration projects; and require states to notify grandparents/relatives when a child is removed from parental custody and explain options to participate in the child's care and placement.

The Kinship Caregiver Support Act was reintroduced in 2005 (S. 985) and again in 2007 (S. 661/H.R. 2188). Since its initial introduction, this legislation has continued to gain bipartisan congressional cosponsors, as well as the support of a variety of organizations that are working toward enactment of this bill.

Caregivers of Older Adults: From Direct Services to Tax Credits

Several pieces of legislation have been introduced to address the growing number of family caregivers providing care for the aging population. Like many of the recently enacted caregiving policies, these initiatives include efforts to provide direct service, financial incentives, and assistance, and to expand consumer choice.

Americans Giving Care to Elders Act

In 2007, the Americans Giving Care to Elders (AGE) Act (S. 2267) was introduced to address the needs of caregivers of older adults. This legislation would provide an income tax credit for eldercare expenses (up to $1,200 each year), extend and increase funding for the National Family Caregiver Support Program, and establish the National Resource Center on Family Caregiving. This Resource Center would identify, develop, and disseminate information on best practices for and evidence-based models of family caregiver support programs; provide timely information on policy and program updates relating to family caregivers; partner with related organizations to disseminate practical strategies and tools to support families in their caregiving roles; convene educational programs and Web-based seminars on family caregiver issues and program development; and provide a comprehensive Internet website with a national searchable database on family caregiver programs and resources in the states.

Alzheimer's Family Assistance Act

In 2007, the Alzheimer's Family Assistance Act (S. 897/H.R. 1807) was introduced to: (a) allow a phased-in tax credit for family caregivers of spouses and dependents that have long-term-care needs; (b) allow a tax deduction for long-term-care insurance premiums; and (c) apply certain consumer-protection standards to long-term-care insurance contracts. Later in 2007, similar legislation was introduced called the Caregiver Assistance and Relief Effort Act, or the CARE Act (S. 2121). This bill would provide similar tax benefits as those proposed in the Alzheimer's Family Assistance Act and would also increase and extend the authorization of appropriations for the National Family Caregiver Support Program, including caregiver support programs for Native Americans.

Alzheimer's Breakthrough Act

The Alzheimer's Breakthrough Act was originally called the Ronald Reagan Alzheimer's Breakthrough Act when first introduced in 2004 (S. 2533/H.R. 4595). This legislation was reintroduced in 2005 (S. 602/ H.R. 1262) and again in 2007 (S. 898/H.R. 1560). The Alzheimer's Breakthrough Act would increase support for Alzheimer's disease research at the National Institutes of Health and authorize grants for a variety of Alzheimer's research areas, including Alzheimer's disease services and caregiving. This legislation also directs the U.S. Department of Health and Human Services to: (a) convene a summit of researchers and other industry representatives on Alzheimer's disease; (b) make grants for public education programs on risk factors associated with cognitive health, Alzheimer's disease, and other dementias; and (c) make grants to community organizations to establish and operate Alzheimer's call centers to provide 24-hour information on Alzheimer's disease.

Community Living Assistance Services and Supports Act

The Community Living Assistance Services and Supports Act, or the CLASS Act, was originally introduced in 2005 (S. 1951) and reintroduced in 2007 (S. 1758/H.R. 3001). Specifically, this legislation would create a national, voluntary disability insurance program (CLASS program) under which: (a) all employees are automatically enrolled, but they are allowed to waive enrollment; (b) payroll deductions pay monthly premiums; and (c) two-tiered benefits are provided, based on the level of disability, to purchase nonmedical services and supports that the beneficiary needs to maintain independence. In addition, this bill would require each state to: (a) assess the extent to which personal care service providers are serving or able to serve as fiscal agents, employers, and providers of employment-related benefits for personal care attendant workers, who provide personal care services to individuals receiving benefits under this Act; (b) designate or create entities to serve such purposes; and (c) ensure that such entities will not negatively alter or impede existing programs, models, methods, or administration of service delivery that provide for consumer-controlled or self-directed home and community services, impede the ability of individuals to direct and control their home and community services, or inhibit individuals from relying on family members for such services. Finally, this legislation would also establish a Personal Care Attendants Workforce Advisory Panel to examine and advise policy makers on workforce issues related to personal care attendant workers.

Expanding the Family and Medical Leave Act

As discussed earlier in this chapter, the Family and Medical Leave Act was one of the first employment-based federal laws focused on the issue of family caregiving. While this law took an important step forward to address the needs of those caring for a family member with an illness or new child, many have identified the need to expand such employment-based federal policies. One of the legislative expansion initiatives that has been proposed in recent years is the Family and Medical Leave Expansion Act, which was first introduced in 2002 (S. 3141), and again in 2003 (S. 304), 2005 (S. 282), 2006 (H.R. 5625), and 2007 (H.R. 1369). This legislation would expand the Family and Medical Leave Act by providing grants to state or local governments to pay for the federal share of the cost of carrying out projects that assist families by providing wage replacement for eligible individuals responding to caregiving needs resulting from the birth or adoption of a child or other family caregiving needs. The Family and Medical Leave Expansion Act would also extend coverage to employees at worksites employing at least 25 people (current law requires 50 employees), entitle employees to leave who are experiencing domestic violence, and authorize a demonstration project in coordination with a federal agency that provides paid leave for eligible individuals who are responding to caregiving needs resulting from the birth or adoption of a child or other family caregiving needs.

In recent years, there has been increasing interest in and support for several of the above mentioned as well as other federal legislative proposals focused on family caregiving. However, much more work remains ahead to increase the profile of family caregiving legislation as a key federal policy priority. Efforts to bring additional attention to and enactment of such federal policies will undoubtedly require tremendous collaboration among a variety of interested parties, including care recipients, family caregivers, researchers, health care providers, advocates, and policy makers.

ADDRESSING THE CAREGIVING NEEDS OF MILITARY SERVICE MEMBERS AND VETERANS

Today, the United States faces both a growing population of aging veterans and an increasing number of military service members returning from the conflicts in Iraq and Afghanistan with physical and mental health challenges. These circumstances have focused a great deal of attention on some of the caregiving issues facing the service member and veteran populations. Evidence suggests that the long-term care preferences of veterans are much like those of their civilian counterparts, with a preference toward home- and community-based options as opposed to institutional care (U.S. Department of Veterans Affairs, 2007a).

The U.S. Department of Veterans Affairs (VA) and the U.S. Department of Defense (DoD) are the lead federal entities responsible for the needs of veterans and military service members. Both government departments are focusing attention on caregiving issues facing their populations. The following section highlights some of the caregiving-related efforts being undertaken by the VA and DoD. In addition, this section also identifies recent recommendations proposed by a presidential commission regarding the caregiving needs of service member and veteran families and provides some examples of federal legislative initiatives that have been proposed in recent years.

U.S. Department of Veterans Affairs

The VA has been a national leader on aging and caregiving issues. Over the last decade, the VA has worked to provide optimal care to veterans who are aging or living with disabilities, with increased attention to promoting independence. Options for home and community based care continue to expand, as do supports for those family caregivers who assist in making home care possible for many veterans. Among the VA services and supports of significance to family caregivers are respite care, adult day home care, home based primary care, medical foster homes, homemaker and home health aide services, care coordination, telehealth, and information and referrals (Edes, 2008).

In 2003, the VA implemented a national care coordination program to apply "care and case management principles to the delivery of health care services using health informatics, disease management, and telehealth technologies to facilitate access to care and improve the health of designated individuals and populations with the intent of providing the right care in the right place at the right time" (U.S. Department of Veterans Affairs, 2007a). In November 2006 the VA Office of Care Coordination published a manual entitled "Innovative Caregiver Practices: A Resource Practice Guide." This resource guide highlights a variety of innovative caregiver practices that are incorporated within the VA system (U.S. Department of Veterans Affairs, 2006). The VA Office of Care Coordination has also hosted an annual Care Coordination and Caregiver Forum focused on caregivers and efforts by the VA to support care coordination between veterans, caregivers, providers, and health-care organizations.

In December 2007, VA further solidified its commitment to family caregivers by allocating nearly $4.7 million to caregiver assistance pilot programs "to expand and improve health care education and provide needed training and resources for caregivers" of veterans who are aging or living with disabilities (U.S. Department of Veterans Affairs, 2007b).

This initiative supports eight VA caregiving pilot programs from around the country focused on a variety of issues including managing patient behaviors and caregiver stress, communicating effectively with health care professionals, using the medical foster home model of care, using computer-based technology to assist caregivers, and providing education and training for caregivers of veterans with traumatic brain injury (U.S. Department of Veterans Affairs, 2007b).

U.S. Department of Defense

The DoD is also making efforts to address caregiving issues of importance to U.S. service members and their families. One example of this is the DoD Caregiver's Guide, which was developed to provide information and assistance to service members providing care to an older adult. This guide addresses issues including the aging process, long-distance caregiving, financial and legal issues, housing options, and community resources. In addition, this resource identifies a variety of DoD resources to assist military families, including family centers, the employee-assistance program staff, Federal Women's Program Managers, and chaplains (Department of Defense, 2007).

Commission on Care for America's Returning Wounded Warriors

In March 2007, the president established a Commission on Care for America's Returning Wounded Warriors. The commission—which was cochaired by Bob Dole, World War II veteran and former Senator, and Donna Shalala, former Secretary of the U.S. Department of Health and Human Services—was instructed to provide a comprehensive review of the care provided to returning service members and deliver recommendations (President's Commission on Care for America's Wounded Warriors, 2007).

In July 2007, the commission released its final report, which included some important recommendations regarding strengthening support for the families of services members and veterans. Specifically, the commission recommended that: (a) Congress should make combat-injured service members eligible for the TRICARE respite care and aide and personal attendant benefits currently provided in the Extended Care Health Option program; (b) DoD and VA should provide families of service members who require long-term personal care with appropriate training and counseling to support them in their new caregiving roles; and (c) Congress should amend the Family Medical Leave Act to allow up to 6 months' leave for a family member of a service member who has a combat-related injury and meets the other eligibility requirements in the law (President's Commission on Care for America's Wounded Warriors, 2007). According to the White House, DoD and VA have responded to the commission report by implementing family caregiver training and are developing a package of employment and health-care options for caregivers of seriously injured service members (White House, 2007).

Proposed Federal Legislative Initiatives for Service Members, Veterans, and Their Caregivers

Several pieces of federal legislation have been introduced in the U.S. Congress in an attempt to assist service members, veterans, and those who provide their care. Among these bills are the Disabled Veterans' Caregiver Compensation Act, which was originally introduced in 2002 (H.R. 4621) and again in 2003 (H.R. 2380), 2005 (H.R. 3777), and 2007 (H.R. 3070). This legislation would authorize monthly compensation to a veteran if and while totally disabled and in need of regular aid and attendance and while unpaid aid and attendance is provided by an adult family member who is dependent upon the veteran for support. Another piece of legislation to address the caregiving needs of veterans is the Heroes at Home Act, which was first introduced in 2006 (S. 3517) and again in 2007 (S. 1065/H.R. 3051). This legislation includes a provision that directs the Secretary of Veterans Affairs to establish a program on training and certification of family caregivers of service members and veterans with traumatic brain injury. A similar provision was later included in the Caring for Wounded Warriors Act (S. 2921), which was introduced in 2008. This legislation would establish two new pilot programs, one to train and certify family caregivers as personal care attendants for service members and veterans with traumatic brain injury and another to train graduate students (in mental health or rehabilitation related fields) to provide respite care for family caregivers of service members and veterans with traumatic brain injury. Finally, the Military Family Support Act was introduced in 2005 (S. 1888) and again in 2007 (S. 1649). This legislation would direct the Office of Personnel Management to establish a program to authorize a caregiver (a federal employee at least 21 years of age capable of providing care to a child or other dependent family member or a member of the Armed Forces) to: (a) use any available sick leave for the provision of such care in the same manner as annual leave is used and (b) use any federal leave available to that caregiver as though that period of caregiving is a medical emergency.

These legislative proposals (along with others) aimed at assisting service members and veterans with their caregiving needs have garnered-support among some members of the U.S. Congress and among many organizations committed to the needs of service members, veterans, and their families. However, it appears that much advocacy will be necessary before many of these legislative proposals are signed into law. With the aging of the veteran population and the increasing number of physically and psychologically wounded warriors returning from the current military conflicts, caring for the needs of military service members and veterans is certain to remain a critically important federal policy issue.

CONCLUSIONS

As the U.S. population continues to age and family caregiving burdens continue to increase, there is a growing need for federal policies to assist family caregivers and their care recipients. In recent years, several important federal policies have been enacted and implemented to address the physical, psychological, and financial challenges of family caregiving. Yet, policy makers, experts, and advocates continue their efforts to build on existing federal caregiving policies by proposing and promoting new federal initiatives aimed at filling the gaps in existing federal law. In addition to the recently enacted and proposed legislative initiatives, it is also important to recognize that several federal agencies and departments have taken important leadership roles on issues of family caregiving (e.g., AoA, CDC, VA, DoD). While strides have been made, a great deal of federal policy work remains to ensure that the needs of family caregivers are appropriately addressed. Federal policy efforts must continue to support and enhance the availability, accessibility, quality, and coordination of much-needed services and resources for family caregivers and the loved ones for whom they provide care.

REFERENCES

Administration on Aging. (2004a). *About NFCSP.* Retrieved October 5, 2007, from http://www.aoa.gov/prof/aoaprog/caregiver/overview/overview_caregiver.asp.

Administration on Aging. (2004b). *The Older Americans Act National Family Caregiver Support Program (Title III-E and Title IV-C): Compassion in action.* Retrieved October 15, 2007, from http://www.aoa.gov/prof/aoaprog/caregiver/careprof/progguidance/resources/FINAL%20NFCSP%20Report%20July22,%202004.pdf.

Administration on Aging. (2005a). *Fact sheet: Aging and disability resource centers.* Retrieved October 15, 2007, from http://aoa.gov/press/fact/pdf/fs_aging_disability.pdf.

Administration on Aging. (2005b). *Mission.* Retrieved October 15, 2007, from http://www.aoa.gov/about/over/over_mission.asp.

Administration on Aging. (2007). *Aging and disability resource centers.* Retrieved October 15, 2007, from http://aoa.gov/prof/aging_dis/aging_dis.asp.

Administration on Aging. (2008). *Older Americans Act of 2006: Frequently asked questions.* Retrieved April 5, 2008, from http://www.aoa.gov/OAA2006/Main_Site/resources/faqs.aspx#7.

Baker, L., & Edgar, M. (2004). *Statewide lifespan respite programs: A study of 4 state programs.* Retrieved April 5, 2008, from http://www.archrespite.org/LifespanRespiteReportFINAL9_30_04.pdf.

Cash & Counseling. (2007). *Program overview.* Retrieved October 5, 2007, from http://www.cashandcounseling.org/about/index_html.

Centers for Disease Control and Prevention. (2006). *About CDC: Vision, mission, core values, and pledge.* Retrieved October 5, 2007, from http://www.cdc.gov/about/mission.htm.

Centers for Disease Control and Prevention. (in press). *Advancing caregiving in America: A public health approach.* Atlanta, GA: Disability and Health Team, National Center on Birth Defects and Developmental Disabilities.

Centers for Medicare and Medicaid Services. (2007). *CMS support for caregivers.* Retrieved October 30, 2007, from http://www.cms.hhs.gov/partnerships/downloads/CMSCaregivers91907.pdf.

Colello, K. J. (2007a). *Family caregiving to the older population: Background, federal programs, and issues for Congress.* (Congressional Research Service Report No. RL34123). Retrieved October 15, 2007, from http://digitalcommons.ilr.cornell.edu/cgi/viewcontent.cgi?article=1327&context=key_workplace.

Colello, K. J. (2007b). *Family caregiving to the older population: Legislation enacted in the 109th Congress and proposals in the 110th Congress.* (Congressional Research Service Report No. RS22716). Retrieved April 5, 2008, from http://assets.opencrs.com/rpts/RS22716_20070907.pdf.

Department of Defense. (2007). *DoD caregiver's guide.* Retrieved October 15, 2007, from http://dde.carlisle.army.mil/tcefm/caregive.htm.

Edes, T. (2008). *Veterans Affairs efforts to support family caregivers.* Retrieved June 25, 2008, from http://videocast.nih.gov/launch.asp?14581.

Elmore, D. L. (in press). The impact of caregiving on physical and mental health: Implications for research, education, training and policy. In R. C. Talley (Series Ed.) and R. C. Talley, G. Fricchione, & B. Druss (Vol. Eds.), *The challenges of mental health caregiving.* New York: Springer.

Feinberg, L. (1997). *Options for supporting informal and family caregivers: A policy paper.* San Francisco, CA: American Society on Aging.

Foster, L., Brown, R., Phillips, B., & Carlson, B. L. (2005). Easing the burden of caregiving: The impact of consumer direction on primary informal caregivers in Arkansas. *The Gerontologist, 45*(4), 474–485.

Foster, L., Dale, S. B., & Brown, R. (2007). How cash & counseling affects informal caregivers: Findings from Arkansas, Florida, and New Jersey. *Health Services Research, 42*(1), 510–532.

MetLife Mature Market Institute & National Alliance for Caregiving. (2006). *The MetLife caregiving cost study: Productivity losses to U.S. business.* Retrieved October 5, 2007, from http://www.caregiving.org/data/Caregiver%20Cost%20Study.pdf.

National Alliance for Caregiving & American Association of Retired Persons. (1997). *Family caregiving in the U.S.: Findings from a national survey.* Bethesda, MD: Authors.

O'Shaughnessy, C., & Napili, A. (2006). *The Older Americans Act: Programs, funding, and 2006 reauthorization* (P.L. 109-365) (Congressional Research Service Report No. RL31336). Retrieved October 5, 2007, from http://www.ncoa.org/attachments/CRSOAAReport.pdf.

President's Commission on Care for America's Wounded Warriors. (2007). *Serve, support, simplify: Report of the President's commission on care for America's returning wounded warriors*. Retrieved October 15, 2007, from http://www.pccww.gov/docs/Kit/Main_Book_CC%5BJULY26%5D.pdf.

Talley, R. C., Crews, J. E., Lollar, D., Elmore, D. L., Crowther, M. R., & Valluzzi, J. (in press). Public health caregiving: Contributions and opportunities. In R. C. Talley (Series Ed.) and R. C. Talley & S. S. Travis (Vol. Eds.), *Multidisciplinary coordinated caregiving: Professional contributions*. New York: Springer.

U.S. Department of Health and Human Services. (2006). *Choices for independence: Modernizing the Older Americans Act*. Retrieved October 5, 2007, from http://www.aoa.gov/about/legbudg/oaa/Choices_for_Independence_White_Paper_3_9_2006.doc.

U.S. Department of Veterans Affairs. (2006). *Innovative caregiver practices: A resource practice guide*. Retrieved June 21, 2008, from http://www.chf-queri.research.va.gov/docs/Innovative_Caregiver_Practices_A_Resource_Practice_Guide.pdf.

U.S. Department of Veterans Affairs. (2007a). *History and rationale for care coordination in VA*. Retrieved October 5, 2007, from http://www.va.gov/occ/history.asp.

U.S. Department of Veterans Affairs. (2007b). *VA announces $4.7 million to help caregivers*. Retrieved June 21, 2008, from http://www1.va.gov/opa/pressrel/pressrelease.cfm?id=1428.

White House. (2007). *Fact sheet: Ensuring our wounded warriors get the best possible care*. Retrieved October 20, 2007, from http://www.whitehouse.gov/news/releases/2007/10/20071016-7.html.

White House Conference on Aging. (2004). *History*. Retrieved October 5, 2007, from http://www.whcoa.gov/about/history.asp.

White House Conference on Aging. (2006a). *The booming dynamics of aging: From awareness to action*. Retrieved October 5, 2007, from http://www.whcoa.gov/press/05_Report_1.pdf.

White House Conference on Aging. (2006b). *The booming dynamics of aging: From awareness to action—Appendix Part 2*. Retrieved October 5, 2007, from http://www.whcoa.gov/press/05_Report_3.pdf.

11

Family Care Planning Services

PATTI AUXIER

As one traveling through a foreign country may well need a guide and interpreter to ensure a successful trip, family members embracing the responsibilities of caregiving for aging loved ones may find their journey less taxing when aided by the expertise and counsel of knowledgeable professionals in the area of care planning. The focus of care planning is frequently directed to the needs of those receiving care, with the caregivers' roles defined only in relation to how they may best serve the needs of the care receivers. Often too little attention is given to the physical, psychosocial, financial, and mental health needs of the involved caregivers. With family members playing an ever-increasing role in the delivery of care to the nation's elder population, care planners may directly assist in the care of older adults by developing tools and strategies that educate, empower, and support the family members providing care. Individual consultations with care planners offer family caregivers the opportunity to explore and discuss areas of concern and to create a plan, not for care, but rather for caregiving, with the emphasis on caregiver wellness.

A shift in perspective to that of development and implementation of programs to enhance caregiver wellness gained momentum with the passage of the federally funded National Family Caregiver Support Program (NFCSP) as an amendment to the Older Americans Act in 2000. Each year the Administration on Aging allocates federal dollars to over 650 regional Area Agencies on Aging to assist local communities in identifying family caregivers through outreach and education efforts and to provide no-cost or sliding-scale services to caregivers including respite, caregiver counseling, support groups, caregiver training, community resource information, and individualized care planning. Area Agencies on Aging have the option to provide these services internally or through contracted providers and may also direct the resources to the areas they determine best meet the needs of their region. Some regions utilize the dollars solely for respite care while others focus on counseling and support groups; therefore, these public-funded caregiver programs vary across the country. The overlying purpose of the legislation is to encourage and sustain the involvement of family members in the care of their aging loved ones so as to avoid transferring the cost of care to the government. Each Area Agency on Aging must evaluate and determine how best to meet this goal for its region while also stretching the reach of limited funding. Many regions are funding positions for *caregiver coordinators* as the most efficient and effective way to impact the greatest number of caregivers. *Caregiver coordinators* serve as care planners by assessing each caregiver's situation and assisting in the development of caregiving plans to address both immediate and long-term needs. This type of care-planning assistance has existed in the private sector for many years as one component of a continuum of services offered by professionals in the field of geriatric care management.

Geriatric care management is a professional service designed to assist older adults, their families, and the professional community with the identification and coordination of services designed to address specific care needs in the home or in other care facilities. These services may be covered by long-term-care insurance, but most often they are paid out of pocket by the individual retaining the care manager and average from $75 to $120 per hour. Care managers may be nurses, social workers, or other human service professionals who have extensive knowledge about the costs, quality, and availability of community-based services as well as many other aging-related issues. Many care managers act as family surrogates for relatives who live out of their loved one's area. A care manager is often involved with a variety of parties including the elder, family members, medical providers, attorneys, and other service providers in the community; however, the primary focus of intervention is the care receiver.

The core components of geriatric care management are frequently defined as assessment, care-plan development, implementation/ coordination of needed services, monitoring, reassessment, and discharge. In order to develop the most effective plan of care, a care manager provides a comprehensive assessment of the care receiver's situation by conducting interviews, reviewing medical records, and directly observing the care receiver in his/her own environment. A multidisciplinary perspective is obtained by collecting information in the following areas: physical health, cognition, daily functioning abilities, social supports, behavioral/ emotional issues, values and preferences for care, financial status, legal concerns, and living environment. In many situations, a care manager may be retained to provide only the assessment and other parties develop a plan of action using the information gained. A quality assessment produces a broad-based, thorough, and objective evaluation of the care receiver's situation, identifies the areas of needed intervention, and drives the development of the care plan.

The care plan itself is a tool, a blueprint for actions that may be implemented by the care receiver, family members, and/or a care manager to direct the steps needed to reach agreed-upon goals (remaining in the home, moving into an assisted-living residence, etc). Care managers utilize their knowledge of services and community resources and programs to develop a care plan that satisfies the values and preferences of the care receiver, whenever possible, and addresses the issues surrounding safety, quality of life, and self-determination. Recommendations for service provision are suggested including the type and frequency of needed services, qualitative information about preferred service providers, costs of services, and projected length of need. Again, at this point, a care manager's involvement may cease and another party may implement the plan's recommendations. In other situations, the care manager may coordinate and implement services and stay involved to monitor the quality and appropriateness of the services on an ongoing basis, reassessing and making adjustments as needed.

Family care planning services incorporate the knowledge, experience, and investigative strategies involved in professional geriatric care management, but they shift the focus to the caregiver as the primary client. Care planners serve as guide and interpreter for caregivers who are often confused by their roles and responsibilities, overwhelmed by volumes of nonspecific information, and anxious about the unknowns that lie ahead. Many caregivers find themselves unprepared for the impact family caregiving will have on their lives. Typically, a trigger event of some kind (illness, injury, hospitalization) draws them into a caregiving, and possibly decision-making, role regarding the welfare of an aging loved one. They are unfamiliar with this "foreign country" and do not know where to begin, what to expect, or what questions to ask. By providing individual care-planning consultations to family caregivers, not only are their specific areas of concern defined and addressed, but also areas of need or action of which they have no awareness or knowledge. Circumstances that overwhelm and often paralyze caregivers are discussed, clarified, broken down into more manageable pieces, and prioritized. A written plan for caregiving involvement is outlined to provide guidance, education, and resources for further assistance regarding each step that may need to be taken. Perhaps most importantly, a relationship is created between the caregiver and care planner, assuring the caregiver that ongoing direction, emotional support, and resource identification are available throughout the caregiving journey to build caregiver confidence and minimize stress.

Unlike a geriatric care manager, a family care planner seldom performs a comprehensive in-home assessment of the care receiver or caregiver, so the care planner must establish rapport and obtain necessary information directly from the family caregiver, always recognizing that the information and observations shared are from only one perspective—the caregiver's. Carefully crafted questions must be asked to enable the caregiver and care planner to explore situations and concerns from several points of view, including that of the care receiver, the involved medical and community professionals, and other family members. The conversation is directed to a discussion of a variety of topics pertaining to both the caregiver and care receiver such as medical and functional concerns, financial and legal issues, formal and informal support systems, options for service delivery, and challenges and rewards of involvement. The most accurate picture possible of the caregiver's and care receiver's needs is pieced together by the care planner in order to help the caregiver obtain a broadened and perhaps more balanced understanding of the care receiver's needs. This somewhat more objective perspective enables caregivers to better identify steps for effective intervention and recognize the impact of their caregiving choices on themselves and others.

This in-depth conversation becomes a concrete, organized management tool with the creation of a written caregiving plan. In its simplest terms, the plan utilizes the information gained to clearly define what needs to be done for the care receiver and then outlines what the care receiver is able to do without help, what the caregiver is able to do to assist, what tasks need to be delegated to others, and what the caregiver is not able to do. Additionally, the plan identifies the persons, programs, and resources available to provide the delegated services and provides the specific steps, contacts, and eligibility criteria required to access the needed resources. A caregiving plan allows caregivers to prioritize what needs to be accomplished, gain a sense of control over situations that initially seemed out of control, and realize the opportunities for self-care. Although specific actions for self-care are included in the plan, as with many family caregiving situations, the caregivers most often put their own needs last and will only pursue self-care activities when all other concerns have been settled. The care planner's challenge transitions from defining the plan to empowering the caregiver to implement the plan, a challenge many care planners are unable to surmount alone.

The implementation of a caregiving plan may work flawlessly, with the family caregiver successfully following the advice and outlined steps of the care planner, and result in an improved caregiving experience for the caregiver and care receiver; however, in many instances, the caregiver may be tripped up by a variety of roadblocks that impede progress and erode confidence. The care planner may become aware of potential implementation problems during the development of the caregiving plan or may learn of difficulties later when making subsequent contacts with a caregiver. Initial warning signs of implementation problems include the following caregiver behaviors:

- negation of every idea or strategy proposed by the care planner
- acceptance of every idea proposed by the care planner without any follow-up or clarification questions asked
- repetition of issues, events, or concerns that have been previously addressed
- reluctance to explore new ways of thinking about caregiving roles
- inability to participate in formulating specific caregiving goals
- resistance to learning more about a loved one's medical/functional needs
- verbalization of emotion-laden problem-solving strategies
- reliance on a variety of excuses to explain the lack of progress

Care planners must avoid taking on the role of "fixer" and encourage caregivers to take responsibility for moving ahead; however, they often lack the expertise to provide *stuck* caregivers with a bridge to the successful implementation of a caregiving plan. Partnerships between family care planning services and mental health professionals specializing in caregiver counseling create this bridge.

The value of family care planning and the impact of caregiver counseling services are multiplied exponentially when combined together for a caregiver's benefit. Each service completes the other. Whether a caregiver first seeks a psychologist to address the emotional strain of caregiving or a care planner to learn of resources to ease caregiver burden, both professionals play a critical part in empowering the caregiver to remain in a healthy caregiving role. Caregiver counselors guide the caregiver down a path of self-discovery and realization, offering tools and coping strategies along the way, affording the caregiver the strength and confidence necessary to execute other actions needed to improve the caregiving situation. As mental health professionals, they may not be knowledgeable about the range and availability of services for caregivers—the expertise offered by care planners. Care planners identify what needs to be done and how to make it happen, but they rely on the abilities of the caregiver to follow through with the plan. As community resource experts, they lack the skills to effectively address and eliminate caregivers' emotional and psychological obstacles. In combination, care planning and caregiver counseling create a powerful and effective system of interventions designed to sustain family caregivers.

Family care planning services, offered through public-funded caregiver programs or as a specialty of professional geriatric care-management providers, serve as a vital linkage for family caregivers to a wide range of services and programs designed to make their caregiving roles easier to manage. The development of a caregiving plan not only clarifies the recommended services and processes required to care for an aging loved one, but it also addresses the physical, financial, and psychosocial well-being of the caregiver. Care-planning services alone may be enough to enable caregivers to effectively execute their responsibilities while also caring for themselves, but many caregivers benefit from the additional involvement of mental health professionals who help caregivers identify and apply strategies, perspectives, and behaviors necessary to implement a caregiving plan. Utilized together, caregiver counseling and family care planning services create an approach to caregiver wellness that provides a framework for accessing ongoing information, problem-solving strategies, and emotional support throughout the caregiving experience and beyond.

12

⟫◆⟪

Caregiver Services: Resources, Trends, and Best Practices

NANCY GIUNTA AND ANDREW SCHARLACH

A central theme of this book is that informal caregivers are providing the majority of long-term care in community-based settings in this country. These caregivers, mostly women, provide a much-needed service to loved ones, but they do so by facing potentially serious financial, emotional, and physical health risks. A paradigm shift is underway in which caregivers are being recognized not only as valuable providers of long-term care services, but also as clients in need of supportive services for themselves. This leads us to ask the question, "What public services are currently available for family caregivers?" This chapter hopes to answer that question from a national and state-level perspective, with special attention to caregiver services supported publicly through federal or state funds.

While states are increasingly recognizing family caregivers as both central providers of long-term care services and as clients of the long-term care system, approaches to caregiver support differ substantially. Variations in caregiver services remain significant in the administrative structure, funding streams, and accessibility of services within the states. In 2004, Family Caregiver Alliance (FCA) published an extensive study documenting caregiver programs in all 50 states and the District of

Columbia. The study report features state profiles that are also search-able online at www.caregiver.org. This chapter draws from the findings of the FCA report and other sources to present current resources, trends, and best practices in caregiver services across the states.

This chapter first will provide an overview of the types of caregiver support services currently available and discuss issues related to utiliza-tion of services. Next, current federal and state caregiver support policies and programs will be presented, followed by a brief history of caregiver support at the state level, describing the earliest innovators address-ing caregiver support as a statewide issue: California, New Jersey, and Pennsylvania. Then, trends across states and associated best practices will be described. Finally, the role of local organizations in addressing emerging issues in the area of caregiver support, and their implications for clinicians, will be discussed.

TYPES OF CAREGIVER SUPPORT

The range of support services available to caregivers across and within the states varies, but generally services include: information and assis-tance gaining access to services (which includes assessment and service coordination); respite; individual and group counseling, support groups, and education; personal care; homemaker/chore services; and ancillary services such as home modification and transportation assistance. These types of services are supported by public dollars through the National Family Caregiver Support Program (NFCSP), other federal/state grant programs such as Medicaid Home and Community-Based waivers or Real Choice Systems Change Grants, or programs supported directly by state funds. Some of these publicly funded services target care recipients, but they also benefit the caregiver. Adult Day Health Care, for example, has been shown to reduce the physical and emotional distress experienced by family caregivers (Gaugler & Zarit, 2001). Sometimes it is difficult to separate out the benefit caregivers receive from such services. At the same time, it is difficult to separate out the benefits to care recipients when their caregivers receive formal support services. Following are descriptions of common caregiver support services available in all states.

Information and Assistance

Information about services available to caregivers may be provided over the telephone, in person, or via the Internet, and it is the most commonly sought and provided caregiver service. Information is often the first service requested by caregivers, and formal information providers serve as an entry into the variety of caregiver support systems available in a community. Caregivers often are unaware of the community services available to them (Maslow & Selstad, 2001; Scharlach, Dal Santo, Lehning, et al., 2006). Despite the availability of information services, caregivers are likely to seek information from health-care providers such as their primary care physician (Feinberg, Wolkwitz, & Goldstein, 2006; Scharlach, Dal Santo, Lehning, et al., 2006).

Assistance accessing services may include assessment and service coordination by a knowledgeable staff member or volunteer. This service also may include family consultation or, in some cases, service coordination to assist caregivers with locating and contacting service providers. Case management, in which there is monitoring and reassessment of a care plan and advocacy efforts to assist families in obtaining services on an ongoing basis, is available to caregivers in some states. Additional assistance accessing services may lead to increased utilization and effectiveness of services compared with simply providing caregivers with information (Weuve, Boult, & Morishita, 2000).

Information and assistance is offered to caregivers through local Area Agencies on Aging (AAA) and other local providers who receive funding from the AAA or other public and private sources. However, the extent of information and assistance accessible to caregivers may be limited due to cultural or language barriers, thus demonstrating the need for more culturally sensitive services. The U.S. Administration on Aging manages an Elder Care Locator website (www.eldercare.gov) to provide information about services for caregivers and older adults, which are provided locally through the AAA network.

Respite

Services that enable caregivers to be temporarily relieved from their caregiving responsibilities can include in-home or out-of-home respite programs. Respite provided out of the home consists of daytime care, such as adult day health care or other day programs, or overnight respite in a care facility, such as a skilled nursing or assisted-living facility. The most commonly used respite is that which is provided in the home. Although in-home respite is commonly requested by caregivers who seek services, its availability is limited due to workforce shortages and cost. In-home respite may help delay institutionalization, especially of individuals with Alzheimer's disease or other dementias (Gaugler, et al., 2000; Kosloski & Montgomery, 1995; Sörensen, Pinquart, & Duberstein, 2002). As mentioned previously, there is also evidence that out-of-home daytime respite (adult day health care) reduces caregivers' physical and emotional distress (Gaugler & Zarit, 2001).

Although respite was one of the earliest types of caregiver support services offered and is currently the most common service offered, the amount of respite available both across the states and within each state varies significantly (Feinberg, Newman, Gray, & Kolb, 2004). Indeed, in-home respite is one of the most expensive services caregivers can receive. However, lower-cost respite options are available through adult day programs and sometimes Medicaid-funded programs targeting care recipients.

Counseling, Support Groups, and Education

Emotional or psychosocial support to caregivers, either through individual or group counseling, is offered through various providers. Individual, short-term counseling has been shown to be effective among caregivers for individuals with Alzheimer's disease who need strategies for coping with intensive caregiving situations (Bourgeois, Schulz, & Burgio, 1996). Determining the type of counseling most effective for treating caregivers depends on appropriately matching caregiver needs with the most appropriate types of counseling interventions (Scharlach et al., 2001). The availability of individual and group counseling varies within and between states.

Support groups offer peer support, information about diseases and disability, and referrals for caregiver support services in an informal, group setting. Support groups are typically offered through local social service provider organizations and are available based on the type of caregiving situation, such as disease-specific (e.g., Parkinson's disease) or relationship-specific (e.g., spouse, partner, adult child) situations. Support groups in some geographic areas may target specific cultural, linguistic, or ethnic groups. Although participants of support groups generally describe them as helpful, there is not strong empirical evidence for improving caregivers' mental or physical health (Scharlach et al., 2001).

Caregiver education is offered through a variety of models, including: workshops and forums on the availability of caregiver services, skill development, and dealing with psychosocial issues; lecture series on specific topics of interest; and technologically assisted forums, including telephone, Web-based, or videoconferencing for sharing knowledge. Technologically assisted programs are especially helpful to caregivers who cannot leave a care recipient alone or who live in rural areas where local programs are geographically inaccessible.

Personal Care

Assistance to care recipients with activities of daily living, including dressing, bathing, grooming, and using the bathroom, can provide a benefit to the caregiver, especially in cases when a caregiver may not live with or near the care recipient or may not have the physical strength to take on personal care responsibilities. Care recipients may also prefer to receive this assistance from someone other than the informal caregiver.

Homemaker/Chore Services

Housecleaning, grocery shopping, preparing meals, or other paraprofessional services are offered through local community programming or purchased privately, but often they are not broadly available under the auspices of caregiver services. Such services may be available directly for care recipients, in which case the caregiver indirectly benefits.

Legal or Financial Services

These services include free consultation with an attorney or a financial planner who specializes in aging, or referral to such professionals. Legal consultation may help plan for a care recipient's potential loss of decision-making capacity. This includes assignment of health-care and financial decision-making authority, estate management, or potential eligibility for public benefits. Workshops or group information sessions regarding these legal or financial issues related to caregiving also may be available. Caregivers who are lesbian, gay, bisexual, or transgender may benefit from legal or financial planning in order to prevent future barriers to care or financial benefits for themselves or the person for whom they provide care.

Supplemental Services

Under the NFCSP, services that may be available on a limited basis with the intention of filling a temporary gap in services are considered *supplemental services*. For example, home modification or transportation assistance may be available to caregivers and care recipients as supplemental services. This category of service may be considered a "catch-all" for service providers whose assistance does not fit into other funding categories, and it varies by state and locality.

In summary, although a wide variety of caregiver services exist nationwide, service availability varies greatly by state and local region. Program administrators face various constraints in implementing caregiver services statewide, such as workforce shortages, need for additional outreach efforts, growing diversity among caregiver needs, and limited collaboration among service providers (Feinberg et al., 2004; Giunta, 2007). Similarly, while types of caregiver support services vary across states and local regions, so does the utilization of services.

UTILIZATION OF SERVICES

Service utilization varies markedly across and within states. The existence of caregiver support programs does not ensure that caregivers will use them. Barriers to service use may include eligibility criteria, lack of caregiver self-identification, lack of knowledge about the services available, cultural norms, or other barriers (e.g., language, cost, lack of transportation) to access services (Scharlach, Dal Santo, Lehning, et al., 2006; Scharlach, Kellam, Ong, et al., 2006). Research on the utilization of social services in general, and caregiver services specifically, has been growing both nationally and internationally.

Self-identification as a caregiver is usually a precursor to seeking services. There is substantial evidence that many family caregivers, especially spouses, perform care tasks long before they identify themselves as caregivers (Aneshensel, Pearlin, Mullan, Zarit & Whitlatch, 1995; Dobrof & Ebenstein, 2004; Montgomery & Kosloski, 2001). The transition to identifying as a caregiver is complex, and the reluctance to self-identify may be due to various emotional, cultural, or socioeconomic reasons. Individuals who identify themselves as caregivers are more likely to be involved in activities helpful to them than are adults who do not identify themselves as caregivers but perform care tasks (Kutner, cited in Dobrof & Ebenstein, 2004). This suggests that caregivers who self-identify may be more likely to utilize formal support services.

Other factors affecting the decision to utilize caregiver support services include the type of services offered by service providers, the cultural context surrounding the choice to seek services, and whether the care recipient is using formal services. Dal Santo, Scharlach, Nielsen, and Fox (2007) found that caregivers were more likely to be using respite services than counseling services if they had more physically demanding care responsibilities or if their care recipients were using community services, whereas counseling service use was less likely among Asian and Pacific Islander caregivers. Drawing upon the same California caregiver data, Giunta, Chow, Scharlach, and Dal Santo (2004) found that formal caregiver service utilization differed by race and ethnicity, as African American and non-Hispanic White caregivers were more likely to use services than caregivers of either Latino or Asian/Pacific Island ethnicities. Scharlach, Giunta, Chow, and Lehning (2008) applied a multivariate model to explore whether there were factors that controlled for, or interacted with, race and ethnicity to better predict caregiver service utilization. They found that race and ethnicity did not significantly predict service use after controlling for covarying factors such as age, education, emotional support, family contribution, care recipient service use, and care recipient impairment, although Asian and Pacific Island caregivers with close family relationships continued to be least likely to use formal services.

Scharlach, Kellam, Ong, and colleagues (2006) further examined cultural variations in formal and informal caregiver support utilization. Through focus groups conducted with caregivers from eight racial and ethnic minority groups, they found that participants rarely relied on formal assistance. Four themes related to limited use of services were identified: (a) caregivers primarily turned to informal supports such as family and friends; (b) caregivers lacked knowledge of formal support services available to them; (c) formal service providers were not trusted to provide the quality of services desired by caregivers; and (d) culturally sensitive services were not available.

Caregiver family and social networks may also play a role in service utilization. For example, Williams and Dilworth-Anderson (2002) found that larger network size and higher family cohesiveness were related to lower utilization of service use among African American caregivers. Caregivers may face higher risks of negative health outcomes if they are less likely to seek formal services as the intensity of care required by the care recipient increases (Williams & Dilworth-Anderson, 2002).

Overall, although caregivers are increasingly utilizing available support services, many continue to experience barriers that make such services inaccessible. Barriers to service use have been attributed to geographic, socioeconomic, linguistic, and cultural factors (Scharlach, Dal Santo, Lehning, et al., 2006). Because of such barriers facing the most vulnerable caregivers, many continue to experience significant unmet needs. Recent federal and state programs such as those described in the next section of this chapter have been introduced to address existing barriers and unmet needs among these most vulnerable caregivers.

FEDERAL AND STATE POLICY AND PROGRAMS TO SUPPORT CAREGIVERS

Caregiver support began receiving attention at the national policy level in the early years of the Clinton administration. During this time, a foundation was laid for more significant national policy developments such as the NFCSP (Fox-Grage, Coleman, & Blancato, 2001). After federal attention to caregiver support increased, the number of state-level policies and programs for caregivers grew, offering caregiver support services from states' general funds. Federal policy developments described in this section include: the Family and Medical Leave Act; the Olmstead Decision; Medicaid Home and Community-Based waivers; and the National Family Caregiver Support Program. State programs described in this section include those earliest innovators that served as model programs for both national and state-level policies and programs. While federal policies and programs target both care recipients and caregivers, state programs tend to target caregivers specifically.

Federal Policies and Programs

The Family and Medical Leave Act

The first national policy to support working caregivers, the Family and Medical Leave Act (FMLA) of 1993, provides employees of companies with at least 50 workers up to 12 weeks of unpaid leave to provide care to a child, spouse, or parent. This national policy does not cover all workers, and it only provides unpaid leave, which many middle- or low-income caregivers cannot afford to take. At the state-level, however, awareness and adoption of policy supporting paid family leave is increasing.

California was the first state to implement paid family leave, which is covered under the state's employment disability program and includes care for a newborn or adopted child or a seriously ill family member. The California program is currently the most comprehensive paid family leave program in the country (Pandya, Wolkowitz, & Feinberg, 2006). Other states have introduced paid family leave policies, but these often only cover the care of a newborn or newly adopted child or require the employee to use sick leave for time off. In 40 states, for example, public employees may use sick leave to care for an ill family member.

The Olmstead Decision

After the passage of the Americans with Disabilities Act (ADA) in 1990, increased numbers of lawsuits were filed by institutionalized individuals wishing to live in community-based settings (Scala & Nerney, 2000). In 1999, the landmark U.S. Supreme Court case, *Olmstead vs.*

L.C., known as *the Olmstead Decision*, concluded that states are obliged by the ADA to provide community-based services for persons with disabilities who would otherwise be entitled to institutional services (Rosenbaum, 2001).

The Olmstead decision required states to comply with the ADA in making reasonable modifications to avoid discrimination on the basis of disability by planning for and implementing the following activities: (a) restructure existing programs and services so that community-based options are accessible for individuals wishing to move from an institution into a community-based setting or for those already in community-based settings wishing to remain there; and (b) design and conduct individualized assessments, often including family caregivers, that support community-based care options.

All states have developed *Olmstead plans*, which vary tremendously in scope and the priority they receive. States with highly developed, highly prioritized plans have seen more rebalancing and restructuring to promote community-based services over institutionalization. Ideally, the community-based options presented in Olmstead plans should include elements for caregiver support. Over the last several years, the Administration on Aging has participated in efforts to help states rebalance long-term care and promote community-based alternatives to institutionalization through Medicaid waivers.

Medicaid Home- and Community-Based Waivers

With approval from the Center for Medicare and Medicaid Services (CMS), states may obtain waivers to use Medicaid dollars to fund long-term care services not traditionally covered by Medicaid. The waiver concept was introduced in an effort to allow long-term care services to be provided within community-based settings, rather than institutions. States apply for approval from CMS to waive the requirement that long-term care services are provided in a skilled nursing facility in order for them to be reimbursable. The purpose of the Medicaid waiver is generally to allow an individual who requires long-term care services to live in a community setting and receive services covered by Medicaid that had been traditionally provided only in a skilled nursing facility setting. This has arguably provided higher-quality services to care recipients and lower costs per client. Caregivers may experience lower levels of distress when the institutionalization of their loved one is prevented, although some have argued that decreased access to institutional care may increase the burden on family caregivers.

Although the primary client for these services is typically the care recipient, the informal caregiver indirectly can benefit from in-home respite care provided through waiver programs. Although the states are given flexibility in terms of administering waivers, the states must comply with program requirements set forth by CMS, which include: cost neutrality; measures to ensure the health and welfare of consumers; adequate provider standards; and service provision in accordance with an individual's plan of care.

There are currently 48 states plus the District of Columbia operating Medicaid 1915(c) waivers. There is no limit to how many waivers a state may operate and no limit to how many beneficiaries a state can serve with waivers. It is required that all beneficiaries be at risk of institutional care; however, the definition of *nursing-home eligibility* is determined by the state. Although it is beyond the scope of this chapter to discuss the outcomes of home- and community-based waiver programs, there is evidence that these Medicaid waivers are an effective mechanism toward reducing Medicaid-funded, long-term care costs (Doty, 2000).

Cash & Counseling

One example of a Medicaid waiver program is the Cash & Counseling program. The Cash & Counseling Demonstration is a consumer-directed model that provides monthly cash payments to adults with disabilities (age 18+) to purchase any goods or services necessary to meet their individual care needs. Consumer direction is a service-delivery approach in which a high level of choice and control is offered to the consumer. In this approach, the locus of control for service-delivery decisions shifts from the service provider to the client (Doty, 2004). In the case of family caregiving, consumer direction provides the caregiver with increased decision-making authority for services that both the caregiver and care recipient may access.

Consumers who do not wish to or are unable to manage their cash payments under this model may designate a representative, most often a family member, to assist them. The amount of the cash payment is determined by the level of need, indicated by the consumer's care plan and history of past claims. Cash payments could be used to hire workers (family, friends, or professionals), purchase supplies or assistive technology, or pay for home modifications.

Originally conceived in 1995, the Cash & Counseling Demonstration was first implemented in three states: Arkansas, Florida, and New Jersey (Phillips et al., 2003; Phillips & Schneider, 2002). A randomized experimental design was used to test the effectiveness of the demonstration. Participants were randomly assigned to one of two groups: (a) the treatment group, in which they received the Cash & Counseling intervention, or (b) the control group, in which they received already existing agency-based services.

Results of Cash & Counseling have been well documented and disseminated throughout the literature since its inception (see Simon-Rusinowitz, Mahoney, Desmond, Shoop, Squillace, & Fay, 1997; Mahoney, Simon-Rusinowitz, Meiners, McKay, & Treat, 1998). Randomized trials resulted in members of the treatment group being significantly more satisfied with their care, having fewer unmet needs, and more likely to be receiving paid care than those in the control group (Carlson, Foster, Dale, & Brown, 2007). Although Medicaid costs were higher for personal care services among treatment-group members, these costs were nearly offset by savings in other Medicaid long-term care services (Dale & Brown, 2007). Higher expenditures among treatment-group members were attributed to individuals getting services for which they were eligible, whereas evidence showed that control-group members were less likely to receive services despite being eligible for them.

Better outcomes for informal and paid caregivers in the Cash & Counseling treatment group compared with control-group members were reported in the initial three states (Foster, Brown, Phillips & Lepidus, 2005; Foster, Dale, & Brown, 2007). In addition to expressing significantly less worry about the care provided to service recipients than caregivers in the control group, treatment-group caregivers fared better in the areas of physical, emotional, and financial well-being.

After its introduction in 1995 in three states, it was expanded to 12 additional states. Since then, empirical evidence of its effectiveness has led to this intervention being written into national long-term care policy as a provision of the 2005 Deficit Reduction Act (DRA). The provision in the DRA allows states to institute a "cash & counseling" type of program (Kent, 2007) without the previously required waiver from the Center for Medicare and Medicaid Services.

Real Choice Systems Change Grants

Another federal/state program administered by CMS, which has also promoted increased services for caregivers, is the Real Choice Systems Change Grants program. In 2001, the Bush administration introduced the New Freedom Initiative to promote community living for people with long-term care needs. One outcome of this initiative was legislation authorizing funds, called Real Choice System Change Grants, from the Medicaid program to develop additional infrastructure, but not direct services, to support people with long-term care needs in community settings.

Consumer-directed personal assistance programs, linkages between personal care and affordable housing programs, and transition programs to assist individuals with moving from skilled nursing facilities into community-based settings are all examples of programs funded under Real Choice Systems Change Grants. Since 2001, all 50 states, the District of Columbia, and American territories have received grants, although the amount each state has received varies. The states that have received the highest levels of funding include Arkansas, Michigan, New Hampshire, North Carolina, Vermont, and Wisconsin ($8 million to over $10 million each). North Dakota, South Dakota, Wyoming, and the American territories received the lowest levels of funding, all under $2 million (Shirk, 2007).

While a number of programming changes have occurred across the states, and promising practices have been introduced, outcome evaluation of Real Choice Systems Change Grants is limited. Although Congress authorized grants to be distributed between 2001 and 2006, the legislation required evaluation only for grants awarded after 2005. Most evaluation efforts of these programs have consisted of descriptions of the program activities (Shirk, 2007).

The National Family Caregiver Support Program

The NFCSP is a federal entitlement program administered as Title III-E of the Older Americans Act (OAA). Introduced as an amendment to the OAA in 2000, the purpose of the NFCSP is to meet the needs of caregivers at the local level through the already-established aging-services network of 56 State Units on Aging, 655 local Area Agencies on Aging (AAAs), and 243 Indian Tribal and Native Hawaiian Organizations (ITNHOs). A caregiver is eligible for services regardless of income if he or she is providing care to an older adult (age 60 or over) or if he or she is a grandparent or relative caregiver over age 55 providing care to a child. As with all OAA programs, states are required to give priority to individuals with the greatest social or economic need.

The NFCSP was modeled after successful state programs in California, New Jersey, Pennsylvania, and Wisconsin and designed with input from family caregivers nationwide. The NFCSP and Native American Caregiver Program (NACP), both funded through the OAA, are administered federally by the Administration on Aging and at the state level by each of the State Units on Aging. Local AAAs and ITNHOs provide direct services to older adults or contract with local service providers to provide services. Local AAAs and tribal organizations can use NFCSP/NACP funds to provide the following services to caregivers (Administration on Aging, 2006, p. I-2): *information* for caregivers about available services; *assistance* for caregivers in gaining access to these services; *counseling, support groups,* and *training* to help caregivers make decisions and solve problems relating to their caregiving roles; *respite* care to temporarily relieve caregivers from their caregiving responsibilities; and *supplemental services,* on a limited basis, to complement care provided by caregivers.

Prior to the NFCSP, not all states funded caregiver support programs. More than a third of states offered caregiver support services for the first time as a result of the NFCSP (Feinberg et al., 2004), demonstrating that this federal policy was an important inducement for states to begin to address the needs of informal caregivers. There were, however, several states that served as innovators in developing statewide caregiver support programs that specifically targeted family caregivers and utilized state funds to do so. These state-level programs are described next.

State-funded, Caregiver-Specific Programs

Caregiver support programs financed by state general funds are not required to comply with federal Medicaid or Older Americans Act funding, thus they can be more flexible in defining types of services, target populations, and eligibility criteria. State-funded programs can explicitly target the caregiver rather than the care recipient as the client of services. Since the implementation of the NFCSP, states have increasingly enacted legislation relevant to family caregiving. Between 2001 and 2003, for example, 23 states enacted such legislation. State funds allocated for caregiver support often include tobacco settlement funds, which have created new revenues for home- and community-based services, including respite for caregivers.

Prior to caregiver support services making it to the national policy agenda, three states, California, New Jersey, and Pennsylvania, were early *models* in the area of caregiver support (Feinberg, 2001; Feinberg & Pilisuk, 1999). These early innovators recognized family caregivers as primary clients or took a family-systems perspective in treating the family as the service recipient rather than seeing elderly care recipients as the only consumer of services. They offered an array of supportive services, including several types of respite options, and many promoted consumer direction, both for care recipients and family caregivers.

California

An exemplary model of a state-funded caregiver support program is the California system of Caregiver Resource Centers (CRCs). California was by far the earliest state to recognize the need for caregiver support. The lead agency in the statewide network, Family Caregiver Alliance, a private nonprofit organization founded in San Francisco in the 1970s, administers state funds and provides technical assistance to 11 CRCs operating throughout the state. State funds for caregiver support in

California were made available as early as 1980, when the single San Francisco agency grew into a system of 11 Caregiver Resource Centers (CRCs) statewide. Since the development of the CRC network, other states have designed their state-funded, statewide caregiver support programs after California's model.

In addition to being the leader in caregiver support statewide, FCA hosts the National Center on Caregiving, a research and public policy think tank that "serves as a central source of information on caregiving and long-term care issues for policy makers, service providers, media, funders, and family caregivers throughout the country" (from FCA website: www.caregiver.org).

New Jersey

The state of New Jersey introduced two statewide programs in the late 1990s to provide increased community support for caregivers in order to delay or prevent placement of care recipients into a skilled nursing facility. The Caregiver Assistance Program (CAP) is a Medicaid Waiver program covering only care recipients who are Medicaid beneficiaries, while the Jersey Assistance for Community Caregiving (JACC) program is a state-funded initiative that serves care recipients who are not eligible for Medicaid but are at risk of nursing-home placement and have limited financial resources. Both programs use a consumer-directed approach, involving individualized care plans that allow care recipients to hire and pay family caregivers to provide in-home services to care recipients. Both programs also cover respite and education programs for caregivers in addition to an array of supportive services to assist the caregiver and care recipient in maintaining a living arrangement at home.

The two programs were established after a reorganization and consolidation effort in which 20 programs serving older adults and caregivers merged into one *senior services* division within the New Jersey Department of Health and Senior Services (Reinhard & Fahey, 2003). The primary purpose of the reorganization was to rebalance the long-term-care service system from providing mostly institutional care to offering home- and community-based services for individuals in need of long-term care and their caregivers.

Pennsylvania

Like California and New Jersey, Pennsylvania was one of the first states to introduce legislation and allocate funding for family caregivers (Feinberg & Pilisuk, 1999). Pennsylvania's Family Caregiver Support Program recognizes both the care recipient and family caregiver as clients. The program uses a family-centered approach that allows flexible spending to meet the needs of both the care recipient and family caregiver, thus supporting the care recipient to remain at home and prevent institutionalization.

In approximately 3 decades, caregiver support policies and programs have grown from radically progressive ideas into more mainstream, widespread interventions. Next, this chapter will describe the current trends and best practices in caregiver support across the United States.

CURRENT TRENDS AND BEST PRACTICES IN STATES

Studies examining the implementation of caregiver support programs and policies have identified a number of emerging trends across states. Three such trends are: caregiver assessment, consumer direction, and collaboration and coordination among service providers (Feinberg et al., 2004, 2006; Giunta, 2007).

Caregiver Assessment

The body of literature on caregiver assessment has grown recently, with increased attention to the need for uniform assessment guidelines for determining caregiver needs. In 2003, less than one-fourth of states used a uniform assessment for their home- and community-based service systems, and only five of them included a caregiver component (Feinberg et al., 2004). However, there is significant support among state-level program administrators for uniform assessment guidelines that include a caregiver component (Feinberg et al., 2004, 2006; Giunta, 2007).

Conducting caregiver assessments changes the paradigm of the care recipient being the only one in need of services and recognizes the caregiver also as a client in need of formal support. Assessing the caregiver provides practitioners an opportunity to begin a dialogue with the caregiver earlier in the caregiving process, recognize the variety of needs experienced by caregivers, and help improve care provided to care recipients (Guberman, in Family Caregiver Alliance, 2006). Although more research is needed to determine the effectiveness of assessment in improving caregiver outcomes, such as decreased levels of burden and depression, increased health and well-being, and quality of life, it is believed that caregiver assessment enhances the practitioner's ability to offer effective interventions to help both the caregiver and care recipient meet their long-term care needs. Policymakers can work with practitioners to ensure that caregiver assessment is included within publicly funded home- and community-based service packages.

Both across and within states, approaches to assessing the needs of family caregivers vary tremendously. However, Feinberg and colleagues (2006) identified best practices in caregiver assessment in five states (California, Massachusetts, Minnesota, Pennsylvania, and Washington). Best practices among these states include: a caregiver interview being part of a state's uniform assessment for Medicaid Waiver participants (Washington and Minnesota); assessing the caregiver as a component to the care recipient assessment, but considering the caregiver as a distinct service user (Massachusetts); including a caregiver component in all uniform assessments administered as part of any publicly funded service for older adults (Pennsylvania); or using a separate, distinct tool for family caregivers when public funds are allocated to serve them (California).

According to Feinberg and colleagues (2006), the caregiving module of an assessment tool should assess the following elements: willingness and ability to provide care; caregiver satisfaction (i.e., unable to continue caring due to decline in health, not satisfied with support received from other family and friends, feelings of distress, anger, or depression); measures of self-reported health; and caregiver strain (e.g., the 13-item Caregiver Strain Index). Including caregivers in the assessment benefits the clinician because it creates a more complete picture of the support network the care recipient relies on, and the process assists caregivers with identifying and accessing services they may need in order to support the care recipient.

Three strategies have been associated with the successful implementation of caregiver assessments (Feinberg et al., 2006). First, the use of mobile technology to enter assessment data directly into a centralized database improves planning and efficiency and allows care managers to spend more time assisting clients. Second, when recommendations from all stakeholders are incorporated into the assessment tool, it will be useful to clients, service providers, and administrators. Finally, technical assistance and education regarding the utility of the assessment tool as well as services available to caregivers provides clinicians with the necessary information for administering the tool correctly.

Consumer Direction

Attention to consumer direction has been increasing as evidenced by increased consumer-directed programs and increased empirical research related to consumer-directed models. The Cash & Counseling demonstration and the Olmstead decision have brought increased support for consumer direction. States with innovative consumer-directed programs specifically for caregivers include: Alabama, California, Georgia, North Carolina, and Pennsylvania (Feinberg et al., 2006). North Carolina, for example, provides caregivers with vouchers they may use to purchase services they need. Services include, but are not limited to, home care, respite, supplies, transportation, and meals.

Consumer-directed support benefits caregivers in several ways. First, there is significant evidence that consumers of long-term care, whether they are caregivers or care recipients, prefer the choice, flexibility, and control of consumer direction over traditional agency-driven service models (Benjamin & Mathias, 2001; Feinberg & Whitlatch, 1998; Simon-Rusinowitz et al., 1997). In consumer-directed models, family caregivers and care recipients have more choice and control over who provides care, which may ensure the provision of more culturally appropriate services. Second, given the growing shortage of direct-care providers, consumer-directed options may increase the hiring pool of potential caregivers by including family providers (Feinberg et al., 2006). Finally, evidence increasingly supports the possibility that consumer direction may be more cost-effective than traditional agency-driven service mechanisms by potentially reducing the need for more expensive interventions such as nursing homes (Stone, 2000; Dale & Brown, 2007).

Interorganizational Collaboration

Statewide and local collaborations between the aging network and health-care systems are part of a trend emerging nationally (Feinberg et al., 2006). Historically, the trend to collaborate or, more specifically, to integrate health and social support, although discussed as beneficial in the literature (Bolda, Lowe, Maddox, & Patnaik, 2005; Bolda, Saucier, Maddox, Wetle, & Lowe, 2006; Marosy, 1994), has not been practiced widely (Aliotta & Andre, 1997; Bolda & Seavey, 2001). Within the context of caregiver policy, Feinberg and colleagues (2006) found that, with the implementation of the NFCSP, community-based service providers began working with health-care providers to help conduct outreach to caregivers in an attempt to address the lack of self-identification among this population. Health-care practitioners may be influential in assisting caregivers with self-identification, a common barrier to service utilization (Montgomery & Kosloski, 2000). Because the primary care physician often is the first and most accessible contact that the caregiver communicates with, efforts to include health-care providers in the caregiver support milieu are underway in several states (Feinberg et al., 2006).

In addition to the need for collaboration between health-care and aging service providers, collaboration and coordination among all local service providers can help break down barriers and inefficiencies created by organizational isolation and funding silos (Feinberg, 2004; Giunta, 2007). Several innovative programs such as those described in the following have emerged from local collaborative efforts. Indeed, states with traditions of innovation or experimentation have shown promising results in offering supportive services for caregivers (Giunta, 2007; Scharlach et al., 2001).

LOCAL ISSUES AND INNOVATIONS

Program administrators face several challenges in implementing caregiver support programs, including the following: shortages in the direct-care workforce; lack of public awareness about caregiver issues and programs; limited access to services in rural areas; lack of culturally sensitive programming to meet the diverse needs of caregivers; and limited utilization of technology for information management (Giunta, 2007; Kietzman, Scharlach, & Dal Santo, 2004; Whittier, Scharlach, & Dal Santo, 2005). Local efforts may be more effective than state or federal initiatives at developing innovative programs for tackling issues such as these because of their ability to tailor efforts to meet individualized community needs.

The following program examples, a selection of recipients of the 2007 National Family Caregiving Awards, were recognized as innovative best practices by the National Alliance for Caregiving and the MetLife Foundation. Although they have not been evaluated empirically, these best practices in caregiver service innovation demonstrate local efforts to address some of the constraints faced by program administrators at the state level. To address shortages in the direct-care workforce and the need for culturally sensitive services, the Asian Community Center in Sacramento, California, offers a "Caregiver Cooperative Model" that enables caregivers to volunteer and *earn* respite time that they can later *buy* from the program. The program is available for caregivers and care recipients of Japanese, Chinese, and Filipino descent.

To address the need for increased public education, the Just Care Caregiver Education Project in Los Angeles, California, offers educational clinics and training for low-income disabled and older adults, and for the professionals who serve them. Multilingual training covers problems and issues regarding the complex laws and regulations governing benefits available to caregivers, among other topics.

Rural caregivers tend to spend more time on caregiving activities than their urban counterparts (Dorfman, 2002; Horwitz & Rosenthal, 1994). To address the needs of rural caregivers, Montana State University Extension, in Bozeman, Montana, implemented a program to educate caregivers of individuals with Alzheimer's disease. Specialists travel to communities across the state and spend a week in each area providing educational workshops for caregivers. Evaluation of this program showed increased self-confidence in caregiving skills among participants.

Rural issues also have been addressed through the use of technology. In Albany, New York, teleconference technology is used in the facilitation of telephone support groups for caregivers who are unable to leave their homes or cannot travel long distances to attend in-person support groups. In Rochester, Minnesota, the Minnesota Help Network is a Web-based decision-making tool used to assess needs, create a plan of care, and help caregivers locate community services. A personal plan based on individual needs is created and can be updated as needs change.

The use of technology to provide information and services to caregivers has grown tremendously through the Internet. Web-based support is available to caregivers in most states through public as well as disease-specific advocacy organizations. For example, Link2Care (www.link2care. net) provides information and support for people caring for someone with memory loss in California. Organizations such as the Alzheimer's Association, American Cancer Society, American Diabetes Association, the National Parkinson's Foundation, American Heart Association, and American Lung Association have websites with an abundance of disease-specific educational materials, discussion forums for caregivers and care recipients, and resource listings for finding supportive services.

In summary, the small sample of local innovations presented here illustrate that local communities are working to meet the needs of caregivers and care recipients. Although these smaller programs have yet to be systematically evaluated, they are attempting to meet the diverse needs of many caregivers within their local communities.

CONCLUSION

Family caregivers are increasingly being recognized as both valuable contributors and clients within long-term-care service systems. Caregiver support policies and programs nationwide—including the Olmstead Act, the Family and Medical Leave Act, the National Family Caregiver Support Program, Medicaid Home and Community-Based waivers, and individual states' efforts—have influenced this paradigm shift. Although the National Family Caregiver Support Program falls significantly short of providing the fiscal resources needed to support caregivers nationally, this federal policy jump-started many states to recognize caregivers' needs and offer support to family caregivers. However, support available to caregivers both across states and within states remains tremendously uneven.

Clinicians play an essential role in supporting family caregivers. The ability to recognize the caregiver as a person in need of services, and the ability to assess caregiver needs, is the first step toward ensuring a caregiver will receive appropriate support. Clinicians can assist caregivers with self-identifying early in the caregiving trajectory so that preventive services can be offered to help caregivers avoid emotional, physical, or financial health problems. Second, the knowledge of support services offered from national, state, and local programs is indispensable, as is the ability to share this knowledge with caregivers in a culturally sensitive manner. Finally, collaborating with other service providers, program administrators, advocates, and policy makers can ensure that knowledge and innovation will spread to create effective programming that breaks down barriers to services. Meanwhile, caregiver support advocacy organizations continue to work to improve resources for caregivers, who are the backbone of the home- and community-based long-term care system.

REFERENCES

Administration on Aging (AoA). (2006). *The National Family Caregiver Support Program resource guide*. Washington, DC: Author.

Aliotta, S., & Andre, J. (1997). Case management and home health care: An integrated model. *Home Health Care Management & Practice, 9*(2), 1–12.

Aneshensel, C. S., Pearlin, L. I., Mullan, J. T., Zarit, S. H., & Whitlatch, C. J. (1995). *Profiles in caregiving: The unexpected career*. San Diego, CA: Academic Press.

Benjamin, A. E., & Matthias, R. E. (2001). Age, consumer direction, and outcomes of supportive services at home. *The Gerontologist, 41*(5), 632–642.

Bolda, E. J., Lowe, J. I., Maddox, G. L., & Patnaik, B. S. (2005). Community partnerships for older adults: A case study. *Families in Society, 86*, 411–418.

Bolda, E. J., Saucier, P., Maddox, G. L., Wetle, T., & Lowe, J. I. (2006). Governance and management structures for community partnerships: Experiences from the Robert Wood Johnson Foundation's community partnerships for older adults program. *The Gerontologist, 46*(3), 391–397.

Bolda, E. J., & Seavey, J. W. (2001). Rural long-term care integration: Developing service capacity. *Journal of Applied Gerontology, 20*, 426.

Bourgeois, M., Schulz, R., & Burgio, L. (1996). Interventions for caregivers of patients with Alzheimer's disease: A review and analysis of content, process, and outcomes. *International Journal on Aging and Human Development, 43*, 35–92.

Carlson, B. L., Foster, L., Dale, S. B., & Brown, R. (2007). Effects of cash & counseling on personal care and well-being. *Health Services Research, 42*(1, p. 2), 467–487.

Dal Santo, T., Scharlach, A., Nielsen, J., & Fox, P. (2007). A stress process model of family caregiver service utilization: Factors associated with respite and counseling service use. *Journal of Gerontological Social Work, 49*(4), 29–49.

Dale, S. B., & Brown, R. S. (2007). How does cash & counseling affect costs? *Health Services Research, 42*(1/2), 488–509.

Dobrof, J., & Ebenstein, H. (2004). Family caregiver self-identification: Implications for healthcare and social service professionals. *Generations, 27*(4), 33–38.

Dorfman, L. T. (2002). Family networks and relationships among rural elders. *Geriatric Care Management Journal, 12*, 16–21.

Doty, P. (2000). *Cost-effectiveness of home and community-based long-term care services.* Washington, DC: U.S. Department of Health and Human Services/Assistant Secretary for Planning & Evaluation/Office of Disability, Aging and Long-Term Care Policy.

Doty, P. (2004). *Consumer-directed home care: Effects on family caregivers.* San Francisco: Family Caregiver Alliance.

Family Caregiver Alliance. (2006). *Caregiver assessment: Voices and views from the field.* Report from a National Consensus Development Conference (Vol. II). San Francisco: Author.

Feinberg, L., & Whitlatch, C. (1998). Family caregivers and in-home respite options: The consumer-directed versus agency-based experience. *Journal of Gerontological Social Work, 30*(3–4), 9–28.

Feinberg, L., Wolkwitz, K., & Goldstein, C. (2006). *Ahead of the curve: Emerging trends and practices in family caregiver support.* San Francisco: Family Caregiver Alliance.

Feinberg, L. F. (2001). *Systems development for family caregiver support services.* Issue Brief for the Lewin Group and U.S. Administration on Aging.

Feinberg, L. F. (2004). The state of the art of caregiver assessment. *Generations*, 27, 24–32.

Feinberg, L. F., Newman, S., Gray, L., & Kolb, K. (2004). *The state of the states in family caregiver support: A 50-state study*. San Francisco: National Center on Caregiving at Family Caregiver Alliance.

Feinberg, L. F., & Pilisuk, T. L. (1999). *Survey of fifteen states' caregiver support programs: Final report*. San Francisco: Family Caregiver Alliance.

Foster, L., Brown, R., Phillips, B., & Lepidus, C. (2005). Easing the burden of caregiving: The impact of consumer direction on primary informal caregivers in Arkansas. *The Gerontologist*, 45(4), 474–485.

Foster, L., Dale, S. B., & Brown, R. S. (2007). How caregivers and workers fared in cash & counseling. *Health Services Research*, 42(1/2), 510–532.

Fox-Grage, W., Coleman, B., & Blancato, R. B. (2001). *Federal and state policy in family caregiving: Recent victories but uncertain future*. San Francisco: National Center on Caregiving at Family Caregiver Alliance.

Gaugler, J. E., Edwards, A. B., Femia, E. E., Zarit, S. H., Stephens, M. P., Townsend, A., & Greene, R. (2000). Predictors of institutionalization of cognitively impaired elders: Family help and the timing of placement. *Journal of Gerontology: Psychological Sciences*, 55B(4), P247–P255.

Gaugler, J. E., & Zarit, S. H. (2001). The effectiveness of adult day services for disabled older people. *Journal of Aging and Social Policy*, 12, 23–48.

Giunta, N., Chow, J., Scharlach, A., & Dal Santo, T. (2004). Racial and ethnic differences in family caregiving in California. *Journal of Human Behavior in the Social Environment*, 9(4), 85–109.

Giunta, N. M. (2007). *Caregiver support programs and policies: A mixed methods evaluation of implementation efforts in 50 states*. Unpublished doctoral dissertation, University of California, Berkeley.

Horwitz, M. E., & Rosenthal, T. C. (1994). The impact of informal caregiving on labor force participation by rural farming and nonfarming families. *The Journal of Rural Health*, 10, 266–272.

Kent, C. (2007). Cash & counseling given a major boost. *National conference of state legislatures state health notes*. Washington, DC: National Conference of State Legislatures. Retrieved April 23, 2007 from http://www.cashandcounseling.org/news/20070307–170540/article.pdf.

Kietzman, K., Scharlach, A., & Dal Santo, T. (2004). Local needs assessment and planning efforts for family caregivers: Findings and recommendations. *Journal of Gerontological Social Work*, 42(3/4), 39–60.

Kosloski, K., & Montgomery, R. J. V. (1995). The impact of respite use on nursing home placement. *The Gerontologist, 35*, 67–74.

Mahoney, K. J., Simon-Rusinowitz, L., Meiners, M. R., McKay, H. L., & Treat, K. C. J. (1998). Empowering the community: Public initiatives in consumer-directed services. In L. C. Walker, E. H. Bradley, & T. Wetle (Eds.), *Public and private responsibilities in long-term care: Finding the balance* (pp. 150–164). Baltimore: Johns Hopkins University Press.

Marosy, J. P. (1994). Collaboration: A key to future success in long term home care. *Home Health Care Management & Practice, 6*(2), 42–48.

Maslow, K., & Selstad, J. (2001). Chronic care networks for Alzheimer's disease: Approaches for involving and supporting family caregivers in an innovative model of dementia care. *Alzheimer's Care Quarterly, 2*, 33–46.

Montgomery, R. J. V., & Kosloski, K. (2000). Family caregiving: Change, continuity and diversity. In M. P. Lawton & R. Rubinstein (Eds.), *Interventions in dementia care: Toward improving quality of life* (pp. 143–172). New York: Springer.

Montgomery, R. J. V. & Kosloski, K. D. (2001). *Change, continuity and diversity among caregivers.* Paper prepared for the U.S. Administration on Aging Caregiver Listserv.

Pandya, S., Wolkwitz, K., & Feinberg, L. (2006). *Support for working family caregivers: Paid leave policies in California and beyond* (Policy Brief). San Francisco: National Center on Caregiving at Family Caregiver Alliance.

Phillips, B., Mahoney, K. J., Simon-Rusinowitz, L., Schore, J., Barrett, S., Ditto, W., Reimers, T., & Doty, P. (2003). *Lessons from the implementation of cash & counseling in Arkansas, Florida, and New Jersey.* Princeton, NJ: Mathematica Policy Research, Inc.

Phillips, B., & Schneider, B. (2002). *Moving to independent choices: The implementation of the cash & counseling demonstration in Arkansas* (Report No. 8349–107). Princeton, NJ: Mathematica Policy Research, Inc.

Reinhard, S. C., & Fahey, C. J. (2003). Rebalancing long-term care in New Jersey: From institutional toward home and community care. New York: Milbank Memorial Fund.

Rosenbaum, S. (2001). *Olmstead v L.C.: Implications for family caregivers* (Policy Brief). San Francisco: Family Caregiver Alliance.

Scala, M. A., & Nerney, T. (2000). People first: The consumers in consumer direction. *Generations, 24*(3), 55–59.

Scharlach, A., Dal Santo, T., Greenlee, J., Whittier, S., Coon, D., Kietzman, K., et al. (2001). *Family caregivers in California: Needs, interventions and programs.* Berkeley, CA: Center for the Advanced Study of Aging Services.

Scharlach, A., Dal Santo, T., Lehning, A., Gustavson, K., Lee, S., Auh, E., et al. (2006). *Caregiving in California: Final report of the University of California family caregiver support project.* Berkeley, CA: Center for the Advanced Study of Aging Services.

Scharlach, A., Giunta, N., Chow, J., & Lehning, A., (2008). Racial and ethnic variations in caregiver service use. *Journal of Aging and Health. 20,* 326–346.

Scharlach, A., Kellam, R., Ong, N., Aeran Baskin, B., Cara Goldstein, M., & Fox, P. J. (2006). Cultural attitudes and caregiver service use: Lessons from focus groups with racially and ethnically diverse family caregivers. *Journal of Gerontological Social Work, 47*(1/2), 133–156.

Shirk, C. (2007). *Trading places: Real Choice Systems Change Grants and the movement to community-based long-term care supports* (Issue Brief No. #822). Washington, DC: National Health Policy Forum.

Simon-Rusinowitz, L., Mahoney, K. Desmond, S. Shoop, D., Squillace, M., & Fay, R. (1997). Determining consumer preferences for a cash option: Arkansas survey results. *Health Care Financing Review, 19*(2), 73–96.

Sörensen, S., Pinquart, M., & Duberstein, P. (2002). How effective are interventions with caregivers? An updated meta-analysis. *The Gerontologist, 42,* 356–372.

Stone, R. (2000). Long-term care for the elderly with disabilities: Current policy, emerging trends, and implications for the twenty-first century. New York: Millbank Memorial Fund.

Weuve, J., Boult, C., & Morishita, L. (2000). The effects of outpatient geriatric evaluation and management on caregiver burden. *The Gerontologist, 40,* 429–436.

Whittier, S., Scharlach, A., & Dal Santo, T. (2005). Availability of caregiver support services: Implications for implementation of the National Family Caregiver Support Program. *Journal of Aging & Social Policy, 17*(1), 45.

Williams, S. W., & Dilworth-Anderson, P. (2002). Systems of social support in families who care for dependent African American elders. *The Gerontologist, 42,* 224–236.

13

A Platform for Intervention and Research on Family Communication in Elder Care

MICHAEL WILLIAMS AND CLAYTON LEWIS

In the transitions to assisted-living and skilled nursing facilities, aging adults can become isolated by a number of factors: health crises, personal decline, or depression. While these transitions increase the need for social support, at the same time they conspire to increase barriers. The elder is removed from his or her familiar environment, so contact with friends and neighbors is reduced; mobility may be limited; and the situation may be complicated by physical and cognitive decline. Electronic communication can help, if it can be made simple enough to operate. New technology is emerging that is simple to use for people with limited backgrounds in modern systems.

Systems built around this new technology are creating an interesting new platform for conducting research into communication by and with elders and its role in maintaining or increasing well-being. In addition to allowing study of family communications, the systems can be used to deploy and study a wide range of interventions, including programs that support three-way communication among elders, family, and facility staff. The systems allow prompting to promote participation. Benefits to researchers include automated data collection, monitoring of participation, and access to geographically distributed participants online. The systems are readily configurable so that new services and interventions are relatively easy to create and adapt. Experimenting with new services can begin with a computer, three graduate students, and an idea.

FAMILY ELECTRONIC COMMUNICATION

Being in touch with other people is not just an amenity as people age; it is a critical factor in survival. Studies show dramatically increased mortality, by a factor of two or more, for people who are socially isolated compared with those with close interpersonal ties (Fratiglioni, Paillard-Borg, & Winblad, 2004). The mechanisms underlying the value of communication are unclear. Communication may promote increased sense of purpose, which may sustain life (Glass, de Leon, Marottoli, & Berkman, 1999). Communication may also promote cognitive activity, which has been found to reduce the incidence of dementia (Verghese et al., 2003).

Elders quickly recognized the value of electronic communication in keeping in touch with friends and family after moving to a retirement community in another area. In principle, electronic communication would also be helpful to elders in an assisted-living, skilled nursing, or rehabilitation facility. But many elders are not getting this potential benefit.

According to 2006 data, 82% of Americans aged 30 to 49 have Internet access, and more than half of people with Internet access use e-mail on a daily basis (Pew Internet and American Life Project, 2007). But data from the same source show that only a third of Americans over 65 have Internet access. This means that the way grandma and grandpa communicate is different from the way their children and grandchildren communicate, posing a challenge for family communication.

While the data show that Internet usage by elders is increasing, there are factors that may limit adoption and lead to some elders who have had Internet access giving it up as they age. Operating a computer is cognitively demanding, and maintaining a system exposed to the Internet, with required updates, virus protection, pop-up blockers, and spam filtering, is difficult.

New technology allows elders to communicate electronically with their families, without the use of a computer. A new class of system is entering the market that supports electronic communication by elders without requiring them to operate and maintain a computer. The Presto Printing Mailbox (http://www.presto.com/) and the Digital Mailbox from CaringFamily, LLC (http://www.CaringFamily.Com) allow e-mail to be sent to an elder and printed out automatically. While both "mailbox" devices contain computers acting as controllers, these computers are not directly connected to the Internet. Rather, they are connected via telephone lines (so that elders do not need to obtain Internet service). Operations are scheduled so that the phone line is used only in the middle of the night, so a dedicated line is not needed. This mode of connection means that the device can be reached only via the associated services by registered users. Elders are thus protected from viruses, spam, and other intrusions. Further, no user interaction is required for printing, so elders do not have to cope with signing on or using menus, commands, or keys to receive e-mail. E-mail sent to the elder can include pictures, which are printed out in color.

While some devices only support incoming e-mail, some allow elders to send e-mail as well, either by replying to messages they have received or by sending messages of their own. Addressing is handled by barcodes imprinted on incoming messages when they are received, in the case of replies, or by the use of stationery preprinted with barcodes designating the recipients. Messages without barcodes are sent to a default recipient for possible rerouting to other family members. This design allows the user interface for the Digital Mailbox to consist of a single send button: The elder places a to-be-sent message in a scanner in the Digital Mailbox and presses "send" (see Lewis, 2007, for an analysis of the Digital Mailbox user interface design). Messages from the elder are scanned, rather than keyed in, so they can be composed in any mode that is convenient, including handwriting, and can freely include snapshots, news clippings, greeting cards, or any like materials elders wish to send.

New Technologies Simplify Linkages for Elders

One service has been operating in trial form since January 2004, with 150 systems deployed across the United States. In these trials, 45,867 messages have been sent by family members to elders (as of mid-December 2007), and 7,947 messages have been sent by elders. The simplicity of the user interface has been demonstrated by the fact that users, including elders, have needed almost no training or assistance from staff in operating the technology.

In a study of the system, funded by a Small Business Innovation Research grant from the National Institute of Aging, usage by seven families was analyzed over an 8-week period. The messages sent during the trial suggested that the system supported general communication within the families, with a very wide range of content. Within the brief study period, messages dealt with weddings, birth, health, illness, death, employment, travel, and holiday greetings, as well as miscellaneous contacts.

Besides the content of these communications, the study showed that family members differ in their communication roles. In some cases, a family member sent messages only on a single topic (e.g., humorous news stories). In four of the eight families, the distribution of message traffic was quite skewed, with a single member originating more than twice his or her proportionate share of messages to the elder. This member may perhaps be the *kin keeper*—the person who takes greatest responsibility for maintaining family relationships, as identified in family studies (Rosenthal, 1985).

In this field trial it was difficult to add or enroll new members, because of the need to obtain consent from research participants. Data from commercial trials show that when enrollment is not restricted, the number of family members who participate grows dramatically, and that growth continues (at a declining rate) indefinitely. The graph in Figure 13.1 shows the viral growth that has been observed. Across all groups, about 20% of members are recruited at the initiation of the caregroup, 50% in the first 20 days, then recruiting seems to continue at an ever-diminishing rate, indefinitely. The largest families (including friends and distant cousins) have 40 to 60 members.

In the description so far, the role of the Digital Mailbox as a simple channel of communication between elders and family members has been presented. But the design of the system in fact makes it possible to automate many communication functions. For example, using a website associated with the service, a family member can select a category of

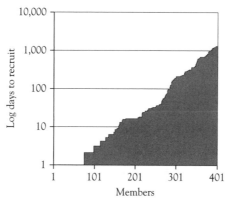

Figure 13.1   Viral Recruiting

message, such as a joke of the day, and ask that a message in this category be sent to the elder each day. The system then sends these messages automatically.

Services Architecture

The potential of the system under review stems from the architecture of the system. The architecture is similar to that of OnStar, the popular program that offers a wide range of services to people in their cars. Like OnStar, the CaringFamily system is built around a database that stores information needed by the services. Software components in the system do not have to communicate directly with one another, but they can communicate only with the database, greatly simplifying software development and allowing new services to be added with minimal, if any, impact on older services.

Basic features built into the infrastructure of the platform include the following.

- Web access to selected database content. For example, messages to and from the elder can be seen by remote family members, if the system is configured to permit this.
- Flexible, role-based permissions that restrict access to data and protect privacy. For example, it is easy to change who is entitled to have Web access to stored messages.

- Content delivery system. Messages to the elder can be formatted into a daily delivery, including layout with pictures. E-mails to other participants can be automatically composed and sent.
- Schedule- and event-driven automation. It is easy to specify that a certain message should be delivered to the elder at a future time. It is also easy to have a message sent to a family member or other participant based on something happening, or not happening, such as a certain number of messages being sent to the elder. This makes it possible to monitor activity in the system conveniently.
- Customizable *dashboards* for viewing system data. Key statistics about system usage can be defined and displayed.

TECHNOLOGY SUPPORT FOR COMMUNICATION

Let us describe just one of these features: the member e-mail delivery system that supports a wide array of communications, such as member introduction to the system, training (e.g., of the multitude of family website features), recruiting (i.e., encouraging the recruiting of new family members), scheduled notifications that members have set to remind them to send their parent a message, and more. The following are the major attributes of this feature:

- *Template driven.* Candidate e-mails are created using a template system with a set of personalization tags. As shown in Figure 13.2, these tags pull information from the collection of system databases to personalize messages to the elder and family.
- Prompting message *sequences*. Message templates can be collected into delivery sequences to achieve various longer-term goals. Thus, there are sequences of messages available to train family members in the capabilities available, to remind family members of holidays or family events, and to encourage expanding of the caregroup membership. To make it easier to create and manage these sequences, the system provides a special editor for this task, as shown in Figure 13.3.

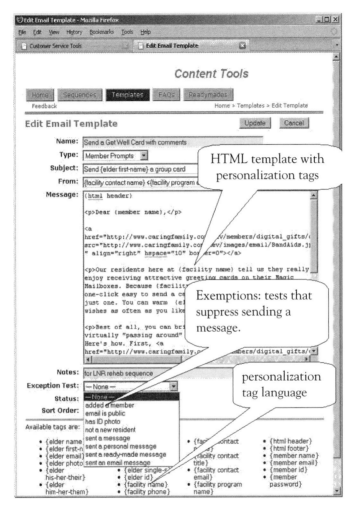

Figure: 13.2   A screen image of the member e-mail template editor. Several things to note: (1) the template language is HTML augmented with personalization and branding tags, (2) the exception tests are database queries used to suppress the sending of the e-mail under specific conditions (e.g., not reminding the member to add an ID photo to their profile if they have already done so, (3) a list of the available personalization and branding tags to facilitate cut and paste.

- *Scheduling.* Messages and message sequences can be initiated upon the registration of a new member, some on calendar events (e.g., holidays, birthdays, facility events), or by customer service personnel.

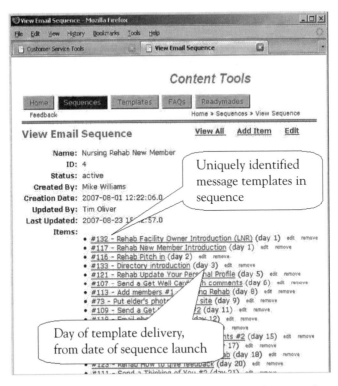

Figure 13.3 A screen image of the member e-mail sequence editor. Two things to note: (1) each item refers to an existing e-mail template; (2) each template identifies a day of delivery, relative to the start day for the sequence.

- Logical *triggering* and *exceptions*. Message templates can be made sensitive to member or caregroup state or activity. For example, there is no need to encourage sending a birthday message if one has already been sent.
- There are a wide array of editors and logs for creating, previewing, managing, and tracking member e-mail templates.

SYSTEM EVOLUTION

A key point about the architecture of the system is that it allows new services to be added and old ones better tuned to user needs, as experience with the system grows. Indeed, the service has developed in stages in just this way.

The original, basic system is shown in Figure 13.4. Family and friends could send messages to the elder and access messages stored in the database via a Web interface. The database also included a variety of control information, used in routing messages to the correct recipients and in determining who is authorized to access information in the system and to send messages to the elder. (Some of this information acted as a so-called *whitelist* for blocking unwanted messages—only messages from authorized users are sent to the elder.)

Once the system shown in Figure 13.4 was in place, a wide range of services were added. Because new services can use the facilities of the database, it is relatively easy to innovate.

Figure 13.5 shows some of the features that have been added to the basic system. Camera-phone access was added to allow users to send pictures taken with a phone camera to the elder. A program was created that can be installed on a cell phone and allows a picture to be taken and sent to a predefined e-mail address with a few clicks. E-mail processing was then modified to handle these e-mails automatically.

An example of an automated component is the *Active Reminder* feature that allows a user to receive reminders, prompting him or her to send a message on a planned schedule. A second example is a newsletter

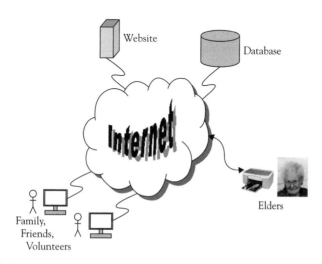

Figure 13.4 The basic system

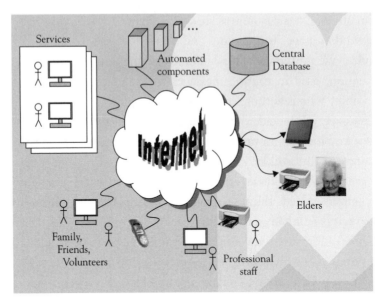

Figure 13.5   Features of a System

generator that automatically creates a summary of recent message traffic, including thumbnails of pictures included in the messages, and sends it to family members.

An example of a service that is not fully automated is wellness director monitoring. This optional feature allows an authorized person in a care facility to get a visual summary of system usage. If usage falls off, this person can see if a problem has developed. In one such case, a usage drop indicated a developing vision problem for the elder.

The fact that services need not be fully automated is important for the evolution of the system. A potentially useful service can be implemented in pilot form using human intervention. If the service is a success, and if automation proves possible, automation can be added later. The newsletter generator was piloted in this way before being fully automated.

Figure 13.5 shows another addition—another mailbox for the use of professional staff in a care facility. Some staff use computers as a core working tool, many use computers infrequently, and some almost not at all. By adding a mailbox for staff use we can support participation by staff who are not computer users. We have found that paper delivered via the staff mailbox can drive staff training and prompting and supply useful tools for their daily work.

AN ADAPTATION FOR SENIOR HOUSING

The Card Display Kiosk, shown in Figure 13.6, is another example of a service component that points to the broad diversity of tools that can be deployed to enhance a service program. A rack of attractive cards and an associated shared mailbox is presented in a public space (e.g., the activities room, the lobby, the physical therapy room). Residents are encouraged to send a card (e.g., holidays, thinking of you, family visit) to their families. Such missives delivered to family via e-mail can be one of the

Figure 13.6   Kiosk card rack and sample card and reply stationery

most effective encouragements to family member communications back to the elder.

The card display kiosk can play an important role in supporting facility activities. In particular, we have found Card Parties an effective tool for stimulating communications from residents as well as for the initial *recruiting* of families into the network.

This kiosk, as a service, is more complicated than one might think at first blush. To the user it looks easy: Take a card, add a FROM sticker, write a note, send. To the developer-operator, multiple issues and opportunities arise. For example, how does one replenish cards and keep them *fresh* in a cost-effective manner? How can autorouting be preserved with shared mailbox devices? The uses of the Kiosk are also more complicated than one might think at first. The Kiosk provides staff with:

- a ready activity to engage any participating resident,
- a basis for family visit cards (where staff take a picture of Grandma's visitors with an instant camera and encourage her to send a memento to her entire social network),
- a basis for creating a unique social event around each holiday (i.e., Card Parties described previously), and
- a mechanism for amplifying any current facility event (e.g., just take an instant photo of granny at the visit by Christmas carolers, apply it to the family visit card, and send).

HOW A SERVICE IS ADDED

The Holiday Cards service illustrates how the basic system has been extended.

Holiday cards have:
- collections of topic-specific cards for occasions like Passover, Halloween, Thanksgiving, or Christmas
- associated e-mail prompting sequences (to prompt sending and to conduct training for new family members)
- associated content-management tools for the cards and the e-mail prompts (the e-mail templating and sequencing tools are briefly described in a previous section)

- a database revision identifying a specific date of a holiday (used to launch e-mails; e.g., some 7 days before, some just 4 days before, some both; also used to post and remove card sets to the family website)
- special family website interface adaptations to make the cards usable in that environment (i.e., e-card sending tools and associated website FAQs)

The development process began with a simple card-content creation and management tool and an appropriate family website–user interface. E-mail prompting began as a task done by hand by our customer service personnel and has been refined and partially automated over time. The content tools were also expanded, refined, and generalized over time (e.g., adding some of the features shown in Figure 13.2—template tags that allow prompting messages to be personalized—and an exception process that suppresses a prompt if a card has already been sent).

Some coding was required to add this service. Specifically, the exception processing specific to holiday cards took about 40 person hours, and modification to the scheduler to handle holiday card delivery took about 40 more person hours.

A LARGE ARRAY OF COMPONENT SERVICES

There are currently over 40 distinct services available on the system. Besides the examples mentioned, these include: a variety of member card services (e.g., holiday, birthdays, thinking of you, guided journals, and more; each of these have distinctive e-mail prompting regimes), member website training, recruiting and awareness prompt sequences, bedside journal, and an assisted-sending card kiosk—a mailbox set up in a common area in a care facility so that staff can help residents send messages. There are also specialized research services in development such as online member consenting and survey prompting sequences.

Selected services can be packaged into Facility Programs, with custom documentation and content. The specific compositions are determined by particular facility and resident situations. Specific programs under development are: (a) Nursing Rehab, (b) Nursing Long-Term Care,

(c) Community Forum, (d) Assisted Living, and (e) Home Health Care. In the case of Skilled Nursing Facility rehab units, for example, the typical 30-day stay, specialized rehabilitation services, and heightened family concerns call for a program with special staff-to-family reporting tools, accelerated family training and prompting, and elimination of many of the long-term elements used in the other programs.

Services can be added to support emerging best practices in care, using technology both to promote these practices and to reduce the cost of providing them. These extensions support three-way communication, involving the care facility staff as well as the elder and family members, as shown in Figure 13.7.

Family Involvement in Care (FIC) is an example of an emerging care practice (Maas et al., 2004). As developed by Maas and colleagues, FIC involves face-to-face interactions between family members and staff to define staff and family roles and negotiate mutual expectations. For example, the electronic communication system described in this chapter could be augmented with message templates to help family and staff carry out a similar process online, in a way that can include family members who live at a distance.

Partners in Caregiving (PIC) (Pillemer et al., 2003) is another emerging practice involving face-to-face interaction between family and staff. Participants in PIC, as currently managed, do role-playing to enhance their understanding of effective and ineffective communication about care of the elder. By using the electronic communication system to provide information about effective communication in elder care, PIC could

Figure 13.7   Communications within the context of a facility

be extended to support geographically scattered families for whom face-to-face interaction with staff is difficult.

Family Stories Workshops (Hepburn et al., 1997) is an emerging practice that enhances staff knowledge of residents. Often staff have little idea *who* the residents in their care *are* because they have limited access to information about residents' past personal and professional activities, their family connections, and the like. Experiments are under way in which information about elders is collected and shared online. By including staff in the process of developing this information, staff can learn more about residents in their care. A variant of this program are the legacy activities (Allen, Hilgeman, Ege, Shuster, & Burgio, 2008) in which elders work with family members to create an enduring family artifact.

The Active Reminder extension mentioned earlier can be broadened to promote better communication between staff and family members. Messages automatically delivered by the system can remind staff when a status update on the elder would be timely and provide a template to help the staff member create an appropriate update message. The same flexible platform for communication can help build communication for and with elder in other ways, as well. For example, pen pal interactions could be scaffolded, as could interactions between an elder or a group of elders and a group of school children in an Adopt a Classroom activity. Connections with hobby clubs or community and church groups could also be promoted. Interactions between family counselors, or other care practitioners, and elders and their families could also be promoted.

OPPORTUNITIES FOR RESEARCH

The ability to track family communication may open up new opportunities for research. Data on message frequency and volume can be collected, and a basic communication matrix, showing who is sending and receiving messages to and from whom and how often, can be generated automatically. Responses to prompting messages, like Active Reminders, can also be tracked automatically. As already mentioned, changes in communication patterns can easily be detected. Examining message content could reveal more subtle phenomena. The fact that operations are online can increase the geographic reach of research studies at reasonable cost.

By adding other assessments, such as questionnaires, the impact of communication on affect and attitudes of elders, family members, and staff can be measured. For example, in a planned study of the impact of the Family Stories activity outlined earlier, the staff knowledge scale developed by Kane and colleagues (1997) and a staff-resident cohesion scale (Lemke & Moos, 1987; Timko & Moos, 1990) will be administered using the CaringFamily infrastructure.

Supporting this kind of instrument is fairly easy, given the e-mail facilities described earlier. Message templates are created that present a form for respondents to fill out and return, either via e-mail (for participants with e-mail access) or via Digital Mailbox. The scheduling features then can be used to determine when the forms will be sent. Triggering features can be used to prompt participants automatically if a response is not received within a planned interval.

As this example illustrates, this emerging technology offers substantial benefits to researchers:

- The technology allows communication among family, care staff, and elders to be efficiently captured and analyzed.
- Because of the use of electronic communication, the logistics of working with today's geographically dispersed families are simplified.
- Because of the features of the mailbox, users, whether elders or care staff, need not be computer users, even though electronic communication is supported.
- Automated features, including monitoring and preprogrammed communication, can increase adherence to research protocols.
- Online consenting and data collection, including surveys, allow very large studies to be conducted economically.
- The database-centered service architecture makes it relatively easy to add new functionality as needed by emerging research.

These benefits can help the research community address a wide range of questions about communication and the status of elders, whose importance increases as the representation of elders in our society grows, and as patterns of living and care for elders evolve.

IMPLICATIONS FOR CLINICIANS

As the transition is made from research trials to widespread deployment, clinicians can expect to see the communication technology described here becoming a practical possibility for the elders with whom they work. As mentioned earlier, a more limited mailbox service is already commercially available to individuals. Installations in care facilities are in the trial stage at the time of writing. Clinicians can think about the benefits the technology can bring and consider how the technology can be shaped to make it more useful.

REFERENCES

Allen, R. S., Hilgeman, M. M., Ege, M. A., Shuster, J. L., Jr, & Burgio L. D. (2008). Legacy activities as interventions approaching the end of life. *Journal of Palliative Medicine, 11*, 1029–1038.

Fratiglioni, L., Paillard-Borg, S., & Winblad, B. (2004). An active and socially integrated lifestyle in late life might protect against dementia. *Lancet Neurology, 3*, 343–353.

Glass, T. A., de Leon, C. M., Marottoli, R. A., & Berkman, L. F. (1999). Population based study of social and productive activities as predictors of survival among elderly Americans. *British Medical Journal, 319*, 478–483.

Hepburn, K. W., Caron, W., Luptak, M., Ostwald, S., Grant, L., & Keenan, J. M. (1997). The Families Stories Workshop: Stories for those who cannot remember. *Gerontologist, 37*, 827–832.

Kane, R. A., Caplan, A. L., Urv-Wong, E. K., Freeman, I. C., Aroskar, M. A., & Finch, M. (1997). Everyday matters in the lives of nursing home residents: Wish for and perception of choice and control. *Journal of the American Geriatrics Society, 45*, 1086–1093.

Lemke, S., & Moos, R. H. (1987). Measuring the social climate of congregate residents for older people: The Sheltered Care Environment Scale. *Psychology and Aging, 2*, 20–29.

Lewis, C. (2007). Simplicity in cognitive assistive technology: A framework and agenda for research. *Universal Access in the Information Society, 5*, 351–361.

Maas, M. L., Reed, D., Park, M., Specht, J. P., Schutte D., Kelley, L. S., et al. (2004). Outcomes of family involvement in care intervention for caregivers of individuals with dementia. *Nursing Research, 53*, 76–86.

Pew Internet and American Life Project. (2007). *Latest trends.* Accessed March 20, 2007. http://www.pewinternet.org/trends.asp.

Pillemer, K., Suitor, J. J., Henderson, C. R., Meador, R., Schultz, L., Robison, J., & Hegeman, C. (2003). A cooperative communication intervention for nursing home staff and family members of residents. *Gerontologist, 43* (Special Issue II), 96–106.

Rosenthal, C. J. (1985). Kinkeeping in the familial division of labor. *Journal of Marriage and the Family, 47*, 965–974,

Timko, C., & Moos, R. H. (1990). Determinants of interpersonal support and self-direction in group research residential facilities. *Journal of Gerontology: Social Sciences, 45*, S184–S192.

Verghese, J., Lipton, R. B., Katz, M. J., Hall, C. B., Derby, C. A., Kuslansky, G. et al. (2003). Leisure activities and the risk of dementia in the elderly. *New England Journal of Medicine, 384*, 2508–2516.

CHAPTER

14

⇒⊷⇐

Personal Health Records for Older Adults with Chronic Conditions and Their Informal Caregivers

Elaine A. Blechman

More effective treatments for infectious and acute illnesses dramatically increased Americans' life expectancy rates in the twentieth century while shifting the leading causes of death to chronic and degenerative illnesses (Centers for Disease Control and Prevention, 2003). Over age 65, heart disease (32%), cancer (22%), and stroke (8%) account for 62% of all deaths (Centers for Disease Control and Prevention, 2006). About 80% of Americans older than 65 have one chronic condition; 50% have two (Centers for Disease Control and Prevention & Merck Foundation, 2007).

Compared to other economically developed countries, the United States spends disproportionately more on health-care services and less on health information technology (Anderson, Frogner, Johns, & Reinhardt, 2006). Compared to their counterparts in other developed countries, older Americans with chronic conditions experience more safety risks, less satisfactory long-term care, and less efficient care coordination

(Anderson & Knickman, 2001; Kane & West, 2005; Schoen et al., 2005). Public health-care spending would be even higher were it not for the *shadow workforce* of unpaid family caregivers who as case managers, medical record keepers, paramedics, and patient advocates protect aging relatives from dangerous gaps in the health-care delivery system (Bookman & Harrington, 2007).

Emerging health information technology could help remedy the crisis of U.S. health care and of family caregivers (Aaron, 2007; Anderson et al., 2006) but not with its conventional, provider-centered architecture. Conventional health information technology, described in the first half of this chapter, involves electronic health record systems (EHRs) for medical providers and personal health records for patients that are tethered to these EHRs (tethered PHRs). Tethered PHRs, also called patient portals, give consumers fragmentary views of the electronic records that doctors maintain in their EHRs. Provider-centered EHRs and tethered PHRs are best-suited for primary-care providers in private practice and their relatively healthy patients who rarely require health or human services from other providers. With conventional EHRs, primary-care providers can maintain comprehensive records for their healthy and self-sufficient patients.

Only 10% of all U.S. medical providers and less than 1% of safety-net providers are equipped with conventional EHRs (Jha et al., 2006). Safety-net providers who accept Medicare and Medicaid payments deliver the bulk of formal care to older Americans. Conventional EHRs and tethered PHRs are of little use to informal family caregivers (acting as case managers, record keepers, paramedics, and patient advocates) in their frequent communications with EHR-deprived safety-net providers.

The second half of the chapter introduces technology for a consumer-centered, interoperable, personal health record platform. A secure, standards-based Internet computing platform supports any number of platform PHRs. Platform PHRs enable confidential health-information exchange among older consumers and their authorized family caregivers, EHR-equipped and EHR-deprived providers. With Platform PHR tools, family caregivers can automatically and continuously consolidate bits of consumer information that are stored in EHRs, tethered PHRs, and health data banks. And, with platform PHR tools, family caregivers can grant and audit user access privileges and enforce consent directives whether users connect via the platform or via external EHRs or health data banks. Finally, with platform PHR tools, family caregivers can partner with many providers to design, implement, coordinate, monitor, and refine long-term care plans. In an illustrative scenario, a woman uses a platform PHR to coordinate care for her 80-year-old husband who has memory loss, high blood pressure, and a history of prostate cancer and strokes.

FAMILY CAREGIVERS

Health care for older survivors of chronic conditions has increasingly shifted from institutional to home settings and from paid health-care providers to unpaid family caregivers (Allen & Ciambrone, 2003; Docherty et al., 2008). In 1998, 23% of surveyed Americans provided unpaid homecare to ill, disabled, or elderly persons (Donelan et al., 2002). Medicaid, which insures low-income and disabled older Americans, pays for home health care except when delivered by relatives (Kaiser Family Foundation, 2007b). Medicare, which insures retired American workers ages 65 and older, covers few home health-care costs (Kaiser Family Foundation, 2007a). This means that older survivors whose incomes are above the poverty line generally depend on family caregivers for long-term home care.

Reliance on unpaid family caregivers saved state and federal governments an estimated $196 billion in 1997 (Arno, Levine, & Memmott, 1999). Family caregivers are estimated to reduce annual government expenditures by about $25,381 for each cognitively impaired person (Zhu et al., 2006) and $18,385 for each elderly male veteran (Moore, Zhu, & Clipp, 2001). Home-based care by family caregivers has been estimated to be significantly less costly than institutional care even when caregiver time is valued at replacement wages (Anderson, Ni Mhurchu, Brown, & Carter, 2002; Chappell, Havens, Hollander, Miller, & McWilliam, 2004). More than 50% of family caregivers are employed full time. Few have access to health-care professionals for guidance in their caregiving efforts or for personal stress reduction (Navaie-Waliser et al., 2001). Many succumb to stress-induced illnesses, causing institutionalization of their relatives (Wolff & Kasper, 2006).

Family caregivers obviously substitute for paid home health-care workers—assisting with activities of daily living, administering medications, and monitoring health status (Donelan et al., 2002; Port, 2006). Family caregivers are a less obvious shadow workforce, supplying unpaid disease-management services including record keeping, case management, multidisciplinary care coordination, and patient advocacy that are otherwise unavailable to chronic condition survivors (Bookman & Harrington 2007; Faxon et al., 2004; Krumholz et al., 2006). Family caregivers unquestionably want ongoing support for daily disease-management and care-coordination activities (Hewitt, Bamundo, Day, & Harvey, 2007; Russell, Thille, Hogg, & Lemelin, 2008).

Family caregivers are the biggest contributors to home care of older relatives. Yet technology that eases their daily disease-management and care-coordination efforts is unavailable. Health care providers contribute the least time to care of older individuals. Yet they have access to electronic health record systems (EHRs) with embedded disease-management tools (Henry, Douglas, Galzagorry, Lahey, & Holzemer, 1998; O'Connor et al., 2005; Schnipper et al., 2008).

Electronic Health Records (EHRs)

Electronic health record systems (EHRs; also called electronic medical records or EMRs) were recommended as a solution for the U.S. health-care crisis in a 1991 Institute of Medicine report (Dick & Steen, 1991). In 2003, Nebeker and colleagues advocated EHRs as a solution for care of older survivors of chronic conditions. EHRs have, however, not improved geriatric care due to the continued fragmentation of patient information. EHRs have, in fact, promoted inaccessible patient information, fragments of which are now scattered in both paper records and incompatibly formatted electronic records. Fragmented record keeping contributes to medical mistakes, excessive costs, and ineffective long-term care for chronic conditions (Asch et al., 2006; California HealthCare Foundation, 2007; Kohn, Corrigan, & Donaldson, 2000).

To counteract fragmented record keeping, President Bush mandated in 2004 a nationwide health information network of local health information exchanges connecting physician and hospital EHRs by 2014 (Brailer, 2005) so that a comprehensive patient record is available at the point of service (IOM, 2003). Local networks, as they become available, will connect providers equipped with EHRs. No one knows when all U.S. private-practice and safety-net providers will adopt EHRs and when all U.S. communities will supply the infrastructure for interoperability among all providers' EHRs (e.g., Berner, Detmer, & Simborg, 2005; Gans, Kralewski, Hammons, & Dowd, 2005).

Personal Health Records (PHRs)

What if consumers had secure, private, comprehensive personal health records (PHRs) that consolidated fragments of information scattered in providers' paper and electronic files and information available only to consumers such as advance directives? Health-care policy makers have described a variety of benefits that might result from consumer-centered PHRs, including better coordinated long-term care for chronic conditions (Liaw, Lawrence, & Rendell, 1996; Tang, Ash, Bates, Overhage, & Sands, 2006; Tang & Lansky, 2005). The idea of a consumer-centered PHR has taken various technological forms.

A transport PHR is a USB (or other media) device that allows consumers to enter, store, and share health information. In a likely transport-PHR scenario, a consumer connects a USB stick to a home computer, enters health history information into a software program on the USB stick, and wears the USB stick in case of emergency. The value of transport PHRs for disease-management and care-coordination is compromised by questionable accuracy of data (e.g., consumers often do not know what medications they are taking) and limited accessibility (e.g., a consumer must hand the USB stick to one provider at a time) (Wright & Sittig, 2007).

A tethered PHR is an Internet portal into a patient's record in a provider's EHR (Halamka, Mandl, & Tang, 2008). In a likely tethered-PHR scenario, a consumer logs on to her health maintenance organization's website, views results of recent diagnostic laboratory tests along with her doctor's recommendations, and queries her doctor about these recommendations. The value of tethered PHRs for disease-management and care-coordination is compromised by fragmented data (e.g., one older consumer with chronic conditions will have bits of information scattered in many tethered PHRs) and by incomplete data (e.g., the consumer will not be able to exchange information with EHR-deprived providers).

A commercial health data bank (e.g., Microsoft Health Vault™ and Google Health™) is an Internet data repository that allows consumers to deposit information and authorize providers and payers to withdraw this information. Health data banks enable consumers to search for information related to worrisome health complaints including diagnosis, treatment, and qualified care providers. In a likely health data bank scenario, a family caregiver searches the Internet for a local provider who specializes in prostate cancer, takes Medicare patients, and communicates with patients via the health data bank. She uses her health data bank account to enter information about her husband's health history and to make this information available to the provider before her husband's first visit with the provider. The value of health data banks for disease-management and care-coordination is compromised by the proliferation of these repositories and other methods of health information exchange among consumers and providers, escalating the fragmentation of consumers' health records. Consumers will soon find themselves exchanging information with some providers via Bank A, with others via Bank B, and with yet other providers via tethered PHRs.

A PHR PLATFORM

A PHR platform supports the health information exchange needs of consumers with chronic conditions, their family caregivers and their EHR-equipped and EHR-deprived, private-practice and safety-net providers. The patent-pending Smart Medical Home Health Information Exchange Platform™ (or the Smart Platform) is a secure, standards-based, Internet computing platform. The Smart Platform is the first commercial implementation of a PHR platform, with installations in varied safety-net test-beds. The Smart Platform was developed to improve on the conventional technology solutions available to consumers with chronic conditions and their family caregivers. No claims are made in this chapter that the Smart Platform is better than conventional technology. However, the Smart Platform offers the only technology basis for the example that follows.

Smart Platform architecture leverages nationwide health information exchange standards (Glaser et al., 2008) now being tested in prototype form (DHHS, 2008). The Smart Platform, however, reverses the usual health-information exchange paradigm putting consumers (and their family caregivers) at the center of the connectivity process rather than providers.

The Smart Platform supplies so-called cloud computing services to users who access the platform from any Web-connected device (including smartphones) without downloaded software. The Platform's relational databases offer Smart PHRs™ for consumers with chronic conditions. The basic record in the Platform's relational database tables is a consumer's Smart PHR. Smart PHRs give consumers and consumer-authorized family caregivers tools for managing access privileges of users who connect directly to the Platform or indirectly via external EHRs, health-information exchange networks or health data banks.

Unlike tethered PHRs, which give consumers access to only one EHR, Smart PHR tools allow consumers to start and stop simultaneous associations with many external EHRs and other information systems. Consumer-authorized users, who connect to the Platform via external EHRs, could inadvertently expose consumer information to users unauthorized by the consumer. Therefore, unique Smart Platform technology enforces consumer consent directives while consumer-authorized users are connected to Platform accounts and when users return to their native external information systems.

Smart Platform capabilities for enforcing consumer-consent directives are intended to create trust, enabling consumers, family caregivers, and providers to confidently share information and effectively coordinate care.

This section describes how a family caregiver might use the Smart PHR to coordinate care. A so-called Internet computing cloud, in Figure 14.1, surrounds a family caregiver, Mrs. Smith, and the people involved in her husband's care. In the cloud's center, Mrs. Smith connects to the Smart Platform and to her husband's PHR via a smartphone (a mobile phone with PC-like functionality); she could also employ other Web-connected devices. On the cloud's edges, authorized users connect to the Platform directly (e.g., friends and family at location J) and indirectly via external systems (e.g., diagnostic and imaging labs at location K). Consistent with their privileges, users may invoke various connectivity options.

The paths, in Figure 14.1, radiating from Mr. Smith's Smart PHR to authorized users on the cloud's edge, indicate user-specific, consumer-authorized and platform-enforced health information exchange. Take the

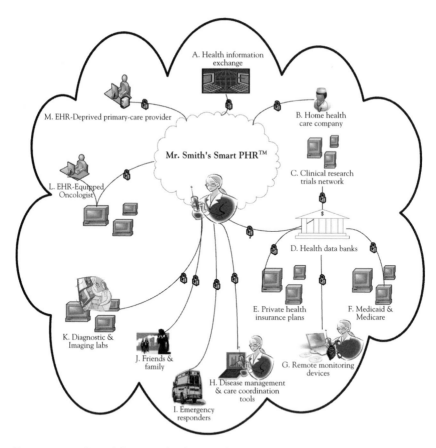

Figure 14.1 Consolidation and Selective Sharing of Consumer Health Information via a PHR Platform

EHR-equipped oncologist at location L. Mrs. Smith has authorized automated exchange of information between Mr. Smith's PHR and the oncologist's EHR in a standardized continuity of care document format. The oncologist can use his EHR to send Mr. Smith's lab results to his PHR with an alert about the update for Mrs. Smith. Mrs. Smith can enter information about a recent allergic reaction in Mr. Smith's PHR and send it to the oncologist's EHR with an alert about the update for the oncologist. Or, consider the EHR-deprived primary-care provider at location M. Before examining Mr. Smith, the primary-care provider can connect directly to Mr. Smith's PHR and view updated lab results (identified as entered by the oncologist) and allergies (identified as updated by Mrs. Smith).

With the Smart PHR, Mrs. Smith can consolidate information scattered in the records of all authorized users. She can then selectively exchange information with one of these users via a health data bank. For example, a private health insurance payer may request claims-related information via health data bank A. Mrs. Smith can use the platform PHR to deposit only the information that the payer requests, without exposing other information in Mr. Smith's PHR.

What follows is a step-by-step scenario illustrated by screen shots of how our hypothetical Mrs. Smith employs her husband's Smart PHR over the course of one day. This is one of many possible scenarios in which family caregivers and/or their delegates (e.g., home health-care providers, geriatric case managers, nurse practitioners) employ such a PHR to facilitate record keeping, disease management, and care coordination.

The local Area Agency on Aging has given Mr. Smith a modestly priced lifetime subscription to a Smart PHR and appointed Mrs. Smith as account administrator with her husband's consent. During a group-training session, Mr. and Mrs. Smith ask about security and privacy and learn about the Platform's software-as-services model and its HIPAA security and privacy compliance enforcement. Data are encrypted during transmission (so that a successful hacker would see garbled, meaningless data) and the system's security is continuously monitored. Without downloading any software, Mrs. Smith accesses the PHR from her home computer, from her daughter Lorraine's laptop, from her cell phone, and from a Web browser-equipped computer at her local library.

During training, Mrs. Smith establishes a convenient daily routine, accessing the PHR for ordinary planning once a day after breakfast from her home computer and accessing it periodically during the day from her cell phone to record observations of disease symptoms and check on milestones.

> ***Step 1.*** After breakfast today, Mrs. Smith logs on from her home computer and lands on her user home page (Figure 14.2). From there, Mrs. Smith (A) checks for upcoming events, (B) schedules appointments with authorized users, (C) securely exchanges messages with them, (D) and then navigates to her husband's PHR.
>
> ***Step 2.*** Mrs. Smith lands on the dashboard of Mr. Smith's Smart PHR (Figure 14.3). From there she could navigate to his (A) calendar, (B) vital information page, (C) care plans, or (D) messages.

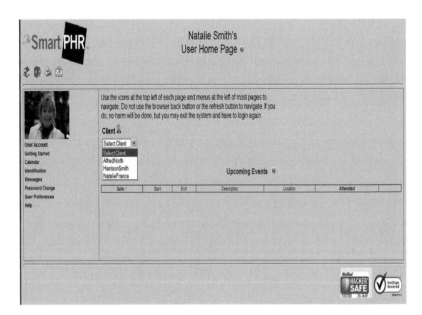

Figure 14.2   Mrs. Smith's User Home Page

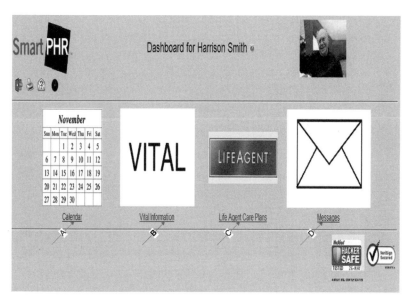

Figure 14.3   The Dashboard of Mr. Smith's PHR

Step 3. On the dashboard of her husband's PHR, Mrs. Smith selects the vital information page and the allergy list (Figure 14.4, A). She decides to add an entry about what may be a new allergy (B). She selects "mold" from the drop-down allergy list (A) and makes a text entry to describe her observations (B). She could attach to the allergy entry a document in any electronic format (C) (see Figure 14.5).

Step 4. Information in Mr. Smith's Smart PHR is accessible to users that Mrs. Smith authorizes, consistent with the privileges she grants them. All data in the PHR are permanent once entered, subject to archiving and removal from view by Mrs. Smith (acting as account administrator), but not to deletion. All data entries are permanently tagged with information such as the user who made the entry and the date and time of entry. Mrs. Smith has various account-administration tools available to her. On the manage-privileges page (Figure 14.6), Mrs. Smith decides to give her daughter Lorraine (A) *read*

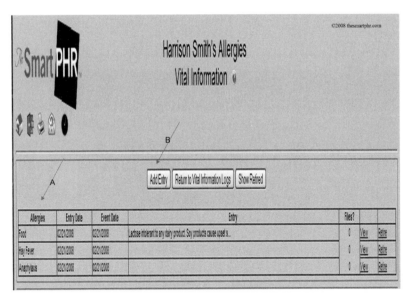

Figure 14.4   Allergy List in Mr. Smith's Vital Information

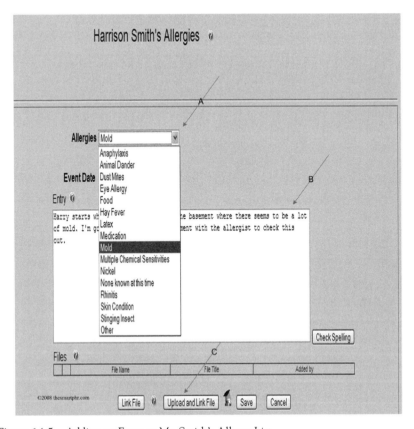

Figure 14.5   Adding an Entry to Mr. Smith's Allergy List

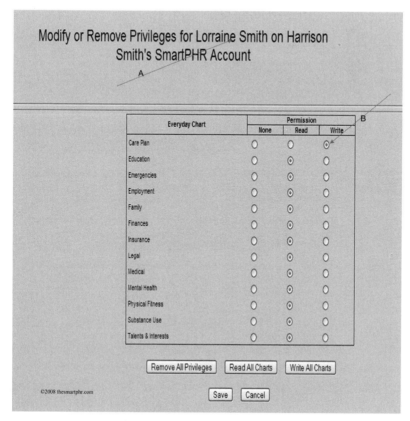

Figure 14.6   Granting User Privileges on Mr. Smith's PHR

privileges for all charts in Mr. Smith's PHR and (B) *write* privileges for his care plan because Lorraine will be taking charge of her father's care next weekend so that Mrs. Smith can travel to visit a childhood friend. Mrs. Smith has previously used the manage-privileges page to grant specific privileges to each individual health-care provider involved in Mr. Smith's care.

Step 5. Mrs. Smith wants to follow through on the possible mold allergy, concerned that neglect of this allergy may weaken Mr. Smith's immune system. She navigates to the vital information page (Figure 14.7), where she stores signed copies of health-care providers' consent forms (A) and their contact

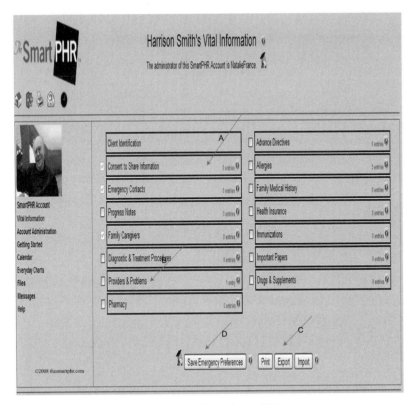

Figure 14.7   Exchanging Information with Authorized Users

information and areas of expertise (B). She finds information about an allergist who treated Mr. Smith a few years before and uses the links to reputable health information sites to find out more about mold allergies. She goes to the message page and sends a secure message to the allergist, asking for an appointment and querying him about the information she has located.

Step 6. On the vital information page, Mrs. Smith exports a copy of Mr. Smith's medical summary (which is automatically updated to include the recent allergy entry) to a USB stick that fits into Mr. Smith's medical ID bracelet. She could also print the medical summary, export it to providers' interoperable electronic health record (EHR), or transport it to a new health insurance plan or health maintenance organization (Figure 14.7, C). Source tags on entries in the medical summary inform providers that Mrs. Smith, rather than an allergist, has suggested a possible mold allergy. Updated vital information, including the possible mold allergy entry, is automatically available online from Mr. Smith's cell phone and on a printed wallet card (D). After completion of allergy tests, there will be a variety of options for the allergist to confirm the mold allergy and to update Mr. Smith's allergy list so that it includes authenticated detailed information. These options include updating of the Smart PHR allergy list via automated messages from the allergist's EHR and from the testing laboratory, and via a manual upload of the allergist's diagnostic report.

Step **7.** As she does every morning, Mrs. Smith navigates from the Smart PHR dashboard to the Life Agent™, a care-coordination tool (Figure 14.8). Each time an authorized user updates information in the Life Agent, an older version is archived (available for retrieval) and the new version is displayed. The Life Agent is shown here in a highly condensed format (A). Some sections are autopopulated from vital information pages, such as background (B), health insurance, and medical summary information (C). Some sections are designed for direct data entry, graphic display, and access from cell phones such as condition-specific treatment plans (D), symptom and side-effect observations (E), and intervention and critical incident milestones (F).

Mrs. Smith has granted Life Agent view and/or update privileges to active members of Mr. Smith's health-care team. They may check the Life Agent from their cell phones or laptops when they receive an emergency call from Mrs. Smith or during a scheduled encounter with Mr. Smith. They may receive alerts, triggered by out-of-bounds observation or milestone values, on their Internet-connected wireless devices. They may, particularly if they are EHR-deprived,

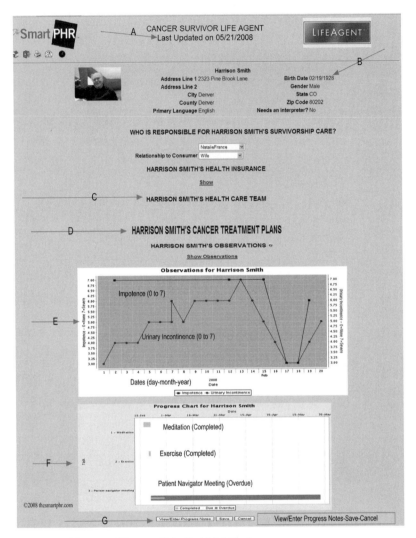

Figure 14.8   View at a Glance of Mr. Smith's Life Agent

enter progress notes and update files related to Mr. Smith
(G). They may share such entries with all authorized users or
they may limit access to authorized users in their own practice or agency.

Step 8. An article in today's paper about new treatments for
prostate cancer encourages Mrs. Smith to take a quick look at
Mr. Smith's cancer treatment plan (Figure 14.9). Mr. Smith

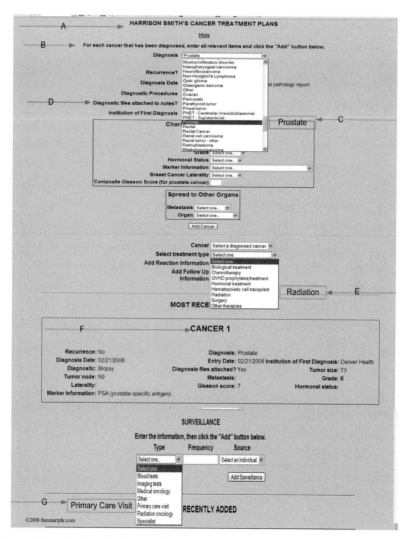

Figure 14.9 Mr. Smith's Cancer Treatment Plans

was diagnosed last year with prostate cancer and is involved in an oncologist-prescribed course of watchful waiting, diet, and herbal supplements. On a recent follow-up visit to the oncologist, the oncologist's nurse educator filled in the Life Agent cancer treatment plan template. The template allows entry of plans for concurrent treatment of multiple cancers and for archiving and retrieval of past plans (A). The template provides decision support to oncology clinicians. It prompts entry of standard data elements and offers comprehensive code sets in diagnosis (B), surveillance (D), treatment type (E), and other dropdowns. And the template allows for uploading of small electronic files (e.g., diagnostic summaries) and for insertion of links pointing to large or specially constructed files (e.g., radiology images). Mr. Smith's primary-care physician has user privileges that allow him to view Mr. Smith's current cancer-treatment plan, to be notified about changes in the plan, and to query the oncologist about these changes in secure messages that are copied to Mrs. Smith. If a change in health-plan coverage requires a shift to another oncologist or primary-care physician, the treatment plan and a history of communication about the plan will be readily available to new health-care providers.

Step **9.** Accessing the observations tool in the Life Agent from her cell phone (Figure 14.10, A), Mrs. Smith enters information about symptoms and side effects (including some specifically identified by Mr. Smith's oncologist) that she has observed (B). The observations graph immediately displays each observation (e.g., urinary incontinence on February 15) and shows trends over time in multiple observations (C). Using the milestones tool in the Life Agent (E), Mrs. Smith enters information about providers' recommendations and other events that may impact symptoms and side effects (F). She could use the milestones tool to delegate responsibilities to authorized users and to automatically remind them about due dates (G, H). Completed milestones, shown as vertical bars in the observations graph, suggest the possible influence of milestones on symptoms and side effects. Introduction of an herbal supplement on February 14 (D) was followed by a brief decline in urinary incontinence and impotence and then by a reversion to previously high levels of these symptoms. This suggests to Mr. and Mrs. Smith and to the oncologist that the herbal supplement is not doing much good.

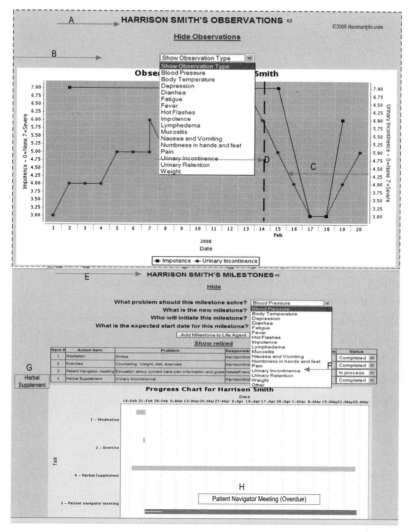

Figure 14.10   Symptoms, Side-Effects, and Milestones in Mr. Smith's Life Agent

CONCLUSIONS

Those who have been optimistic about information technology as a mechanism for health-care culture change may be wrong. Despite four decades of encouragement, about one in ten health-care providers have adopted interoperable, electronic health-record systems (Berner et al., 2005). Despite distribution of millions of tethered personal health records (PHRs) to Kaiser Permanente and Veterans Affairs health-plan members, two pilot studies suggest that the people who actually use their tethered PHRs are young, affluent, healthy, and presumably in little need of health information (Weingart, Rind, Tofias, & Sand, 2006).

On the other hand, optimists may be wrong only about the proper fit between end user and information technology that is needed to transform our health care culture. About one in four Americans has been or will be a family caregiver to frail relatives. Some family caregivers will make extraordinary sacrifices for decades to disabled children, parents, and partners. Some family caregivers are so devoted that they will do anything, including using unfamiliar technology, if there is a chance that it will help. Because family caregivers operate off the health-care system grid, their potential as health information technology end users has been overlooked. The Smart PHR is the result of a what-if thought experiment that may result in a new generation of platform PHRs. What if the family caregivers who are the hardest working, least recognized suppliers of health-care services got technology that supported their solitary disease-management and care-coordination efforts? My colleagues and I are just beginning to examine the clinical and culture change potential of platform PHR technology in the hands of survivors of chronic conditions and family caregivers.

REFERENCES

Aaron, H. J. (2007). Budget crisis, entitlement crisis, health care financing problem—which is it? *Health Affairs, 26*, 1622–1633.

Allen, S. M., & Ciambrone, D. (2003). Community care for people with disability: Blurring boundaries between formal and family caregivers. *Qualitative Health Research, 13*, 207–226.

Anderson, C., Ni Mhurchu, C., Brown, P. M., & Carter, K. (2002). Stroke rehabilitation services to accelerate hospital discharge and provide home-based care: An overview and cost analysis. *Pharmacoeconomics. 20*(8):537–552.

Anderson, G. F., Frogner, B. K., Johns, R. A., & Reinhardt, U. E. (2006). Health care spending and use of information technology in OECD countries. *Health Affairs, 25*, 819–831.

Anderson, G. F., & Knickman, J. R. (2001). Changing the chronic care system to meet people's needs. *Health Affairs, 20*(6), 146–160.

Arno, P. S., Levine, C., & Memmott, M. M. (1999). The economic value of family caregiving. *Health Affairs, 18*, 182–188.

Asch, S. M., Kerr, E. A., Keesey, J., Adams, J. L., Setodji, C. M., Malik, S., & McGlynn, E. A. (2006). Who is at greatest risk for receiving poor-quality health care? *New England Journal of Medicine, 354*, 1147–1156.

Berner, E. S., Detmer, D. E., & Simborg, D. (2005). Will the wave finally break? A brief view of the adoption of electronic medical records in the United States. *Journal of the American Medical Informatics Association, 12*, 3–7.

Bookman, A., & Harrington, M. (2007). Family caregivers: A shadow workforce in the geriatric health care system? *Journal of Health Politics, Policy, and Law, 32*, 1005–1041.

Brailer, D. J. (2005, January 19). Interoperability: The key to the future health care system. *Health Affairs Web Exclusive, W5-19-21*.

Bush, G. W. (2004, April 27). *Executive Order 13335: Incentives for the Use of Health Information Technology and Establishing the Position of the National Health Information Technology Coordinator*. Washington, DC: The White House.

California HealthCare Foundation. (2007). *Uncoordinated care: A survey of physician and patient experience*. Oakland, CA: Author.

Centers for Disease Control and Prevention. (2003). Public health and aging: Trends in aging—United States and nationwide. *Morbidity and Mortality Weekly Report, 52*(06), 101–106.

Centers for Disease Control and Prevention. (2006). Trends in Health and Aging. Accessed December 8, 2007 from http://www.cdc.gov/nchs/agingact.htm.

Centers for Disease Control and Prevention & the Merck Company Foundation. (2007). *The state of aging and health in America 2007*. Whitehouse Station, NJ: The Merck Company Foundation. Accessed December 12, 2007 from http://www.agingsociety.org/agingsociety/pdf/SAHA_2007.pdf.

Chappell, N. L., Havens, B., Hollander, M. J., Miller, J. A., & McWilliam, C. (2004). Comparative costs of home care and residential care. *The Gerontologist, 44*, 389–400.

DHHS. U.S. Department of Health and Human Services. (May 31, 2008). Summary of the NHIN Prototype Architecture Contracts. hhs.gov/healthit/healthnetwork/resources/summary_report_on_nhin_Prototype architectures.

Dick, R., & Steen, E. B. (Eds.). (1991). *The computer-based patient record. Institute of Medicine*. Washington, DC: National Academy Press.

Docherty, A., Owens, A., Asadi-Lari, M., Petchey, R., Williams, J., & Carter, Y. H. (2008). Knowledge and information needs of family caregivers in palliative care: A qualitative systematic review. *Palliative Medicine, 22,* 153–171.

Donelan, K., Hill, C. A., Hoffman, C., Scoles, K., Feldman, P. H., Levine, C., & Gould, D. (2002). Challenged to care: Family caregivers in a changing health system. *Health Affairs, 21,* 222–231.

Faxon, D. P., Schwamm, L. H., Pasternak, R. C., Peterson, E. D., McNeil, B. J., Bufalino, V., et al. (2004). Improving quality of care through disease management: Principles and recommendations from the American Heart Association's Expert Panel on Disease Management. *Circulation, 109,* 2651–2654.

Gans, D., Kralewski, J., Hammons, T., & Dowd, B. (2005). Medical groups' adoption of electronic health records and information systems. *Health Affairs, 24,* 1323–1333.

Glaser J., Henley, D. E., Downing, G., Brinner, K. M., & Personalized Health Care Workgroup of the American Health Information Community. (2008). Advancing personalized health care through health information technology: An update from the American Health Information Community's Personalized Health Care Workgroup. *Journal of the American Medical Informatics Association, 15,* 391–396.

Halamka, J., Mandl, K. D., & Tang, P. C. (2008). Early experiences with personal health records. *Journal of the American Medical Informatics Association, 15,* 1–7.

Henry, S. B., Douglas, K., Galzagorry, G., Lahey, A., & Holzemer, W. L. (1998). A template-based approach to support utilization of clinical practice guidelines within an electronic health record. *Journal of the American Medical Informatics Association, 5,* 237–244.

Hewitt, M. E., Bamundo, A., Day, R., & Harvey, C. (2007). Perspectives on post-treatment cancer care: Qualitative research with survivors, nurses, and physicians. *Journal of Clinical Oncology, 25,* 2270–2273.

IOM. Institute of Medicine. (2003). *Committee on data standards for patient safety. Key capabilities of an electronic health record system.* Washington, DC: National Academies Press.

Jha A. K., Ferris, T. G., Donelan, K., DesRoches, C., Shields, A., Rosenbaum, S., & Blumenthal, D. (2006). How common are electronic health records in the United States? A summary of the evidence. *Health Affairs, 25,* 496–507.

Kaiser Family Foundation. (2007a, December). *Medicaid and long-term care services and supports* (Publication No. 2186-05). Accessed January 13, 2008 from http://www.kff.org/medicaid/upload/2186_05.pdf.

Kaiser Family Foundation. (2007b, June). *Medicare spending and financing* (Publication No. 7305-02). Accessed January 13, 2008 from http://www.kff.org/medicare/upload/7305-02.pdf.

Kane, R., & West, J. (2005). *It shouldn't be this way: The failure of long-term care.* Nashville, TN: Vanderbilt.

Kohn, L. T., Corrigan, J. M., & Donaldson, M. S. (Eds.). (2000). *Committee on Quality of Health Care in America, Institute of Medicine. To err is human: Building a safer health system.* Washington, DC: National Academy Press.

Krumholz, H. M., Currie, P. M., Riegel, B., Phillips, C. O., Peterson, E. D., Smith, R., Yancy, C. W., Faxon, D. P., & American Heart Association Disease Management Taxonomy Writing Group. (2006). A taxonomy for disease management: A scientific statement from the American Heart Association Disease Management Taxonomy Writing Group. *Circulation, 26,* 1432–1445.

Liaw, T., Lawrence, M., & Rendell, J. (1996). The effect of a computer-generated patient-held medical record summary and/or a written personal health record on patients' attitudes, knowledge and behaviour concerning health promotion. *Family Practice, 13,* 289–293.

Moore, M. J., Zhu, C. W., & Clipp, E. C. (2001). Family costs of dementia care. Estimates from the National Longitudinal Caregiver Study. *The Journals of Gerontology Series B: Psychological Sciences and Social Sciences, 56,* S219–S228.

Navaie-Waliser, M., Feldman, P. H., Gould, D. A., Levine, C., Kuerbis, A. N., & Donelan, K. (2001). The experiences and challenges of family caregivers: Common themes and differences among whites, blacks, and hispanics. *Gerontologist, 41,* 733–741.

Nebeker, J. R., Hurdle, J. F., & Bair, B. D. (2003). Future history: Medical informatics in geriatrics. *Journal of Gerontology, 58,* 820–825.

O'Connor, P. J., Crain, A. L., Rush, W. A., Sperl-Hillen, J. M., Gutenkauf, J. J., & Duncan, J. E. (2005). Impact of an electronic medical record on diabetes quality of care. *Annals of Family Medicine, 3,* 300–306.

Port, C. L. (2006). Family caregiver involvement and illness detection among cognitively impaired nursing home residents. *The Journals of Gerontology Series A: Biological Sciences and Medical Sciences, 61,* 970–974.

Russell, G., Thille, P., Hogg, W., & Lemelin, J. (2008). Beyond fighting fires and chasing tails? Chronic illness care plans in Ontario, Canada. *Annals of Family Medicine, 6,* 146–153.

Schnipper, J. L., Linder, J. A., Palchuk, M. B., Einbinder, J. S., Li, Q., Postilnik, A., & Middleton, B. (2008). "Smart Forms" in an electronic medical record:

Documentation-based clinical decision support to improve disease management. *Journal of the American Medical Informatics Association, 15*, 513–523.

Schoen, C., Osborn, R., Huynh, P. T., Doty, M., Zapert, K., Peugh, J., & Davis, K. (2005). Taking the pulse of health care systems: Experiences of patients with health problems in six countries. *Health Affairs, W5*, 509–525.

Tang, P. C., Ash, J. S., Bates, D. W., Overhage, J. M., & Sands, D. Z. (2006). Personal health records: Definitions, benefits, and strategies for overcoming barriers to adoption. *Journal of the American Medical Informatics Association, 13*, 121–126.

Tang, P. C., & Lansky, D. (2005). The missing link: Bridging the patient-provider health information gap. *Health Affairs, 24*, 1290–1295.

Weingart, S. N., Rind, D., Tofias, Z., & Sands, D. Z. (2006). Who uses the patient Internet portal? The PatientSite experience. *Journal of the American Medical Informatics Association, 13*, 91–95.

Wolff, J. L., & Kasper, J. D. (2006). Caregivers of frail elders: Updating a national profile. *The Gerontologist, 46*, 344–356.

Wright, A., & Sittig, D. F. (2007). Encryption characteristics of two USB-based personal health record devices. *Journal of the American Medical Informatics Association, 14*, 397–399.

Zhu, C. W., Scarmeas, N., Torgan, R., Albert, M., Brandt, J., Blacker, D., Sano, M., & Stern, Y. (2006). Clinical characteristics and longitudinal changes of family cost of Alzheimer's disease in the community. *Journal of the American Geriatrics Society, 54*(10), 1596–1602.

Future Directions in Family Caregiving: Clinical, Policy, and Research Initiatives

STEVEN H. ZARIT

Family care of older persons has been a prominent issue for clinical practice, research, and policy for many years. It has become impossible to escape the repetitive drumbeat of the media about the aging of the Baby Boomers. The real-life stories are poignant tales of prominent and humble people alike who find themselves caught up in arduous and emotionally draining circumstances. As we build on the perspectives presented in this volume and look to the future, perhaps the overriding consideration is that caregivers must be viewed as a central component of geriatric care. It is neither a luxury to address family concerns, nor a distraction from treating the older person. Rather, clinical and policy initiatives need to be anchored in the premise that the well-being of older people depends to a large extent on the functioning of their families, and that addressing the needs and strains experienced by family caregivers will be a cost-effective strategy in the long run.

CLINICAL INITIATIVES

Clinical interventions with family caregivers are effective. As discussed in this volume, clinically oriented treatments that are flexible, that address caregivers' individual needs, and that also involve the larger family network have been found to reduce feelings of strain, burden, and depression. Of course, more research is needed to refine and expand these findings, but clinicians have an ample toolbox from which they can draw for treatment of caregivers.

The main challenge for the clinical field is dissemination. More clinicians need to learn the concepts that guide caregiver interventions and the skills involved in providing effective treatment. And physicians and other health-care professionals must understand that the problems that family caregivers experience require skilled treatment.

The typical approach used by many professionals is to give the caregiver advice and information. As research shows (see S. Zarit, Chapter 7 in this volume), giving people advice and information or sending them to a website is not generally effective in lowering strain and burden. Caregivers instead need to explore the options they have with an empathic, nonjudgmental, and knowledgeable clinician. Additionally, the clinician must have the skills to help caregivers overcome the emotional barriers and other obstacles they may face in learning new skills for the care of a parent and in implementing an overall plan for care. Over the years, I have seen many well-meaning and inadequately trained people become stymied when they give caregivers information and tell them what to do, only to have the caregiver reject their advice and fail to make any changes. Caregivers who are ready to use information will often find and implement it on their own. When caregivers are stuck, depressed, and overwhelmed, information is not the answer. They need instead to work with a professional who has the skills to help them identify and unravel the emotional knots and family dilemmas that are holding them back.

Treatment of family caregivers is rewarding. Most are willing and eager clients and make rapid progress. Issues around the care of their relatives, such as managing behavioral and emotional problems, are challenging but often solvable. The family dynamics they describe are always fascinating and, as described by J. Zarit and by Qualls and Noecker (Chapters 6 and 8, respectively, in this volume), are usually workable within the framework and goals of a caregiving intervention.

Of course, clinicians also need to be rewarded monetarily for their efforts. The level of reimbursement for this kind of treatment has been inadequate and is growing worse as Medicare and other insurers make across-the-board cuts in payments for mental health services. The social value of treating caregivers must be matched by the payment given for it. The general public, politicians, and policy makers need to have a better understanding of what we do and what we accomplish, that we do more than hand-holding, to have skills that facilitate behavioral change and thereby help caregivers meet the many challenges they are facing.

I want to add that the emphasis on family caregivers should not lead us to overlook older people who do not have family members to assist them. The Baby Boomer generation is noteworthy both for high rates of marriage and high rates of divorce. Family ties may be strained or absent in middle and old age. In the American piecemeal system of human services, the person without family who can be a strong advocate is likely to get inadequate help (Shea et al., 2003). At times, the clinician may have to become an advocate, and also help the older person contact appropriate legal and social services professionals who can play that role (Zarit & Zarit, 2007).

PUBLIC POLICY INITIATIVES

The inadequacies of the American health-care system are well-known—large numbers of people without health insurance, large inequalities in access to care, runaway profits of health-care and drug companies. These problems are on the public agenda, as is concern about the rising costs for Medicare and shrinking base of working-age people who are supporting it. There are likely to be lively political discussions of these issues in upcoming years. The particular danger that mental health clinicians who work with older persons face is that their services, which have traditionally been undervalued, will get such severe cuts as to make practice economically unsustainable. We all need to be advocates for our profession and the people we serve. Our clients are not "greedy geezers" or their entitled children. They have genuine problems that we can help with, and the solutions we offer will support them and the older person they are caring for, sustain their health and well-being, and contribute to the well-being of their whole family. Helping politicians and the general public understand the value of this type of work will be a challenge.

The debates over health care often overlook one of the most important gaps in the current system—the lack of a national program of long-term-care insurance. Private insurance is available, but it can be expensive and the number of people who are covered is relatively small. Compared to other economically advanced countries, we are woefully behind in development of a national program that makes long-term-care services affordable and accessible to older people and their families. Even Japan and Korea, which have cultures steeped in ancient Confucian principles that families care for their elders, have recognized that modern life places so many demands on the family that outside help is sometimes needed. Both countries now have programs of universal long-term-care insurance.

The cost of such a system in the United States is likely to be contrasted with other obvious needs, such as universal health insurance for children. Yet the current piecemeal system of services and funding streams is wasteful and fails to deliver help to the people most in need (Davey et al., 2005). Although an efficient and comprehensive system would cost more, there would be potential savings by helping more people remain at home or in less costly settings, such as assisted living, and by working in collaboration with families to share the burden of care.

The advantages of universal health and long-term-care services for family caregivers are enormous. A simple, user-friendly system would allow them to identify quickly the types of help that are available and to access those programs and services that are most appropriate. A coordinated system of care could support and complement the help caregivers provide (e.g., Shea et al., 2003), rather than serving as just another source of stress, as is often the case currently.

Two issues may be critical for the success of long-term-care reform. First, a new system should have choices. One approach in the field has been to recommend services for older people and their families based on a structured assessment. A rigid formula of matching services, however, may overlook individual differences and preferences. Adult day care, for example, works well for some caregivers, but not for others (Zarit, Stephens, Townsend, Greene, & Leitsch, 1999). People need to be able to choose from various services and providers, an approach facilitated by the Cash & Counseling program described by Elmore and Talley (Chapter 10 in this volume).

Second, quality of care will improve only when the workforce is well-trained. There are many qualified and dedicated people who currently work in long-term care, but their numbers are dwarfed by those employees who are indifferent and have no idea of what constitutes quality care. High rates of staff turnover, particular at the nurse's aid level, have been a disincentive to service providers to improve training.

A promising program to improve the workforce in preschools may serve as a template for long-term care. This program, Keystone Stars, was developed by the Department of Public Welfare in Pennsylvania (Pennsylvania Early Learning Keys to Quality, 2008). The program lays out a series of steps that preschools can take to improve quality. Included is a detailed program of education for teachers that addresses the knowledge and skills that are critical to working with young children. Preschools are awarded between one to four stars from the state, depending on how many staff meet the educational and other requirements of the program. And more importantly, the state increases its payment to the preschool for low-income children in the program based on the number of stars it has earned, which goes toward improved salaries for teachers who have met the training requirements. A comparable approach to long-term care would reward programs for staff training and would help retain the better-trained people.

RESEARCH INITIATIVES

Many interesting and important research questions about family care need to be addressed. There is much still to learn about the effectiveness of treatments for caregivers. We need to know more about what treatments are effective with which caregivers and how various combinations of treatment work—for example, counseling and adult day care. Much of the available treatment research is relatively short term. More systematic longitudinal studies can help identify sustained benefits of interventions (e.g., Mittelman, Roth, Coon, & Haley, 2004).

Given the importance of family to the success of caregiver interventions, more studies are needed that examine the roles, contributions, and perspectives of various family members. Newer statistical approaches (e.g., multilevel modeling) make it possible to study multiple members within a family and to consider both how families differ from one another and how factors common to most families contribute to particular outcomes.

A major gap in our knowledge is how caregiving unfolds. Most research is based on people who have been caregivers for some time. With early diagnosis of dementia becoming the norm, there is an opportunity to look at how both the caregiver and the patient react to diagnosis and the decisions they make at that point that may affect long-term outcomes. Interventions may also be used in a preventive way by preparing patient, caregiver, and the wider family for the challenges that lie ahead (e.g., Whitlatch, Judge, Zarit, & Femia, 2006).

Finally, it is important to incorporate the care receiver's perspective into caregiving studies (e.g., Femia, Zarit, Stephens, & Greene, 2007; Teri, Logsdon, Uomoto, & McCurry, 1997). The goal of interventions ultimately is to support the well-being of both the caregiver and the older person receiving care. At times, caregiver and care receiver may have diverging interests; but well-constructed interventions should generally help address each person's needs and goals.

CONCLUSIONS

The chapters in this volume have provided a broad look at family caregiving in society today. We hope to have given clinicians a solid foundation on which to build their interventions and to have stimulated researchers to ask new and more-focused questions. The role and importance of family care will only grow in the coming years. Skilled clinicians are needed to meet the challenges that lie ahead and to help families manage age and disability in a manner consistent with their values, to maximize positive outcomes for the care receiver, and to reduce the emotional and physical costs on the caregiver.

REFERENCES

Davey, A., Femia, E. E., Zarit, S. H., Shea, D. G., Sundström, G., Berg, S., Smyer, A., & Savla, J. (2005). Life on the edge: Patterns of formal and informal help to older adults in the United States and Sweden. *Journal of Gerontology: Social Sciences, 60B,* S281–S288.

Femia, E. E., Zarit, S. H., Stephens, M. A. P., & Greene, R. (2007). Impact of adult day services on behavioral and psychological symptoms of dementia. *The Gerontologist, 47,* 775–788.

Mittelman, M. S., Roth, D. L., Coon, D. W., & Haley, W. E. (2004). Sustained benefit of supportive intervention for depressive symptoms in caregivers of patients with Alzheimer's disease. *American Journal of Psychiatry, 161(5),* 850–856.

Pennsylvania Early Learning Keys to Quality. (2008). http://www.pakeys.org/ Accessed June 20, 2008.

Shea, D. G., Davey, A., Femia, E. E., Zarit, S. H., Sundström, G., Berg, S., & Smyer, M. A. (2003). Exploring assistance in Sweden and the United States. *Gerontologist, 43,* 712–721.

Teri, L., Logsdon, R. G., Uomoto, J., & McCurry, S. M. (1997). Behavioral treatment of depression in dementia patients: A controlled clinical trial. *Journals of Gerontology Series B: Psychological Sciences & Social Sciences, 52B(4),* P159–P166.

Whitlatch, C. J., Judge, K., Zarit, S. H., & Femia, E. E. (2006). A dyadic intervention for family caregivers and care receivers in early stage dementia. *Gerontologist, 46,* 688–694.

Zarit, S. H., Stephens, M. A. P., Townsend, A., Greene, R., & Leitsch, S. A. (1999). Patterns of adult day service use by family caregivers: A comparison of brief versus sustained use. *Family Relations, 48,* 355–361.

Zarit, S. H., & Zarit, J. M. (2007). *Mental disorders in older adults* (2nd ed.). New York: Guilford.

Author Index

Subject Index